THE REAL DEAL

Joselito
THE REAL DEAL

José Miguel Arroyo

Translated by Brian Harding

First published in Spain in 2012
as *Joselito el verdadero* by Espasa Libros, S.L.U.

First published in Great Britain by
the Club Taurino of London, 2015

The right of José Miguel Arroyo to be identified as the author of this
work has been asserted by him in accordance with the Copyright,
Designs and Patents Act 1988

Copyright © José Miguel Arroyo Delgado, 2012
Copyright © Francisco Aguado Montero, 2012
Copyright © Espasa Libros, S. L. U., 2012
Copyright © English translation, Brian Harding/
Club Taurino of London, 2015

Editing and documentation of original text: Paco Aguado

Cover photo: Tristan Wood
Cover design: Lindley Smith

Interior photos: Archivo de JMAD, Archivo Espasa,
Archivo Escuela de Tauromaquia de Madrid, Agencia EFE, Mateo,
Roland Costedoat, Brian Harding, Mike Penning, Tristan Wood.

ISBN: 978-0-9932716-0-1

Printed and bound in Great Britain by Berforts Ltd.

Club Taurino of London
PO Box 58515
London SW13 3AF
UK

www.ctol.org.uk

CONTENTS

FOREWORD

José Miguel Arroyo, known as *Joselito,* was one of Spain's leading matadors – some bullfight aficionados would say, *the* leading matador – in the latter part of the twentieth century and the first few years of this century.

I first read this autobiography in the original Spanish version, published in 2012. A bestseller in Spain, the book had already reached its third edition by the time I bought it.

When I finished reading the book – a tale which brought me to tears – I was convinced an English language edition was merited. To my mind, this was the most important book published by a matador since the autobiography of the legendary Juan Belmonte (available in English as *Juan Belmonte – Killer of Bulls* since 1937 in a translation by *The Saint* author Leslie Charteris). *Joselito*'s book takes a similar format to Belmonte's, which used the matador's own words but was carefully woven together by the journalist Manuel Chaves Nogales; in this case, the taurine writer and journalist Paco Aguado was involved in its creation.

The voice and views of *Joselito* are clearly expressed in this remarkable book. Matadors are a mystery to most people, aficionados included. Their performances in the bullring are generally mute affairs (brief interviews are given for television or radio audiences) and their interactions with the media tend to be stylised, rather like those of politicians, so getting an understanding of the real man wearing the 'suit of lights' rarely happens. In these pages too, the workings of the modern 'mundillo de los toros' – the tight-lipped world of bullfighting – are revealed.

Rumours and insinuations – some too vile to be repeated here – encircled *Joselito* throughout his professional career. Here, for the first time, he reveals the truth about his boyhood on the streets of Madrid, his relationships with his birth family and his manager, Enrique Martín Arranz, who became his second father through adoption, and the dedication and sheer hard graft involved in becoming a successful matador.

Readers new to bullfighting may be surprised at *Joselito*'s description of himself as an artist. The English-speaking media tends to characterise bullfighting in a number of ways – as an act of uncivilised savagery, or as a (blood) sport, or merely as a misguided and archaic entertainment. Yet, at its heart – when at its very best – it is none of these things. Rather, Spanish culture has turned the everyday act of humans killing animals for their meat into a spectacle that can attain the heights of artistry, as a man, armed merely with a piece of cloth, risks his life to confront a wild animal bent on destroying him, and, in doing so, creates emotion by expressing the very nature of his being, and demonstrating the shared intelligence and creativity that enable us to overcome the challenges we face in our lives.

Despite *Joselito*'s assertions in this book that his professional bullfighting days are over, the entreaties of another matador led him to make a one-off appearance at Istres, in South-East France, in June last year. Aficionados from all over the world packed the town's modest bullring, witnessed a memorable performance from *Joselito*, and saw him carried out of the ring in triumph by fellow spectators at the end of the corrida. *Joselito* has nevertheless insisted the event did not herald a resumption of his bullfighting career, and, to date, he has continued to resist impresarios' offers to finance further appearances.

Married into a Madrid family and a long-term '*joselitista*' (follower of the matador) himself, Brian Harding was the obvious person to do this book justice in English. Thanks to the care taken by Brian (and my co-editor, Helen Windrath), *Joselito*'s story has lost nothing in translation. It is fitting, too, that this book is published, in its 56th year of existence, by the Club Taurino of London, of which José Miguel Arroyo has been Honorary Vice-President since 1995.

Tristan Wood
March 2015

TRANSLATOR'S PREFACE

This translation was not my idea at all. In May 2013, just as I was about to set out on my annual pilgrimage to the San Isidro Fair in Madrid, I received a phone call from Tristan Wood, one of the editors of the magazine of the Club Taurino of London, and my companion at many corridas in Spain and France. He was unusually excited and asked me if I had read the autobiography of José Miguel Arroyo *Joselito*, which had just been published. According to Tristan this was the best writing about a matador since Juan Belmonte. He wanted to know if I would be prepared to help him translate it for publication. I looked at my half-packed suitcase and said I would consider the idea and let him know.

There was no time to have a copy posted to me, but I bought a download of the eBook of *Joselito el verdadero* and determined to read it on my iPad while I was away.

Which is what I did, sacrificing my mornings in Madrid and a few evenings too, in the cause of finding out what made Tristan so excited. It didn't take long to realise that this was an exceptional story, well-written with a liberal use of Madrid street-slang, impenetrable to the average English-speaking reader. My advantages are that I have married into a large Spanish family; I have a weak knowledge of Spanish grammar; and I've never taken an exam but have learnt what I know by listening to conversations in family gatherings, business meetings and bars. As an aficionado, my vocabulary about the bulls is quite good too.

What immediately impressed me about José's book was that I could clearly hear his own voice speaking to me – I have met him several times. I learnt that his co-writer, Paco Aguado, had based the book on a series of recorded, intimate interviews with José, which were subsequently edited down as words on the page. The language used by José in telling his story is of great importance; it traces his progress from working-class streets to Royal Palace, in his struggle to reach the top of his profession. It was this obsessive ambition which saved him from the fate of most of his childhood friends, who sank into the morass of drug addiction, endemic in Madrid at the time he was growing up. I have tried in my translation to respect the tone of the original by replacing East Madrid slang with East London slang. This may be difficult at times for readers not familiar with the vernacular I grew up with, but it gives a flavour of the language of José's original text. I apologise in advance if I have been over-zealous on occasions.

English language publishers were unwilling to take on this book. They were worried about what the animal activists would do. But the Club Taurino of London rose to the challenge and this English translation is the result.

I couldn't have completed it without the support and help of many people. First is Tristan Wood, who started the project, then stepped back to let me get on with the task of translation, after which he finally edited the finished manuscript. I am very grateful to Helen Windrath who co-edited the text and presented it in a form that modern printers would recognise. Paco Aguado was always ready and willing to explain the more obscure passages to me. Members of my extended Spanish family were particularly helpful in remembering the names of forgotten street games and the correct terminology for drugs on the street. Special mention must be made of my sister-in-law,

Amalia Martínez and her husband, Carlos Escalona, who displayed an encyclopaedic knowledge of street games, gypsy argot and just about everything illegal. And immeasurable thanks go to my wife, Juanita Martínez, who made it all possible.

Brian Harding
March 2015

For those who love me and
for those who hate me.

INTRODUCTION

If I hadn't become obsessed with the idea of becoming a bullfighter, by now I would be either in jail or dead from an overdose. This is something I say a lot, because when I was twelve and I lost my father, my life was about to fall into a bottomless pit of crime and drugs. And that's not just empty words: it's a fact.

Now that I have retired from active bullfighting, and for the first time in my life I have a stable family life, and can enjoy the proceeds of what I have earned from fighting bulls, I feel I should look back and tell the story of what I have lived through.

I don't want to moralise, and I won't, because that's not in my character: I never liked laying down the law about anything. But now that so many kids are growing up at a loose end in so-called 'dysfunctional' families, maybe my story can serve as an example to someone else.

It would be enough just to show that you can get out of even the most desperate situation if you really want to, or have enough ambition to refuse to accept the inevitable, to rebel and fight against your fate, even if you're just a kid, by going all out for it, one hundred per cent.

Throughout my career, there have persistently been the most

bizarre and morbid rumours about my personal life. So, mainly because of them, many people have the impression that I am an enigmatic individual. When my career was starting to take off, a critic once described me as 'the torero with a sad face', and even as a teenager there was talk of my 'irrational, melancholic personality'. And I admit there was something in that. Because, even though most of these comments were wrong, there were others which came close to reality. But no more than close.

I have never before wanted, or been in a position, to speak so clearly about all this. I used to feel very nervous when I was asked to reveal the most insignificant details of my personal life, perhaps because the experiences that lay behind my circumstances were so grim that subconsciously I was ashamed to bring them out; I thought that it was a weakness that shouldn't be shown to my enemies.

I am now over forty and I have hung up – I hope for ever – my suit of lights. No one should think, as some other professionals have done, that I am telling all this in order to set up a campaign for a comeback; that's all in the past. Quite the opposite, in fact: I have waited until now, when the cheers and the 'olés' are just a distant echo in my head, and I have finally closed all the doors to my profession.

Time has passed by; I think it's fair to say that I have been successful, both in the world of bullfighting and in my private life. And now is a good time to look back without regrets to consider with a degree of pride where I've come from and where I've got to, in spite of my own inner struggles. If it's true that my childhood and teenage years were complicated and tough, it's also true that later on I was able to enjoy my chosen profession to the full, and I found an art form in which to express myself and to achieve creative fulfilment. Being a bullfighter was not just a means of making money for me: it also gave me a philosophy for life. It became like a religion that demanded great sacrifices, but gave me great rewards in return. I owe everything I am to the bulls, because that's where I learnt the values which have helped me to become a better person, and a better artist.

I want people to know my story. And I especially want my daughters to know it, because they are thankfully growing up in a healthy and happy environment, very different from the one I knew when I was their age, and which almost swallowed me up for ever.

1

A NEIGHBOURHOOD TO
THE EAST OF EDEN

Although I grew up in the district of La Guindalera, which is to the East of Eden of Madrid, I was actually born in the heart of Madrid's up-market Salamanca district, on 1st May 1969, May Day, the Day of the Workers. That's two paradoxes: my parents weren't so well off as to have money for a posh clinic, and they didn't even live there in some poor concierge flat, it's just that in those days the Social Security used to send women from some of the suburbs to give birth in a maternity clinic in Calle Montesa.

So it happened that, while General Franco was officiating at the parade of his phoney 'trade unions' in Real Madrid's Bernabeu Football Stadium in the rain, and while the state police were clubbing the real workers who were on protest demos, I first saw daylight in the posh district of Salamanca.

My parents weren't at all well-off. In reality, they lived in the working-class district of Alcorcón, where they moved to after they got married. Both of them were emigrants, just another couple among the thousands of men and women who fled their villages to escape from the misery and poverty of the years of development. Many of them landed up in shanty towns, or hoped for better luck in the outskirts of Madrid.

My father, Bienvenido Arroyo de la Llana by name, came from a village called Villanueva de Alcorón, in the mountains of Guadalajara, between Molina de Aragón and Beteta, near to the provinces of Cuenca and Teruel. I went there on holiday as a child once or twice, not often because Bienve had little contact with his family there.

And my mother was from Villamor de Órbigo in the province of León. I don't really know that, but I assume she was from there, because that's where her parents lived. Her name was María Encarnación Delgado Vega. Maybe that is still her name, because as far as I know she is still alive.

They met in Madrid, and I don't know why they went to live in Alcorcón. We lived in what is now known as the old quarter, but then it wasn't known as such, because the cottages of the old village were still standing, before they were cleared to make way for the blocks of flats which turned it into just another one of those dormitory satellite towns which surround the capital.

The only memory I have of those childhood days is of me sitting on a balcony with my legs dangling down, with my little brother, Roberto Carlos. And there was a very big, multi-coloured plastic snail, which we both played with. That's all I can remember. And neither can I remember my older sister, Maribel.

I can't recall a thing about my mother in those days either. I can't even put a face to her. If I were to cross by her in the street, I wouldn't recognise her. Over the years, I have only ever seen her perhaps three times, and she has left no impression on me whatsoever. I have no sense of pining for that woman, and no feelings of affection.

I have a vague memory from there of her holding my brother in her arms, and taking my clothes out of a bedside cabinet. Suddenly, my father came into the room, took my hand, and led me away. It must be the day they broke up for good.

There were two years between all of us children. My grandparents took Maribel, who was five, to their village in León. I was three, and I stayed with my father. My mother, for the time being, stayed in Alcorcón with my little brother, who was just one year old. Later on, she left him with some neighbours, a couple who had twelve children of their own, and were family of the man she was starting a new life with.

I never knew why she abandoned us. My father never told me, because he never talked about her, and I didn't ask. I wasn't worried about not knowing. Understanding him as I do now, I suppose they just didn't get along together, because he was not an easy man to live with.

I came to terms with it in my own way. At first it was about feeling rejected, but then I tried to understand her, and deep down I grew to forgive her. But to this day, I still can't understand how a mother could walk out like that on three small children. Her marriage must have been a living hell for her to come to a decision like that. Or maybe they just couldn't afford to bring up all of us – who knows? For sure, it couldn't have been easy or pleasant for her.

My father, who was a good person at heart, lived his own life with no lines drawn or responsibilities. He didn't think ahead. He was just a prick. But it was him who stayed by me, and brought me to Madrid.

It was like the world suddenly opened up for me, because although I was only three, I can remember very clearly our arrival on the scene. First we caught the bus from Alcorcón, known locally for some reason as *La Blasa*, and then we got a tram, which went along the Avenida de los Toreros, near the Public Baths where later we used to go for a shower every Saturday. And then we walked from the Plaza San Cayetano to Calle Eraso, where our new home was.

It was an attic room of about eight or ten square metres, not much more than a cupboard at the end of a corridor, in one of those typical Madrid houses with balconies around a central patio. And right in front of our door was a miserable WC, which was for the shared use of the other four attic rooms on our landing. In our room, which hardly had space to move around in, we had a small coal-fired stove and a granite sink, where we washed with water heated by the stove.

We also had a sort of sofa or mattress, tucked under the sloping roof, and that was where I slept. Although I wasn't very big, I had to be careful getting up, or I would bang my head. And there was also, obviously, a big double bed where my father slept with his new partner, Pepita; she came to live with us, and I think there was already something going on between them when he was still with my mother. The three of us lived there for a couple of years. It was all a bit unsafe, and we were unbelievably cold, but I couldn't say that I had a sad childhood. My father spelled the new situation out to me: he knew that I would soon be going to school, and that the other kids would do their best to get at me by repeating the gossip they had heard at home, so he told me very clearly me that this woman who lived with us wasn't my mother, and I accepted that.

The house had a biggish patio with lots of light, where the neighbours did their sewing and things, and where we kids played. Not far away, to the east, which is now the M-30 motorway, it was then open country. From a little window we could see a local dairy and smell the cows; they sold the milk in metal churns. Nearby was a bakery, with much nicer smells of freshly baked bread and cakes. And there was a garage workshop where they repaired second-hand cars. And nearby there was a spooky, two-storey house, locked-up, almost in ruins, which had a patio with trees, and where we kids would get inside and frighten ourselves silly.

Over to the west lay the Plaza San Cayetano and the Calle Cartagena, which was the edge of civilisation, represented by the outskirts of Francisco Silvela, standing like an imaginary wall between the wealthy district of Salamanca and our working-class slum of La Guindalera. That was how things still were in Madrid in the mid-1970s.

My father, Bienve, felt immediately at home, like a duck to water. As I said, he was a decent bloke, although a bit wild, and a bit of a freeloader. He was a nice chap out on the street, but a disaster at home. He went his own way, came and went as he pleased, living a disorderly, untogether lifestyle. I don't suppose for a minute that it could have been easy scraping a living in those years, but I have the impression that hard work didn't appeal to him – he just didn't like it.

He was a dreamer, everyone's friend and a bit fly. He was well known in all the bars, and he liked to strut his stuff, well-dressed, slicked back, combed hair, shiny shoes, and he'd play cards and pull strokes... In a word, he was a player.

When we were living in Alcorcón, I think he drove a school bus, and when we moved to Madrid, he got a job delivering for a pastry shop in the Carmen district, on the other side of the bridge of Ventas. He must have done all right there, because he bought himself a little van. But that wasn't because he was earning well, so much as because he took up with Crescen, the woman who owned the shop.

We got to know about it, because one day she called home, and the cat was out of the bag. There was a huge row, and Pepita went to stay with a friend in Moratalaz for a few days; this friend was married to a Police Commissioner. By one of life's strange coincidences, it was that same policeman who, years later, helped me to falsify my papers so that I could start bullfighting before I was legally old enough.

My father was fired from the pastry shop, but he kept the van. Although he didn't pay for it, he had conned his 'floozy' into putting it in his name. Pepita came back, and from that point on, they began to have terrific fights. I slept like the hares do, with one eye open, because all the time they were at it hammer and tongs, and my father would end up hitting her. Many nights the police would come knocking at the door, because the neighbours had complained. When he was all right, Bienve was a decent bloke, but I don't know if he was just putting it on, or if he had an aggressive streak. I was only little and I didn't know enough to work out what was going on, but I do know that sometimes things got seriously out of hand.

Because he was out of work, he sold the van and we rented a taxi, a Seat 1500, which we had for a while. I say 'we' because he often took me along on the job with him. I asked him to get me a blue shirt, which was the uniform of taxi-drivers in those days, and dressed like that I used to sit on the front bench seat with him, when all the taxis were like that, black with a red stripe along the side. I would put down the flag and take the money. I had a great time.

And my father too, since the clients would leave a good tip because of the funny kid.

By then, we had moved to a house in Calle Cartagena, two blocks from the covered market of La Guindalera. It was – and it still is, because I kept it for years afterwards – an apartment of just over thirty square metres, with a WC, a shower, a kitchen and three small bedrooms. After the shoebox of the Calle Escaso, this was real luxury. My father bought it equal shares with Pepita. Things were going better between them, and I had started pre-school in a building next to the studios of Madrid-Film, and I was now in the junior school doing EGB, which stands for Basic General Education.

LEARNING IN THE STREETS

When I was a kid, I was a good student. In the first few years, I passed everything with top marks. I studied hard, and kept myself in good order. But as I was growing up, with all the disorder at home, I used to come and go as I pleased. I had my own set of keys in my pocket, and when Pepita – who didn't take much notice of me anyway – got a job in a restaurant, there was no one to keep an eye on me.

I did hardly any schoolwork, and because I was a bit sharp I could get by with bits and pieces that I heard in class. I was learning more outside school than in it. And like all us kids at that time, I grew up living in the street. When the teachers let us out, we ran straight to play in the park, or to the open spaces, or the empty building sites, because there were plenty to choose from. We were like a wave of noisy sparrows flying from one place to another. We had stone-fights with the kids from the other side of Calle Cartagena. We played 'rescue', catch, whip-and-top, and 'steps', a sort of torture where we all stood in a line, and one of us had to pass through it while the others whacked him on his neck. And there was also 'arropa que hay poca', hide-and-seek, marbles, bottle-tops, running races, or games of football, picture cards, 'nails' if it was muddy...

I was really good with a spinning top. My father brought me one from the village, made from an amazing hardwood, and I beat everyone with that. At least until they brought out one made of plastic, and that was that. Sometimes we played with yo-yos, and I was pretty good at that too. There was a special type which let me do all the tricks, like 'walking the dog', 'swings', 'pistols', 'Eiffel Tower', and all those other things you did with the string, without moving the round bit.

In the summer, we built little soapbox carts made of wood with a plank across, car wheel rims, and a sort of rudder for steering with the feet. It was great to race them flat out down slopes and embankments, although more than one of us would lose a few teeth, and we all got covered in cuts and scratches. Us kids from poor districts or villages didn't need expensive toys to play with; a bit of imagination was all that was necessary.

And, of course, we played football, nearly always in the playground of Caldeiro School in the Avenida de los Toreros. A few boys from our neighbourhood went there, and we went in with them until the priests kicked us out.

We were all Real Madrid supporters, and my favourite player – I don't know why – was the German, Uli Stielike. And Miguel Ángel, of course, the goalkeeper, with a big moustache and those very short shorts that were all the rage. And Del Bosque. Those are the footballers I remember from those days. I always asked to be Stielike, but because I wasn't very good and a bit on the weak side, they put me in goal most of the time. Until one time I got the ball right in the face, and they had to take me to A & E to get stitches. That's when I decided that football wasn't for me.

As we got bigger, we turned into hooligans. We broke streetlamps with our catapults, tipped over the dustbins, rang all the doorbells on the entry-phones... One day the local police caught us breaking streetlamps, and they took us down to the police station, and gave all of us in the gang a good hiding: there was Ángel and Rafa, who were twins; *Surjo* and his little brother, Carlitos; Pablito, Vitín, Roberto, Javi...

We loved fireworks: we would put them on the window-sills of the flats on the ground floor, or stick them in a dog shit and let them off; we terrified the old age pensioners. It was just stuff that kids did in those days. And to act older than we were, we smoked the dog-ends that we picked up off the floor in the bars too – yuck! Our time was filled with all these 'extra-curricular' activities, and we didn't have much time for anything else. We hardly watched any television.

And when they pinched my bike from outside my front door, I learnt to steal too. It was a really neat Orbea bike which my father had bought me. So to even things up, an eye for an eye, I stole another bike from outside a nearby house, changed the saddle and used one from a Chopper which I thought looked really cool, and I painted the whole bike another colour. No one ever found out.

And when I was nine or ten, bold as brass, we would go out 'on the rob' with a gang of kids from school. Álvaro was the boss, a real tearaway, and we used to run amok. We would 'streak' through shops stealing stuff, but it was all a bit pointless, because we couldn't take things home for fear that our parents would find us out, so we ended up by dumping them in wastepaper bins.

I remember that what we liked most were the accessories for a range of figures called 'Clicks' made by Famobil, those and boxes of toy soldiers. We stole for the fun of it, not because we needed to, because, although we were all from poor families, we didn't really go short of much. When my father began his dodgy dealing, he even bought me a Scalextric, which did not come cheap, and a terrific racing bike, the only one in the neighbourhood.

But we also made money for ourselves, and so, to afford slot machines and billiards and table-top football games, we'd go and pay a visit to the collecting boxes of the Christian charity, Domund, and the Red Cross. We would go over to the Salamanca district, because on our side people hardly ever made donations.

When the collecting box was full, we would put a knife in the slot, turn it upside down, and the coins would come tumbling out, or else we would break the seam and re-seal it by melting the plastic with a lighter. When they came to empty the boxes, we would put on a sad face and say what a shame it was that people were so tight with their money.

We used to go to the continuous showings in the local cinemas. There were plenty of them: not like now. We had a great time. We would spend dull afternoons up in the Circle, and if the film was boring, we would start throwing things, and annoy the people down below, until the attendant came and started flashing his torch at us, and we would roar with fits of laughter and go and hide in the toilets.

We liked Westerns, but our favourites were the karate movies with Bruce Lee: *Fury of the Dragon, Karate to the Death in Bangkok...* When we left the cinema, we didn't leave a single wastepaper bin or dustbin standing, because we would attack them karate-style and kick them to bits, giving our karate cries like we'd just seen in the film.

We staged fights among ourselves, doing the 'cobra', making a 'tiger face', and we even made up our own kind of *nunchako* – sticks with chains, swivels and broom handles which we wrapped with black insulating tape. Our heads were covered in bumps and cuts from trying to learn how to fight with this 'deadly weapon' with the same speed as the Master of the martial arts.

I was always a bit clumsy with girls. My first love was a very pretty local girl. Her name was Patricia, and we were all after her. Her friends told me that she would like to be my girlfriend, so the very next day when I was out on my bike with my friends from school, I saw her come round the corner of Calle Cartagena, headed in my direction. 'This is my chance,' I thought, and I went to show off by doing a wheelie, but I overdid it and fell flat on my back right in front of a taxi which was coming up behind. What an idiot!

Even so, she became my girlfriend. The most I did was to give her an awkward kiss on the cheek. And I was very proud of myself after that. Because that meant that 'Chestnut' José, *el Moreno* – and they called me that to differentiate me from the other José in the gang who they called 'Blondie' José, *el Rubio* – that I was the boyfriend of Patri. A very big deal. But she grew bored with that over-shy kid, and she dumped me and took up with an older boy, who – it was said – touched her up while they did French kissing with tongues in the stairwell.

*   *   *

When I finished at the junior school, they sent me to another school nearby called Juan de Valdés, a church school, either Evangelist or Protestant – I can't remember which. I don't know why, but in my class there were lots of Africans and Argentinians. I was there for three years, but even without leaving my neighbourhood I learnt about the existence of other cultures and ways of life different to mine. My limits were those of the district around Las Ventas, bounded by Avenida de America. I learnt a lot from the fact that I got to know a wide variety of kids from other countries: what nowadays they call a multicultural experience.

But where I really got to learn stuff was in the streets; that's where my eyes were truly opened to what was going on in the world. And from early on, I found myself in some tricky spots. On the same day that I reached the age of ten, I began to get interested in the bulls, which is something that toughens you, and makes you grow up fast, no choice about it. I went on about it so much that my father, who was already an aficionado, and liked the idea, signed me up in the Madrid School of Bullfighting, which was a new centre of learning for bullfighters, set up by a bunch of crackpots, headed up by someone called Martín Arranz. I didn't know it at the time, but this was to prove my way out of the tunnel into which my life as an adolescent was about to be leading me.

WITH THE DRUG DEALERS

Flitting from one scam to the next, my father had got fed up with the taxi, and bought himself a small yellow Mercedes van to set himself up in a little business doing deliveries and removals. But I think he didn't get a single job, so he took on a contract delivering electrical goods for a shop in the district of Vallecas. The owner – I think her name was Carmen – was a big, blousy woman, attractive, blonde, big boobs, quite a livewire. And Bienve knew how to get to her. If he could have become a Muslim, I think he would have done so, because he found the idea of polygamy very attractive.

One day, my father came to collect me from school. A famous matador, *El Cordobés*, was on at the Fallas Fair in Valencia, and because he was a big attraction and there would be a high demand for tickets, my father got the idea of doing a bit of business as a ticket tout for that corrida.

He got the idea because the previous year in 1979, the day of a comeback by Manuel Benítez *El Cordobés* in Benidorm, Bienve went there and came back with a pile of money he'd made as a ticket tout. He also pulled one of the tassels off the torero's suit of lights as he was carried out on shoulders, and he gave it to me as if it were a precious jewel. I scored quite a few points flashing that glittering bib-bob around in school.

Anyway, it so happened that, because they had yet another row, Pepita had left home again in that month of March, and my father didn't have anyone to leave me with in Madrid. So he took me out of school, put some clothes in a bag, and the two of us set out together, happy as Larry, driving to Valencia in a Seat 124 sportscar that he had to show off in. On the way out we stopped in Calle Alcalá near Calle Goya, and he told me to get in the back seat, because there suddenly appeared the aforementioned Carmen, wearing a fur coat; she was also the one who had put up the money for the earlier deal in Benidorm.

In Valencia, we stayed in El Saler, in one of the bungalows. And for three or four days we travelled to the bullring so my father could sell the wad of tickets he had got hold of. It was there that I got my first job. Doing the three-card trick. As I was left to my own devices, I met up with some spivs, who were doing the rounds with their little table and three cards. They knew Bienve, and they offered to take me along as part of the act to bring in the punters. But first of all they very carefully explained to me how it all worked.

'We give you five hundred pesetas to place bets. When it's quiet, you place bets and start to win, but when the punters turn up, you clear off. If they leave, you come back. And if the cops arrive – beat it! Everyone goes their own way, and no-one knows anyone else. We'll meet up again later, somewhere or other.'

I was with the three-card boys for a couple of days, and we did well, because seeing me winning brought in the punters in droves. I picked up a fair bit of money, and I watched the corrida of *El Cordobés* from the last row of the seats, what they call in Valencia the *naya*, which means 'highlands'. I'll never forget the performance that man put on, not just with the bulls, but going around the ring on a circuit of celebration afterwards. Quite a superstar, the guy they called *El Pelos*, 'Longhair', because of his Beatles' haircut.

When we got back to Madrid, and Carmen saw my house full of electrical appliances, she lost her rag with my father and told the whole story to Pepita, and I don't know how she put up with it all. Even so, Pepita still stayed with him, probably because she couldn't afford not to, although she had been working for a while in a restaurant in the Delicias district, cleaning and washing up.

Then Bienvenido got the idea to take over the lease of a baker's shop over that way, near the railway yards of the Atocha train station. The female railway workers came by every morning to buy baguettes to make their sandwiches. And it was Pepita who ran things most of the time, alternating between the shop and the restaurant.

Every Sunday, my father took me with him to poke around in the Rastro, the flea market, and I think that between there and Vallecas were his two main stomping grounds. Then we would go to Casa Picardías in the Calle Cruz to eat a dish of really tasty bean stew. Afterwards, he would meet up with some people there and play a few games; that's where I learnt how to be really good at dominoes and rolling the dice, just by watching him.

I became a wizard at all kinds of table-top games, except cards, because he didn't want me around when he was betting at cards. He set up a game with one Pedro Romero – not the historic bullfighter, but a barber from Calle Cartagena, either in Bar La Pista or the Mesón Gallego. And whenever I stuck my nose in there, I was amazed at the piles of one thousand peseta notes stacked up on the table.

I can't remember exactly when my father decided to take up dealing in drugs, although at first it must have been gradual, and he just got caught up in it. He would call into all the little bars and dives around there. And at night, all the clip-joints, and especially El Cisne Negro (the Black Swan), a dodgy night club where people went to 'get laid'. A bit like the famous Pasapoga in Gran Via, but in La Guindalera. Because he was such a chancer, he used to spend his idle moments playing poker. There were some days – not many – when he came out on top, and others when he lost, big time. He would come home with his tail between his legs, stiff as a board. I suppose it's only natural that, in that setting, with a drink here and a drink there, puffing a joint here, doing a spliff there, losing again, needing money fast, the time must have come when he said to himself, 'Why am I breaking my balls working like mad, when, if I sold a bit of dope, I would make double what I can with hard graft, and then I could live the life I want to?'

He began by dealing a little at a time, and our house began to fill up with drugs. In every cupboard, in the kitchen, in every drawer – even in the loo – there were kilos and kilos of hash stashed everywhere. And every kind of user came to call, some of them looking seriously dodgy... I soon got to know every small dealer in the district, and further afield, and all their nicknames. They came to score dope for themselves, or to get supplies to sell on for Bienve. He was smart, and moved on from dealing in the street to having his own team of dealers. They would take twenty-five grams, small bags, whole bars... They brought my father the balls of hash as they put it 'straight off the boat from Morocco', and he would prepare it at home with a few mates. First they flattened it, and compressed it by rolling it out with a butane gas cylinder, and then they would cut it up and put it into packets.

They were all night people, and they dressed like Camilo Sesto, the singer: long, heavy hair; shiny shoes with a Cuban heel; tight-fitting, bell-bottomed trousers; tight jackets; and wide shirt-collars outside the lapels. My father dressed the same. And his business was doing bloody well; he bought himself a second-hand Mercedes to be more conspicuous. It was dark red, but he had it painted bright blue so it stood out more. You could see him coming from a long way off.

And I saw all this low-life going in and out of my home. They liked listening to rumbas played by Los Chicos and Los Chunguitos. Especially if the words were about drugs and life in prison. And because they were into everything, some of them had their own 'shooter', their own unregistered gun, to ensure they got respect in the dangerous world they moved in. One day, someone shot up my father's Mercedes while it was parked outside our front door. He told me it was the police who did it...

I got used to all this because I was seeing it on a daily basis. And I loved it. For a kid from the streets like me, these people were fascinating: just seeing how they walked, how they lived, how they dressed, with those massive chains round their necks, engraved bracelets, huge rings, and everything in gold. And the fistfuls of money they handled, the imported cigarettes, branded whiskies, their way of talking in patois, a mixture of Madrid and gypsy... It was like having the house full of characters from American gangster movies. Except these were real flesh and blood. I saw them every day, and they were my heroes. I didn't feel that they were a bad influence, and I still don't. But they were.

In the bars where they'd hang out, there was always music and an atmosphere of high spirits, and they would always ply me with quantities of food and drink: clams, anchovies, olives... 'Give Bienve's kid, the little bullfighter, whatever he wants.' I even got bottles of beer. And vermouth. Nowadays just the smell of it makes me feel giddy, and I've no idea how I managed it when I was only ten years old. And as if that wasn't enough, the bar owners used to give me the key to play on the pinball machines or Space Invaders.

THE COLDNESS OF THE PRISON AND THE CEMETERY

But one day, the police finally caught up with my father. It happened in the Calle Ibiza, with a couple of his mates; I remember it was a few days either just before or just after the attempted coup led by Tejero on 23rd February 1981. Someone must have grassed him up, because the cops followed them and then nabbed them in a car with three kilos of 'chocolate', and half a kilo of cocaine. Or it might have been heroin, I was never really sure. They were on their way to pull off a big deal.

He was inside for a few months. Pepita went to visit him in prison in Carabanchel once or twice a week, to take him food and other stuff. I went with her several times. We had to walk up from the metro station at Aluche, followed by a long wait in the queue, and it was bitterly cold in those open spaces around the prison. On average there were two or three thousand people waiting to visit their relatives inside. All sorts, all kinds, and especially lots of gypsies, loads of them. They would start queuing at daybreak, because the sooner you arrived, the sooner you were let in.

In school, I said that my father was sick, but he didn't really get ill until later on. Life went on as usual. Until he was let out on bail, Pepita and I kept the baker's shop running between us. On the days when she went to visit him in the nick, she left home at six or seven in the morning to get a place in the queue. And I had to sleep on a sofa in the shop to wake up in time for when the van came with the delivery of fresh bread, and then I had to start selling it. If Pepita didn't get back on time, I had to go to the restaurant to stand in for her doing the cleaning. From there I would go every evening in the metro to the Bullfighting School.

My father didn't want me to see him in prison. On all visits only Pepita went in. But when I saw it was going to be like this for a long time, eventually I asked if I could go in with her. This was on 2nd May 1981, and I don't remember the date because it was the day after my twelfth birthday, but because that was the day when my friend from Bullfighting School, Gitanillo Vega, who I knew also from the district of Delicias, made his debut in the ring of Las Ventas. I was very disappointed not to be able to see him in the ring that day, because they said he was very good with the cape.

On the other hand, seeing my father behind bars without being able to touch him...that was a really hard blow. When I walked into the room, my heart sank into my boots. I placed my hand on the glass screen, like I had seen in the movies, and I heard his voice down the phone telling me not to worry, that he would soon be out, and that he was doing okay inside. But it really made an impression on me. Carabanchel Prison was a gloomy, frightening place. To reach the interview room, you had to cross the empty quadrangles after waiting in the overcrowded queue. I was only a kid, but I knew what was going on there; you only had to look at the inmates and you knew they were muggers, robbers, pickpockets, pimps, drug dealers...

Another time I went with Pepita to the first face-to-face that they let me have with my father. Because he was still doing business inside prison, he asked us to bring in some hash and a few pills, and we hid it by sewing it inside our trouser bottoms. But the silly woman wrapped them in silver paper, and when we went through the metal detector, the alarms went off. We were shitting ourselves, but apart from taking the stuff off us, they didn't do anything else, and they still let us make the visit. Well, only Pepita, because I gave my father a couple of kisses and then stayed outside talking to the 'screws', while I imagine they were having a shag.

I went to see him again, and, there in prison, my father was even more of a hero for me. Because he was always good to me, he made my life that much easier and more comfortable. When he was on the outside, we were always having fun. I didn't go short of anything, and even less when he was in the money. All that was missing was the discipline that you normally get from a father, because he wasn't much worried about what I was or wasn't up to.

I saw him around the bars more than at home, where he only went to sleep or to prepare his drugs. In the daytime he stayed in bed, and when he got up for a pee, he would walk through the house stark naked, whoever was there, to the amazement of my friends who came to play with the Scalextric he bought me. But that's the way he was: he didn't give a monkey's about anything like that.

He was locked up until the month of July. And for all those months, Pepita and I had a rough time, and we hardly had enough to eat. Whatever was left over after giving my father his money, she spent in the bingo hall; he needed quite a bit to live reasonably and have money to play cards on the inside. We had to take him cash and drugs for dealing. And as we had to keep the business ticking over, I had to do it myself sometimes, because he used me as a courier between his mates.

One time that I was running one of these 'errands', I bumped into a demo some students were holding near Atocha Station, and the cops started beating people with their night sticks. Just in case, I popped down into the metro station, because I didn't want to get caught with the hash on me, and if I dumped it, I would get an even harder time from my father. I waited until I thought it was safe to go back up to the street, and then I was able to deliver it to the bloke I had been told to. He gave me the cash and said 'See ya!'

Nothing worried me. And I had even started doing a bit of dealing for myself. When they cut up the 'chocolate' at home, there were always a few bits left over, little balls, trimmings. And when they made up the bars of dope from the tablets, from the ends, the odd-shaped ones were kept for personal consumption. I got some of that too, and I sold it to my mates in school, *Pituco*, José Manuel, for a 'ton' a ball, one hundred pesetas.

I was a dealer before my time. I knew just about everything about it, and knew every variety of hashish. The best one was the Lebanese, reddish, but there was another one, greenish, Moroccan, very good stuff. And another darker one. And one made out of the pollen from the flowers. And 'Maria' – marijuana... A lot depended also on how it was prepared. At home, I'd seen it prepared so many times that I knew as much about it as my father did. Still today, I can tell the different types by their smell when I pass someone smoking dope in the street, even from a long way off. But I didn't smoke, although I tried it. One time, to show off, I took my 'Smoking' brand cigarette papers, my metro ticket to make a holder, my ball of hash and my Virginia tobacco to roll a spliff in school. I knew all the paraphernalia, but when it came to rolling it, I dropped the lot on the floor. My mates split their sides laughing. I took it as a warning, and I never tried to smoke a joint ever again.

Around that time, heroin and cocaine started to show up in the neighbourhood, 'smack' and 'coke'. I imagine that my father, seeing that he would make more money by dealing in them, tried to include them in his business, and that's when the problems began. I'm sure that someone must have blown the whistle on him for sticking his nose into something that wasn't his business. But the real problem wasn't that he was selling cocaine, so much as that he began using it himself. Orange tubes from Bic ballpoint pens started appearing all over the house, cut down and empty. At first, I thought they were part of the process for handling the gear, but I gradually began to realise that he was using them himself to snort cocaine.

The year before, he took me to Pamplona for the San Fermín Fair. He told me it was to tout tickets, because there's always a good market there. But it was also for dealing. I remember that, one night when we were sleeping in the van, he woke up, sick as a dog, and I realised that something else was going on.

Three months after getting out of jail, they arrested him again, but they didn't lock him up this time. Shortly after, he became very ill. Terrible pains in his stomach. They took him into hospital, at first to operate on his gall bladder, but things got more complicated. I suppose he must have had cancer. After a few weeks in hospital, they sent him home, but he got bad again almost immediately. When he came home, he had another row with Pepita for the hundredth time, and she left, never to see him again. That's how Bienve came to make his own favourite dish: although they had told him to keep to a light diet, he made a stodgy dish of mashed potatoes with onions and carrots. He stuffed himself silly. He kept going around the bars, and he overdid it on wine and fried ham. Then one evening I arrived home and he wasn't there. He had gone back into hospital as an emergency.

Unaware of this, and thinking that, like before, he would turn up again when he felt like it, I carried on with my normal daily routine, but the next day some relatives I hardly knew turned up when I came out of the Bullfighting School. And they took me to my Aunt Evelia's house: she was my father's sister and lived in Leganés, or Alcorcón – I can't remember which. That's where I met my sister.

I hadn't seen her, or so I thought at the time, since we'd been separated, and I couldn't remember her at all. My father, although he never mentioned my brother, was very fond of Maribel. Whenever he could, he would go to see her in the village in León, and he tried to bring her to Madrid, but my grandparents would never let him. One time I went with him to León, but all I can remember about it was the cows they kept, and how they did the milking. Of my sister – nothing.

I already knew that Bienvenido was on his way out, because they brought Maribel in haste to the same place they had taken me. Our aunts and uncles were very nice to us for the three or four days we were there, but we hardly spoke because we didn't know what to say. And then one morning, while I was washing my feet in the first bidet I had ever seen in my life, and had no idea what else it could be used for, my aunt came in and told me very tactfully that my father had died. There in that strange bathroom, I turned to stone. I tried to put on a brave face, but I broke down in tears, blubbing. My uncles and aunts tried to take my mind off it, and to make things better they bought me a pair of white, canvas John Smith trainers, which we boys thought were the bee's knees. I spent that night there, and the next morning, still wearing my new trainers, they took me to the hospital morgue. In those days there were no chapels of rest.

I didn't want to see the body of my father, or rather I didn't dare to, because I didn't want to have that image with me for ever. When they took me to the burial in the cemetery of La Almudena, it was freezing cold, even though it was already the month of March. All around, among the gravestones, talking among themselves in low voices, I could see some of our neighbours, and I knew that a lot of my father's brothers and sisters were there, and some of my cousins who I didn't know. There were also the teachers and some students from the Bullfighting School.

When the priest finished his bit, they made me stand in a row with the others to receive condolences from those present, but I couldn't manage more than two or three mourners. I did a quick about-turn, and told them all to go to hell. Perhaps I knew what was coming, because, only minutes later, standing before the fresh grave of my father, my future was going to be decided. The future of a twelve-year-old kid, left all alone in the world, like in a cheap novel.

At least it wasn't raining... It was 9th March 1982, an important year for Spain and for me. It was the year the football World Cup was held in Spain, the Rolling Stones played in Calderón Stadium, the Pope flew in from Rome, the socialists won the elections...and I was left an orphan without any prospects.

I have almost blanked out the memory of what happened that morning. I can't remember who I stood next to, or who took me to the cemetery, because I don't suppose it mattered. The one memory I have, as powerful as if it were yesterday, is the circle of my aunts and uncles, seven of the brothers and sisters of my father with their respective partners: Isabel, Nicolasa, Clemente, Pedro, Emilio, Doroteo...I am not sure of all their names because I hardly knew them.

They were arguing among themselves about who I should live with, but they each had an excuse for it not being them: that they had more children than the others; that they didn't earn enough to afford another mouth to feed; that, this or that. I heard everything that was being said there, right in front of me, because they didn't have the decency to talk about it somewhere else. Someone even put forward straight out the idea of putting me in an orphanage. I had this terrible sensation, like in a bad dream, that it was me down there in the grave waiting to be pulled out. I looked up towards the sky, and all their faces were looking down at me saying no, none of them could offer me a hand up.

Until suddenly, Enrique Martín Arranz appeared, my much-feared head of the Bullfighting School, to put an end to the squabbling. He did so in a stroke by asking them if they didn't feel ashamed of themselves, that this was not the time or the place.

'Decide whatever you want,' he said, 'but not in front of the boy, with your brother just buried.'

They didn't answer.

Later, just like my own father would have done, Enrique took me by the arm and led me away from that noisy mob. He put me in his car, asked me where I lived, and dropped me at my front door. That rough individual, who was so hard on us boys who were playing at being bullfighters, had never before that day had any dealings with me or shown me the slightest affection.

It was midday, but for me it seemed like night, a pitch-black, dark night, as I took my key out of my pocket, opened the door and went into my empty house. The blinds were down, and all the rooms, which had no heating, had that damp, clammy cold of an apartment that has been closed for days. It was then, in the silence and all alone, that I finally began to realise what had just happened to me. I saw the unmade bed, and knew that my father would never again be sleeping there, that I would never again have fights with him or laugh with him. I was alone. I was not yet thirteen, and I was truly alone.

Trembling with the cold and fear, I threw myself on my bed, crying out of confusion and anger. It took me some time, but, in despair, I pulled myself together, and picked up the phone to call Pepita in Moratalaz. After the last row, she hadn't gone to the burial. And through tears, sobbing, I asked her, begged her to come home, and not leave me alone. Even though streetwise and a rebel, that kid – which is what I was – still needed someone to help him grow up. And that same evening, Pepita made me dinner.

2

THE SCHOOL OF LIFE

My father was also a big bullfight aficionado. He had two season tickets in the Las Ventas bullring of Madrid, in the last row of seats in Tendido 4, next to Tendido 3. Tendido 4 is priced as Sol, the sunny side, which are the cheapest seats, but because he used to go every Sunday and knew the layout very well, he bought these seats because he knew that, when the first bull came out, he would already be in the shade. In other words, he was paying less for what others paid more. He knew his way around.

From time to time, he would take me with him to junior bullfights, novilladas, but I admit that I got bored easily, and I would play bottle-tops on the stone seating. The only time I paid attention was when things went wrong, the odd scare when something unusual or frightening happened in the ring; like the appearance of an espontaneo – a spectator jumping into the ring – or the bull leaping into the callejón, the corridor behind the fence, or the picador's horse being knocked over, or someone getting tossed...

And I liked repeating a cry which often used to be heard in those days, 'Down with Pimpi!' – he was the contractor for the picadors' horses. Whenever it went quiet, I would shout it out, to the amusement of my father's friends. Although I found the bulls boring because I didn't understand it, despite those who like to present themselves as supposedly protecting children by saying seeing bullfights is a traumatic experience, it wasn't for me, and it didn't turn me into a violent human being either, as argued by those who want to ban children from going to a bullring.

Bienve's favourite matador was Luis Segura, from Madrid, a man of great style, who died from a heart attack while appearing in an event in Valdemorillo. My father was always telling me about him. In fact, he told me about many others too: Antonio *Bienvenida*, Paco Camino... But Segura and *Miguelín* from Algeciras, they were his heroes. And he would defend them loudly in discussions in bars. Although I never saw them fight, I inherited a great admiration for those two.

But my father never managed to get me interested in the bulls. Until one day, playing football with my gang in the surroundings of Las Ventas, I saw a group of people milling around one of the doorways. We thought it was a fight, and we ran over to join the melee. But no, it wasn't a fight, just a bullfighter arriving with his cuadrilla, his team of assistants. I don't know who it was. Anyway, we thought it was cool, and we even plucked up courage to touch the embroidered suits, giggling as we did so. But whether or not it was a laugh, seeing a bullfighter close up, surrounded by admiring faces worshipping him, made a big impression on me. It was a revelation.

I didn't play any more football that day; I left my friends and began to think about what I had seen. So much so, that, when I got home, I said to my father that I wanted to go to the bulls again. 'But you don't like it, you little bugger!' he said, taken aback, all the more so since he had stopped taking me because he was fed up with the kid who kept shouting, 'Down with Pimpi!' and eating salami sandwiches without ever looking at the ring. 'Okay Dad, but I'm over that now,' and I told him what I had felt that afternoon.

Before that day, I always told people that I wanted to be a lawyer when I grew up, without really knowing what that meant. I must have heard someone say it, so every time I was asked, typical of kids, I said the same: a lawyer.

There was another spell when I wanted to work in the Mint, when I learnt that's where they made the money. Even more so, when I saw on television the speed at which the coins and notes shot out of the machines. It must be marvellous to work there, and when clocking off, pick up a bag and take a little bit of the money home; no one would notice with all that cash flying around. But my father put me straight on that when he told me that they frisked you as you left, so you couldn't get away with anything. That's why I decided that it wasn't worth thinking about my future there.

I was serious about being a bullfighter, and I said so. And I believed it. That's why Bienvenido took me back to Las Ventas on my tenth birthday, 1st May 1979. Another novillada. The afternoon went by as usual, and although this time I forced myself to pay attention, I couldn't see anything different from before. Until suddenly, a young matador, a novillero, wearing a suit of sky blue and gold, was tossed in the air by the bull. I can remember the scene very clearly: the novillero fell on his backside and was left sitting on the sand, as the bull turned round and charged at him again, with the horns passing very close to his head. Despite the shock, the guy got to his feet and began to work the bull with his small muleta cape really well, like nothing had happened.

I didn't know that the novillero was Juan Mora until some years later, on the day I had the ceremony of grading up to a full matador, my alternativa. After the corrida, where he had acted as official witness in the ceremony, I was telling him the story, and he told me that it was him. I thanked him because what I saw that afternoon, the way he responded to being tossed by pulling himself together with such character and elegance, and the way the public reacted to that by cheering 'Olé' like crazy, that impressed me like never before, and motivated me to want to try to do the same.

I began to spend my free time working the cape indoors at home, using the kitchen cloths, and although my father was delighted to see that at last I was becoming an aficionado, he told me that I could never be a bullfighter because I was scared stiff, and that I would cry my eyes out if I got the slightest scratch. Bienve didn't take me seriously; he thought it was just another silly childish fad. But because I went on and on about it, he took me one day to the park of Casa de Campo where the professionals used to train in the open air, so I could see for myself. They were grown-ups, all looking very serious, and it didn't mean much to me. But I kept nagging, and, at the next corrida in Las Ventas, we met by chance Pedro Simón, a novillero who my father knew, and who was at the Madrid School of Bullfighting, which had just opened in the same Casa de Campo. And he was the one who gave Bienve the idea to take me there.

One Sunday morning in early June, we turned up, and I liked what I saw. In a small bullring, there were a bunch of boys of my own age working their capes, and they made it look like a game. And because Bienve liked what he saw too, he asked questions about the set-up, and when he got the answers, he signed me up to start the next week.

When I went to give my details and to pay the first lot of subs, the head of the School asked me with a very straight face if I was just another one of those worthless gits who wanted to skip lessons, like all the others there who were just time wasters. 'Take him away, he's taking you for a ride,' he said to my father. That's how Enrique Martín Arranz greeted all new students, so they knew this wasn't a joke. I was taken aback, and I left the office full of embarrassment, but I suppose that Bienve must have been holding in his laughter.

When I'd finished signing up, the same day I started to train with the others; my father had already been to the Rastro flea-market, and bought me all the gear: the large cape, the capote, and the smaller one, the muleta – which were both too big for me – a dummy sword, the support stick for the muleta, and even a large cloth with squares to make a typical bundle like the maletillas, the itinerant toreros, carried. I think he enjoyed it all more than I did.

When I pulled the muleta out of the bundle, I began to swirl it round without really knowing what I was doing. I could have done with a book of instructions. But after a while, one of the boys came over and showed me how to hold it, and insert the support stick; and when I was about to start waving it around again – I didn't have the slightest idea what I was doing – one of the teachers came up and told me to put the cloth down, and to start walking. I was going round and round the ring until the class ended. Two whole hours! Then they showed me how to fold the capes properly, I tied them into my patterned cloth and they sent me home. The next day, the same thing happened: I assembled the muleta by myself, and as soon as I began to practise passes, they said the same to me again: put that down and start walking. And once more, walking and walking until the end of the day. This went on for three days. Later on, when I had made some progress, I plucked up courage to ask our teacher, don José de la Cal, why he made me do that.

'Because you didn't know how to walk, because you didn't walk like a bullfighter, a torero,' was his answer.

And he was right, because I walked like a cocky little street kid, on the balls of my feet and rolling my shoulders. A bit of a swank. Until he saw me walking with a straight back, and putting my feet flat on the ground, he wouldn't let me pick up a cape. Learn to walk properly, that was the first lesson they gave me in the Bullfighting School of Madrid. In a sense, those were my first steps in the world of the bulls.

MY FIRST TIME

I was just over ten years old but I made my own way to the school in Casa de Campo by myself. My father took me twice to show me the way, which metro to take, where to change trains. 'Remember this carefully,' he said, and on the third day he gave me the twelve pesetas the ticket cost and said, 'Off you go. You know the way. You don't need me along.' I don't know if it was because he was bored, or if it was to put me to the test, but he didn't stand on ceremony. It worked out for me and gave me confidence. I needed to go out into the world, and my father took me to the metro so I could do it on my own.

The classes at the Bullfighting School brought about a big change in the way of life I was used to, which was mainly drifting around La Guindalera, doing whatever took my fancy, mixing with older people; you couldn't mess them around, because they'd see through you immediately. It was like cutting the umbilical cord which held me to the neighbourhood. And at first it was hard to give up what I was used to, so, after a month or so, I stopped going to the Casa de Campo. I skipped classes for about ten or twelve days, and my father told me that, if I was tired of going to classes, I should say so, more than anything because he would stop paying for lessons, which must have been about a hundred or two hundred pesetas a month. But I thought long and hard, and went back. I decided that I really liked this bulls business.

They also gave us classes of physical education, under Salcedo as teacher. The first time they made us do running, I ended up out of breath, because I was overweight. I tried to wriggle out, saying that I had had rheumatic fever a few years back, and the doctor had told me that, if I overdid it, I could put a strain on my heart. But they didn't buy it. At first I didn't take it seriously, but the teachers soon showed me that it wasn't a laughing matter.

One time, they put up a poster saying that becoming a bullfighter isn't easy, and that it takes a miracle to become a star bullfighter. There were also photos of horn-wounds which scared the pants off us. When I saw Juan Mora that time on my birthday, I didn't think that a bull could kill you, but I quickly learnt that I was entering a tough world where to succeed you had to put your arse on the line, even if you were just a kid.

The hardest of them all was the head, Enrique Martín Arranz. He was born in the province of Segovia, in Riahuelas, a village near Riaza, and he'd become a bullfighter by taking the hard route of the maletilla, an itinerant going around the toughest amateur events in villages. He went through a lot before he got to wear a suit of lights, and because there were things he wasn't happy with in the system, he became a representative of novilleros in the trade union under Franco. He'd also been a student at a bullfight school in the town of Zamora. It had been set up at his own expense and in his own house by a lawyer, Manuel Martínez Molinero; as well as working as a bullfighting correspondent for the *Informaciones* newspaper, he was crazy about the bulls. In the mid-1960s, a large number of would-be bullfighters from all over Castille passed through his school. Some say he had as many as fifty students.

It was a brilliant idea, a terrific alternative for kids learning to become a bullfighter at a time when thousands took the risk in order to escape from poverty. But Molinero lacked the means to carry on with his project. Martín Arranz was always at his side encouraging him to keep going, because it was the best way to help young bullfighters, and to avoid all the bad experiences that he had gone through himself in the past.

During his time in the trade union, Enrique pioneered the idea that the Minister, Juan José Rosón, should establish a national bullfighting school under the leadership of Martínez Molinero. But, after a series of knock-backs every time he put the idea forward, eventually he decided to form a cooperative with other small-time bullfighters. Among many other activities, like having a specialised tailor to make low-cost bullfight clothing, and putting on novilladas, he finally got to realise the school project he had dreamed about obsessively.

With visionary strength, Martín Arranz kept on at the politicians so much that they finally gave him premises at the site of the International Country Fair in the Casa de Campo, which included a small bullring and other out-buildings for offices and classrooms. The place was almost a ruin when they took over, and they rebuilt it themselves. They did such a good job that, in no time at all, it was used to put on a benefit event for the Communist Party. Underneath the stands they built bunk-beds for students who came from outside Madrid, and a dining area, classrooms and professional training spaces, because the idea was always to give the students an education beyond the bulls as well.

With hardly any money, The National School of Tauromachy, as it was then called at the time, began to function at the same time as the political transition in Spain, in October 1976, and the novilleros of the cooperative were the first students, swiftly followed by a load of other kids who signed up in a short time.

When I joined in 1979, I was already number 181 at the School. In just over two years, many hopefuls had already passed through the School, some of them no more than kids, others grown men, all with the dream of becoming a torero. Several had already made a start in the profession, but three junior becerristas stood out, and they were the best shop-window for the school: Julián Maestro, Lucio Sandín and José Cubero *Yiyo*, who were known as 'The Princes of Bullfighting'.

After a year spent learning to move the capes and familiarise myself with the whole business, the first time they actually put me in front of a heifer was a few days before Madrid's San Isidro Fair in 1980, on 4th May, in one of the classes which they put on for the public on Sunday mornings. I was a bit scared when the teachers told me that at last I was going to face a heifer, but not because I was frightened of the heifer, so much as the thought that I could make a fool of myself in front of the others. Because I knew full well that I didn't yet know enough.

Before they let the heifer out, as was the usual practice, the boys drew lots for the order we were to appear in the ring. I was number eleven, and *El Madrileño* was number twelve; he was another one of us who was going to face a heifer for the first time, and his father was encouraging him from a seat behind the fence. While the others had their turn, I was panicking and hiding in a position of safety, sticking my head out from time to time and listening to the people's laughter inside my head. The last thing I was worried about was the heifer.

When my turn came, I was so nervous that I immediately told *Madrileño* to take my place. I was so embarrassed that I thought, because there'd already been a lot of boys before me, the animal would get tired and the teachers would cut things short, and leave me for another time. I'd just made up my mind that's what would happen when they called out, 'Next! Number twelve!' And there wasn't anyone else for me to change places with.

Swallowing my fear of being ridiculous, as if I was performing a duty, I went slowly out into the ring. I was wearing a sweater, a pair of jeans, and trainers. Nothing like a torero, because I wasn't one.

I walked slowly up to the heifer, looking straight into its eyes, which were fixing me with a menacing stare.

I called it, and with a chest pass, just like they told me would happen, the heifer passed close by me without touching me. It turned, and more confidently than before, I called it again, but this time it hit me cleanly in the hip. It didn't hurt. I took up position again, and it knocked me over again. Five more times it did this, and I only managed to get two clean passes. The only picture I have of this day is not of a pass, but of one of the times it hit me.

I suppose that the teachers were happy to see that I had held my ground and hadn't panicked, because at last they told me to leave the ring. That was the test they set for us youngest students that morning. They didn't say anything to me, neither good nor bad. But, although I was hardly aware of what had happened, I felt relieved because at least no one had laughed at me. I folded up my muleta, and went straight to the toilets to check if the calf had caused me any damage. When I dropped my trousers and saw that little horn-wound on my thigh, scarcely a scratch really, for the first time I felt like a torero. I had a cornada and they had applauded me. I grew at least two metres. It was the best day of my life.

IDOLS AND MASTERS

After that first time, that marvellous experience, I just kept improving, learning quickly and more keenly, and with growing interest. Like when you find out about sex, and you stop being afraid of it. I was so into it all that, soon afterwards, I put my name down for a competition organised by the Las Ventas bullring in Madrid, without saying anything to anyone; the jury included the top matadors Domingo Ortega and Paco Camino, as well as the bull-breeder, Victorino Martín.

There were lots of other boys entering, and the Acevedo brothers came all the way up from Seville to the ranch in El Escorial. First prize was a capote, a muleta, and an appearance in a junior event, a becerrada, they were putting on in the Las Ventas bullring. And I went and won it! Second came Álvaro Acevedo, who is now a taurine critic, but his father argued that we should share the first prize, not so much for the sake of the capes prize as that he wanted his son to appear in the becerrada, which was organised by a group of people who didn't see eye to eye with the teachers at the School.

When Enrique Martín Arranz heard that I was appearing in the event, because they asked him for my credentials, he called me into the office, and he asked me very coldly who I had spoken to about entering the competition. He told me that appearing in the Madrid bullring, even if it was only a becerrada, was a very serious business, and that I wasn't ready for it. So he banned me from appearing in Las Ventas, or else he would have me expelled. So what happened was that, although my name was on the posters, I didn't actually appear in that becerrada event. Later, I would have many more opportunities to appear in that same bullring, and I would reach the very top.

As I was already crazy about the bulls, my father took me as well to capeas, informal events in the countryside. He was from Guadalajara, where there were lots of capeas, so he liked to go to spend the day with his mates, and go around with the novillero Manolo Gómez, who was the brother of one of his cronies.

The people who ran those rough and ready events were José Luis Sedano and Aurelio Calatayud, who had a huge team of South Americans who fought those monster bulls in crude bullrings with a fountain and a lamp post in the middle, fenced off in the old style with carts and trailers. The so-called toreros did what they could in those dangerous circumstances, and then they would bring me out to show off a few passes without a bull, to entertain the crowd, and at the same time, just as I had done in my father's taxi, to encourage them to give more generously when they 'passed the hat', with their capes spread out to catch the coins the public threw.

Luckily, because it would have been a disaster, I never got to fight in those capeas in Guadalajara, but that's where I began to really admire and respect what those men did with the bulls, especially Manolo Gómez, who was like a god to me. He showed me photos of his first appearance in Mexico City, in that huge bullring of Plaza

Mexico, and when I saw him standing up in front of those frightening animals, he looked every inch a hero.

One day, he lent me a capote to give four or five verónica passes to a calf, and that pleased me: to think that the capote which I was just pretending with had already been used in a real event – it even had a mark made by the horn of a novillo – a young bull. I was as proud as hell when I showed it off at the School.

Because I was already a junior torero, neighbours and friends of my father from the bars around organised an event in the countryside, up in the mountains, just for me. But the animals were so 'experienced' that they caught me out time after time, and I lost it, and forgot all about what toreros call 'sitio', my self-confidence when in front of an animal.

When they started up again with practical classes in the School, I couldn't keep my feet still, not at all. When they saw this, the teachers realised what had happened, and they warned me not to perform by myself again. When you're starting out, and you don't know enough about it, it's very easy to lose that delicate mental state that you need to control your fear over the danger.

Those madmen who taught us made us learn about bullfighting with great patience; one step at a time, as it should be. Martínez Molinero, who was a great aficionado, had a considerable natural gift for teaching. He was the one we liked best: he was a diamond. When he died in 2011, it made me very sad, because he was a genuinely decent man.

I can still see him immaculately dressed in a suit and tie, showing he had self-respect, and demanding respect in return. What I would call every inch a torero, although he had never actually been one. He always wore an impeccable black felt Cordoba hat, without fail. You had to be quite a character to wear a Cordoba hat in the street in those days.

In his classes, using very detailed illustrations which he had made himself, Molinero took it upon himself to teach the youngest students the culture of the bullfight: its history, the detail of the rituals, the order of priorities in the parade, the process of dominating the bull, where to stand in the ring, the various acts, the passes, the terrains...

He had never fought a bull, at least not professionally, but he knew a great deal about them, and, in a friendly manner, he put across even the most difficult ideas for a child to take in, so we never got bored, which was quite an achievement. We learnt to walk out on the sand with the proper bearing; how to wrap the special cape used in the parade around ourselves; how to dedicate the bull; how to wear a suit of lights; to behave properly in the street; and to give older toreros the respect they deserve. He even set us tests about these things, and to keep up our motivation, he organised competitions on Sundays and paid out cash prizes from his own pocket: for the best pair of banderillas, for the most varied series of passes with the capote... He taught us exercises which were very much his own, such as moving our capes all together and marking the rhythm with a whistle. A few clever-dicks laughed at him, but that was the best way to keep us concentrated and synchronised.

It wasn't easy to teach a gang of forty or fifty uncivilised teenagers. But Molinero managed it with style. His aim was to ensure that, when we went out to perform, whether in the countryside or in a bullring, we should know all the time exactly where to stand, and that we would always behave with the dignity of a torero, with that mix of arrogance and formality. That's why, when I went to my first event testing calves, a tentadero, in Salamanca, everything went as sweet as a nut. In theory, I had already done the same thing three hundred times with Maestro Molinero.

Enrique Martín Arranz was the same when he took us out into the countryside to perform with heifers. He wouldn't let us repeat a finishing pass with the capote, to position them in front of the horse, because if you did repeat it, or if you went into the same exit, or burladero, already occupied by your companion in the tienta, he sent you to wait up at the top. We weren't even allowed to talk when there was a heifer in the ring. One time, I remember, because someone said something in a whisper, he made him hitchhike home to Madrid.

You had to be quick on your feet, and not miss a chance, always thinking of the correct procedure, and concentrating hard on the behaviour of the heifers, because, if you followed on from a mate and you started with the horn which had already shown itself to be tricky, or if the animal caught you because you did something silly, he would pull you out of there immediately, so that the next time you would be more on your toes.

Another one of the teachers who left his mark on me was José de la Cal, who'd been a novillero before the Civil War, and then a banderillero with several top matadors. Although he was getting on, he was another one of those men who you only had to look at to know that they had been a torero. He too always wore a tie, with a handkerchief showing three points sticking up out of the top pocket of his jacket, with his long-peaked tweed cap, his trousers with turn-ups, and a pair of handmade country-style boots. In the winter, he wore a coat with a fox-fur collar. He never lost his air of a veteran torero: someone to be admired.

When he retired as a banderillero, Don José worked as the secretary of the Fighting Bulls Breeders' Association, because he knew all there was to know about toros bravos, fighting bulls. He knew all about the breeding-lines and origins of every herd, and that's what he taught us about: the bloodlines, the hide colours, the horn types, the physiques, the behaviour characteristics of every line… Fundamental knowledge for every torero. He also set us exams. Many years later he said that he remembered very well the only two students he had awarded ten out of ten to: *Yiyo* and me. He made it a condition that we had to pass his exams to be allowed to face the heifers, and maybe that's why I paid so much attention in his classes.

De la Cal spoke to us a lot about the way things were with the bulls when he was young. He taught us about the character, behaviour and those qualities which are so hard to define in being a torero. But he had it. He told us about Marcial Lalanda, Félix Rodríguez, *Cagancho*, Victoriano de la Serna and all the other great toreros from his times, and always with such energy and enthusiasm that he made it seem like he had them standing there in front of us. He knew how to communicate that magic of the bulls, which we felt when they showed us old films. Because on Fridays in the winter, when it was cold and we stayed indoors, we were visited by Pepe Gan and Domingo, his assistant, who had an amazing film library.

The first time I saw a film of *Manolete* was one afternoon when they showed us the famous documentary about his first appearance in Mexico, with the lame man with crutches lolloping up the stairs to get a seat, with people jumping up and clutching their heads in their hands, seeing *Manolete* perform in the ring...

For some reason, I asked Gan, who was a Cordoban through and through, who this guy was, and he went berserk, 'Are you asking who he is? Listen sonny, Manuel Rodríguez *Manolete*, that's who it is, the greatest torero in history! Now do you understand? Aren't you ashamed to ask such a question?'

I begged his pardon after such a telling off and I sank back in my seat. But when I saw that super-hero creating a storm, and how the bull gave him a serious cornada, a horn-wound, and how he remained standing as if nothing had happened, and with all the crowd throwing their hats into the ring, and the ring becoming a mad-house, I realised that Gan was quite right. I was very excited about *Manolete*, his stillness, his personality... This was another of my early moments of revelation, one of the most powerful, which stayed in my memory and inspired in me a passion to become a torero. From that day on, I looked differently at that ragged copy of *El Ruedo* magazine, the special issue with the death of *Manolete*, which my father bought in the Rastro flea-market.

When I was a kid, I didn't know why Bienve kept that scruffy bundle of paper like it was a treasure, but after seeing the film, it became a sacred object for me too. At the same time, after seeing the crowds of fired-up spectators, I fell in love with Mexico for ever. Who could have told me then that fifty years after the triumphs of my idol, I too would cut the maximum trophy of a tail in the Mexican capital?

With those films, the teachers succeeded in giving us a passion for the bulls, and made us admire the all-time greats. The same thing had happened to us with Bruce Lee, but instead of leaving the cinema practising our kicks, we now began copying the great matadors we had just seen: *Manzanares, Rafael de Paula,* Curro Romero, Pepín

Martín Vázquez, Paco Camino… They inspired me so much that in school I amused myself by drawing bullfight posters with my name next to those of the giants. I imagined myself appearing with those great maestros from the years of the Republic. I acted out wrapping myself in the jacket of my Adidas tracksuit, placing the stripes like the braid of the special parade capes, and I imagined myself waiting in the plaza surrounded by legendary matadors. My biggest hero was Victoriano de la Serna, probably because of Martín Arranz, who rated him highly and, like him, was from Segovia; he showed us one hundred thousand times how that genius performed his mythical verónica pass.

That's how those madmen passed on the magic of forgotten times to a distant generation of kids who were so very different. My idols of those years were not footballers or pop singers, like normal kids. Not even the toreros of my time. My real idols, although I hadn't seen them, were those giants of long ago, with their legendary aura.

I'm sure that all this went on to influence my own style in the ring. Because unconsciously I had developed a feeling for the way things were. I would have given everything to be able to perform with the mythical figures from those times. When I stepped into the ring, without knowing it, I was trying to realise all those images from the past and the solemn faces which the older teachers told us about; they inspired a passion for the bulls in us, and they showed us how to dream.

We were also lucky enough that hanging in the cupboards at the School were several suits for use in becerradas. They were old and worn out, but for us they were like sacred objects. It was fantastic to put on a jacket in secret, touch the faded gold thread in the tassels, and slip on the taleguillas, the trousers, although they were far too big for us. What a marvellous way to feed a dream.

With all of this, almost without noticing, even though we were still children, we entered into a real world that was much tougher than what awaited other boys of our age. Because they not only taught us how to fight bulls, but they also taught us about strength of character, intelligence, commitment, the importance of sacrifice, to respect those who had gone before us, to stay true to type all the time, even when we were scared stiff, even when things didn't work out. To maintain at all times the dignity of a torero.

Strangely enough, although I was a streetwise hooligan, it was no trouble adapting to the harsh regime of my apprenticeship. I don't know if it was because they knew how to get the best out of me, or because I could already see that this was a good way to get on, but that's how they sorted me out and put the finishing touches. Those values engrained in me by those teachers, that way of how to behave in the face of the bull, and in life too, will be my guidelines until the day I die. Because, as the years go by, following their example, I have won the day many times and in many ways, especially in the most difficult circumstances.

LIVING IN THE JUNGLE AT CASA DE CAMPO

Although they had very little money, the Madrid School of Bullfighting in those days worked incredibly well. Additionally, everything was run on democratic lines, and almost all decisions – except for administrative ones – were taken by the students, voting by a show of hands. For example, that's how we decided if one or other of us was ready or not to face heifers in training sessions. There was even room for a bit of rebellion, like when we stood up against Andrés Vázquez, one of the ex-matadors we had as a teacher.

Because he was the godfather of Luis Miguel Calvo, the son of one of his banderilleros, Andrés openly favoured him above the other students. When there were heifers to perform with, he fiddled the order to make sure his godson had a go, or else – because that was the sort of individual he was – he would have a go himself to keep himself fit, for when he decided to make a comeback. 'This is how it should be done!' he would say to us, when we should have been out there instead of him.

But because we were all supposed to be on an equal footing, that didn't go down well with any of us. Until one day, all down to me, the bomb went off. Andrés Vázquez himself told us that if we didn't feel like practising with the cape, or with the carretón (a simulated bull's head on wheels), we shouldn't do it, because there was a danger that we could pick up bad habits or develop faults. So, one day, when he was teaching us how to enter for the kill, it came to my turn and I refused to do it.

'Hey you, Pastyface,' which was what he called me, 'pick up the sword!'

'No, Sir. You have told us that we shouldn't do something when we don't feel like it, and today I don't want to practise killing,' I answered, a bit cheekily.

We had a few words – would I? wouldn't I ? – until he got fed up, turned on his heel and stormed off towards the office. In five minutes, he was back, bringing Enrique Martín Arranz with him, looking very serious. The head came straight up to me, grabbed me by the arm and took me aside. And he explained something that I have always remembered:

'Look. In life there are two types of people: those who give the orders and those who take them. Right now, you take orders, and the maestro hands them out, and today he has the upper hand. In life, you should always try to be the one in charge, but only when you're up to it. For now, you are expelled for three days.'

That was just one clash I had with him, but my fellow students all had problems with Andrés. And things went from bad to worse. So, when the teachers called us together for our monthly grievances meeting after the incident of my expulsion, we all complained about him. I suppose I led the revolt, because I thought his behaviour was unfair, not only with me but with all the others too, so I didn't mind sticking my neck out. Because Andrés had already done other stuff favouring Calvo, and contrary to the principles of the School and against certain students, he was made to leave. I was sorry, because he wasn't a bad person. And what's more, he was a great torero.

That's how it was in the Madrid School of Bullfighting then. We respected discipline, but we also expressed our own opinions about all sorts of things. And the parents didn't complain to the teachers, because that would have created problems for their kids. We were a very special family group. At least in the early years, because, later on, things changed...

The teachers got on very well together. The original members, and those who arrived later: *Serranito*, Luis Morales, Gregorio Sánchez, *Tinín*... But the only one who kept us all in order was Enrique Martín Arranz. Because he was so strict and so direct, he reflected the real toughness of the bullfighting world, the harsh realities. We were all terrified of him, and he knew how to take charge with a single look. He was as hard as iron. He had to be: without discipline, the whole project would have been impossible. In those days, the School had students from every kind of background, different lifestyles, from very different levels of education, with different kinds of ability. Like you get in military national service. We were forty or fifty boys of all ages, twenty or so on days when there were normal classes, and the whole lot when there were heifers to be fought, because no one failed to turn up then.

Some came from a distance, and slept there, like *Chinorri*, *el Hueverito* and Miguel Murillo, who came from Extremadura in the west of the country, and they were more than twenty years old. There were people from France like Stephan Pons, and Loren *el Rubio de Paris*, who's a painter now. And there was *el Sevillita*, and *Manolete*, who was from Galicia and wore pebble-glasses and was never without a transistor radio clamped to his ear; *Illuminado*, who's now the caretaker at the School; Picornell, a Catalan weighing one hundred and twenty kilos; *el Avestruz*... I'll never forget *Ropero*, a street kid who worked as a labourer, and did all the little repair jobs in the School. He used to tell anyone who would listen that, one day, he was going to change 'the paleta for the muleta' – the trowel for the muleta. He always wore a sweater, in summer and winter, and he kept away the cold by stuffing his sweater with newspapers...and by getting out of his head on cheap aniseed liquor. There were also older novilleros, who'd already fought quite a few bulls, like Luis Miguel Villalpando, Vicente Yestera, *Chocolate*, Fernando Galindo, the Cubero brothers, Pedro Simón, Luis Miguel Campano, Gitanillo Vega, and then, of course, the ones already on the road to success: *Yiyo*, Sandín and Maestro...

Every one of them was an individual, all different, but each of them was looking for a way to deal with life and their passion for the bulls, and it didn't always turn out well. I remember Pablito Nevado, a becerrista working with young calves, from Valencia de Alcántara, who we called *Paulita* because his style was very artistic. He was a rough diamond. But in him we saw the effect the city can have on a country lad; a few weeks after his arrival, he was already going around in a leather jacket, with his Ramones T-shirt, dark glasses... He just lost it.

There were all sorts there, all right, and more than one crook. But while at the School, they concentrated on looking for a job, especially those who slept there. A few businessmen who were also aficionados, like the one who owned Peña Tiles, used to give them part-time jobs.

It was like a jungle. As well as being on your toes with the bulls, you had to watch your back, because the others were constantly trying to put one across on you all the time. There was a lot of competition, and there were gang leaders, on one hand the day students, and on the other the older boys who lived in; it was a feudal system. Enrique made them responsible for what happened when they were left on their own. If there was a problem, he would call them to book, and handed out punishments like cleaning the lavatories, or else he would expel them. It was just like being in the army.

Because I was streetwise, I knew instinctively how to deal with such wildlife. To start with, because I was on the small size, I wasn't considered as competition by the top dogs, and they treated me as some kind of mascot: I was known as *Lentejita* ('Little Lentil') because I was on the chubby side... *Yiyo* gave me that name, and he made me wheel the carretón for him all day long for him to practise his capework. Until the time when I began to play a more important role, and I even became a top dog in my own right, in every way.

Apart from training, in most other things we were pretty much hooligans. In class, we were supervised and disciplined, but you can't take the street out of a street kid. All said and done, we were still kids, and what we loved most was being vandals. And just like wolves, when we were in a pack, we were dangerous. We had a go at everything.

My best mate, or the closest to that, was Perea, Pedro José Perea, not forgetting Luisito Adán, who was always around. We were inseparable. Luisito and I stole a muleta which Curro Vázquez had given to some friends for a country capea. They wouldn't let us join in the capework, but at least we got something out of it. Tomás, the sword-handler in charge of the equipment, had invited us, and we drove him crazy looking for that missing muleta.

But as well as my buddies, another one in the team was Ramón García, who we called *Soro*, and who is now a television cameraman. Then there was *Manili* and *Caye*, who joined the Civil Guard. We used to meet up to pinch bikes and to fight with other gangs.

There was also a bunch of kids from the districts of Carabanchel and Useras – a right lot: Fernando José Plaza, Juan Patricio González, *Cachas Negras*, *Montenegro*, *Mestizo*... And there was a bunch from Fuenlabrada and thereabouts: the *Fundi* brothers, *Portu*, Sandoval, *Ocho y Media*, another blond kid who did break-dance... The only one who didn't fit in was Carlos Neila, who lived in the up-market district of Salamanca, and went to a religious school. As he was so prissy, we used to take the mickey, 'What, you don't ever have a wank? Well, fuck me mate!'

You had to be quick on your feet, or they would have you. As soon as you arrived, they would look you up and down, and the wise guys, when they spotted your weak points, would give you a nickname that you could never shake off. We called Juan Carlos Belmonte '*Super*' because one day he was telling us a story and he said he was saved by 'el instinto de supervivencia' – his instinct to survive. Curro Cavas was very quiet, and always said that he had to leave at half-past eight, so it wasn't hard to work out why we gave him the name *Ocho y Media* ('Eight-Thirty'). Nearly all the names, including my own, were dreamt up by *Yiyo*, who was a complete comedian. He was a really good guy, and great fun, but got up to all sorts of scrapes. He knew all the dirty tricks, and he liked nothing better than putting the wind up the youngest ones.

A SHORT ACCOUNT OF SOME OF OUR MISCHIEF

We didn't have a single good idea. Among dozens of others, the stunt which got us most noticed was what we did to the windows of the conference building next to the School. It went something like this: there were these enormous windows right next to where twenty or so boys passed their spare time... Sometimes, especially in the holidays, we would take our sandwiches there, or even take food and cook it there. *El Chinorri* used to make a dish of potatoes and chickens' feet – not drumsticks, the actual feet! – and it tasted marvellous. Stuck in the School from nine in the morning until seven at night, we got really fed up with training, and suddenly we would start to laugh and muck about: we would douse one another with the water-hoses, have races with the carretones...

One of those evenings, towards the end of spring, bored with everything, I went for a walk and arrived at the conference building where they had just finished filming *Carmen*, and I saw the huge windows... I stood looking at them for a while, and then just for the fun of it, wondering what sort of noise it would make, I threw a stone and *crash!* The sound of the broken glass falling to the ground must have been heard miles away, because in an instant all my mates were there: *Mestizo, Luisito*, Perea, Bote, *el Fundi*, the Felipe brothers, who we used to call '*Los Pelaillas*'...

'Whassup?'

I couldn't help myself. 'Did you see that, it's fantastic!'

I picked up another stone, and did it again. Maybe I threw another one, but, when I did, the noise was like an artillery bombardment. We didn't leave a single window untouched. Unluckily for us, we'd forgotten there was a police station about a hundred metres away, and they heard the racket too.

When I reached the School, I saw one of the *Pelaillas* boys running like blazes trying to hide in one of the rooms, because behind him was a policeman with an iron bar in his hand. And then I saw Perea trying to hide behind some bushes.

The way with our bunch was that, whatever we did, if one of

us was caught, he didn't know anyone else. It was his problem, and he had to deal with it on his own. But the cop caught *Rati*, Perea, whose father was a Civil Guard, and he screamed at him '*Sonofabitch*, let me go, you fucking bastard!', while he was being dragged along by one leg.

We all went up to get him, to make him let go, but the cop had that iron bar and we couldn't get close. And he took Perea off to the station and, very shaken, the rest of us went home.

The next day, there was a corrida in Las Ventas, and we used to meet up before the corrida at a doorway of the plaza so that Martín Arranz could take us inside. When I was close enough, he gave me a clip round the ear, which still hurts.

'Tell your glass-breaking friends I want to see all of them back here after the corrida; make sure they all turn up,' he hissed.

And he named each and every one of the culprits.

I found them easily enough, because, at that time, the boys from the School handed out the corrida programmes.

'Perea must have grassed us up,' I told them nervously, 'because Enrique knows who we all are.'

After the corrida, Martín Arranz told us to be at the Casa de Campo at seven o'clock the next morning, so that we would still have time to go to day school. I told them at home that I had a tentadero and had to leave early.

When I woke up, I grabbed my bag and books and left for the Bullfighting School on the first metro train. They were all there, scared shitless, some crying and blubbing that their father was going to kill them. Enrique arrived almost immediately and at once asked who it was who began the damage. No one spoke. A minute went by which seemed like an eternity before I plucked up courage to take the first step.

'I started it, but I only threw three stones. That's all I did. I don't know what anyone else did, because I went back to training and left them there.'

Luisito Adán began to laugh nervously, but Sheriff Arranz scared him into silence. Then José Luis Bote spoke up that he had only thrown one stone, at a piece of glass on the ground. The ratbag! And one by one, the rest of us owned up.

Enrique's punishment for us was that, during the San Isidro Fair, we had to go to the School at seven every morning for class, and leave for day school directly from there. When school ended at six, we had to go back to Casa de Campo to paint the plaza. We didn't dare to drop out. That was the San Isidro in which *Yiyo*, for the first time, was carried out on shoulders after a great triumph. The only one of us who saw it was José Luis Bote; because he was a neighbour of *Yiyo* in Canillejas, and he escaped that day and took refuge in a seat up in the gods.

We were lucky. When we left the telling-off, we thought that they would make us pay for the replacement windows. I skipped day school, and knowing that at home we didn't have two coins to rub together, I went with Perea to the Calle Leganitos, parallel to Gran Vía, to get an idea from a glazier's there of what it might cost. We told them that our parents had asked us to get a quote for windows of such and such a size and shape. It came to a whole packet of money! We were terrified. And because we couldn't tell our families that they had to pay out all that money, we talked about going to Alicante to get work, and sleeping on the beach. But as time went by, it was all forgotten. I think it must have been that no one had to pay for the windows – because it was a municipal building, and because they knew that kids had vandalised it, they must have put it down to general maintenance.

That wasn't the only spot of bother we got into. We pulled a lot more strokes, some of them really crazy, which is what we were at the time. One time, Perea said that he had been to the Waxworks Museum, and there was a whole room dedicated to famous toreros. It was all the rage at the time for aficionados to have a tassel from a suit of lights on their keyring, so we went to the museum the next morning. We met up very early, when there weren't many people around; there was Perea, the *Pelaos, Madriles* and me, each of us with a pair of scissors in his pocket. We bought tickets, and when they opened the doors, we shot straight to the room which Perea had told us about. We set about pinching the tassels from all the suits of lights on the waxwork figures, from the jackets and the trousers. We missed one, because we heard a museum attendant coming. Even the tragic scene of the death of Granero didn't escape our attentions.

On some days after classes, we'd go down to the lake in Casa de Campo. Someone noticed that the attendants always left the motorboat out in the middle of the lake overnight. One evening when it was already dark, we had the mad idea of getting out to the motorboat. We broke the padlock of the kayak school hut, took out a boat, rowed out to the motorboat, and started to play at pirates, fighting one another to board the boat. Obviously, some of us fell in the water. After that business, they put on a night security man.

Another time, we had a go at the refreshment kiosks by the lake. The owner of one of them was friendly to us, and, because he was an aficionado, he gave us credit. But the bill got too big, so he asked us to pay it off. We tried to think of ways to do that: we went to the kiosk next door, grabbed one of the chewing gum machines, the type with coloured balls, and *Mestizo* and Luisito kicked it like they were possessed, until the coins started to come out. The three of us robbed it, squabbling to get the coins just like when you see shops looted in a riot on TV. We got over one thousand pesetas, which was enough to pay off what we owed, and with enough left over to have a few more celebrations as well. Similarly, all the other chewing gum machines from all the other kiosks in Casa de Campo went the same way.

In the station of the metro line which passed right in front of the School, we got up to our usual tricks. We would hide behind the wall next to the park, waiting for the front of the train to pass by, so that, as soon as the driver couldn't see us, we ran down towards the track to get in the carriages. We used to hold the doors open so they couldn't close, we climbed from one carriage to the next... We died laughing, but we didn't know that we were risking our lives. The metro people got wise to us, and one day they set a trap for us with the police, but we saw them first, and had the bright idea to pelt them with stones; we did the same thing, throwing stones at the windows of the carriages from time to time. We were a danger to the public at large.

I spent more time with that wild gang than I did with my father or Pepita. I suppose they were like the brothers I didn't have. We had a great sense of team spirit, and we would sacrifice ourselves, and fight for one another as if it were for ourselves. With the exception of the days when there were heifers to fight in the School; on those days, there was no such thing as friends. Our faces changed and it was every man for himself until the end of the session, then we went back to getting up to our mischief.

MY BOOTS WERE PAID FOR OUT OF IMMORAL EARNINGS

That was one of the best periods of my life, because I escaped from the problems at home, and because I was on my own, I learnt the value of friendship. When I became a full matador, I always liked to have in my team, my cuadrilla, people who had been in the School: like Juan Cubero, Antonio Romero, Venancio Veneros, David Pirri, Victor Hugo... Not just out of friendship, but also because the students had been taught the job well, and they were good professionals.

Critics of taurine schools said that they were like factories churning out toreros by the dozen, all identical. Not true. In the Madrid School, none of us was like any of the others. Each of us developed our own personality over time, with as much variety as possible, and above all, having a fantastic apprenticeship in the profession.

But in those early years is when I started to experience the gloom which all toreros have from the beginning. In the conversations and long walks with my friend Perea, we were always grumbling about the unfair way we were dealt with at the School.

Both of us liked classic bullfighting, and we thought we were the best. We only saw faults in the others, and we happily kept our distance from them. Inevitably, our sense of competiveness created, deep down, a sense of pride and arrogance, and the concerns felt by anyone who puts themselves in front of a bull.

Two years went by between starting at the School and my first becerrada. Although I'd appeared as sobresaliente, a substitute, a week earlier in Aranjuez, and got to give a few cape passes and placed a pair of banderillas, the date of my real debut in public was 7th June 1981, in the bullring of Trujillo, with José Luis Bote and a local lad. We couldn't get a hotel, or use the Town Hall or school building, which is what usually happened in villages, so we had to get dressed into our bullfighting clothes in the actual bullring. Before the corrida, we decided to have a nap lying on our capes in the passage from the ring to the infirmary. The three of us laid down there – *el Fundi* had joined us as sobresaliente – when we noticed a large dried blood stain which led up to the door of the infirmary. We knew at once that the blood belonged to *Morenito de Maracay*, a matador who had received a serious goring there a few days earlier. That was a terrible way to start your first appearance in a bullring!

My clothing may have been borrowed, but the boots I wore that day had been bought for me by a group of prostitutes from my neighbourhood. Because my father was 'inside', Pepita and I didn't have enough money to buy a pair of boots. But that was no setback, because the 'little torero' was already well known in La Guindalera.

Ever since I started at the School, whenever I walked home from the metro, the local 'working girls' would stop me as they stood in the doorways to the clip joints, or I might be looking inside for my father; they would invite me to a lemonade while I told them all my adventures with the bulls. A group of them, together with the owner of the La Pista bar, had the idea to make a collection to buy my boots for me, the cheapest ones in Los Guerilleros in the square of Tirso de Molina.

My first calf in Trujillo was a one-year-old from the ranch of Ángel Ortega, or at least, that's what they said it was. This was the first animal I got to kill, and also the first one I caped from the outset, because in Aranjuez I had just given a few odd passes, and in the School the older boys got to cape them before me.

Performing passes well with the big cape, the capote, is harder than with the smaller muleta, because you have to coordinate both arms together perfectly. I could do it in practice, but I didn't really have a feeling for the texture or the weight of the material. So the calf gave me two or three whacks almost before I got started.

As a souvenir, I still have a mark on my left hand from where it stepped on me.

During the days before my debut, I was full of doubts, because I didn't know how things would turn out: because I had never before caped a bull from the outset, I had never faced a male calf, and above all, because I had never killed before. Performing in public didn't worry me so much, because I'd already performed in public on many occasions. And I could manage well enough with the muleta, because I'd already done that with ten or fifteen calves in the School. Luckily, I got through it all quite well, and I even got the sword in first time, and the calf dropped like a stone. I felt good when they gave me the trophy of two ears.

On the way back with Martín Arranz and a friend of his, I didn't feel like talking. I pretended to be asleep in the back of the car, and they began to talk about me and my performance. They decided that I was coming along, and that I had the makings of a torero. They dropped me off at the School, and I picked up my bag and went home, pleased as Punch. When I opened the door, reality hit me, and my spirits sank: I couldn't tell my father about it, because he was in the nick in Carabanchel and wouldn't be let out until the middle of July. Later on in the summer, when I came home after my first time in France, at Mont-de-Marsan, I found him there, sitting on the sofa. And, that day, we could talk sensibly about the bulls, not like the previous time when he walloped me for contradicting what he'd said about a torero, and I told him he was a joke.

Those first trips to appear in junior bullfights, and to get to know the world, were like the holidays I never had. I remember that, when I was little, we went once or twice to stay with a friend of Pepita in Alicante. And another year, we went to my father's village for the annual fiesta, but I broke my shoulder-bone and we had to leave almost immediately. As I was growing up, and started school, the other kids would brag that they had been to this place or that, to the seaside, or to England, but I hadn't even been outside Madrid. On the very hot days in summer, I sneaked into the swimming pool at the Casa de Campo Lake, got changed behind a hedge, hid my clothes, and went for a dip. So, when the kids at school started to go on about their holidays, I puffed out my chest and told them that, in a few short years, when I was a torero, I would have a huge car so I could go wherever I pleased.

I said it with great confidence, because in those early becerradas around the villages, I was already seeing a bit of money. We didn't get paid, but we cottoned on to the idea of dedicating the bull to the well-off spectators, or to the toreros who went to see us, because we knew that they were certain to give us something by way of a tip: two hundred, a thousand, five hundred pesetas... And, one time, Curro Vázquez even gave me five thousand smackers.

When I had saved up my first two thousand pesetas, I knew exactly what I was going to spend it on. I had seen in the shop window of a local shoe shop, just up from my house, a pair of Yuma trainers which were all the rage, and they were on special offer for 1,999 pesetas. I saw them when I passed by every day, and, for me, they stood for something special: quality trainers, not like the cheap rubbish I usually wore.

When I finally got the money together, the very next day I left school running so I got to the shoe shop before they closed. I arrived out of breath just as they were closing the door, and I asked for the pair of Yumas I'd been dreaming about.

'What size?' said the shopkeeper.

'Thirty-seven.'

'Haven't got it,' he said, 'only one pair left, two sizes smaller.'

'I'll have them,' I said abruptly.

I squeezed them on, very tight, but because I really wanted them, I took a deep breath and wore them home. I wore them for more than two years, until they fell to pieces, worn out because they were too small. My toes are still squashed, like a geisha girl's, but I didn't care. Buying those trainers was an important achievement: a symbol that I could get things by myself, paid for with the first honest money I had made from bullfighting...or the first of any kind, for that matter.

By the end of that season of 1981, I had already killed twenty-four calves. I was one of the top students at the School. Knowing that is the thing that got me through the winter until the death of my father. My natural mother didn't go to the funeral, but, shortly after, she phoned home. I picked up the phone myself, and, although at a distance, I had the first conversation with her that I'd ever had in my life. It was so nasty that I will never forget it.

'José, it's your mother. Tell that bitch who lives with you that I will be coming to the house in a few days, and the two of you can clear out, because the apartment belongs to me.'

I asked her to repeat what she had said, because I couldn't believe what I was hearing. The way things were, because I had just buried my father, I went on the offensive, and answered her back even worse, 'If you've got balls enough, come round here, because I'll give you such a kick in your fanny that'll knock you all the way down the stairs! Are you still coming round here to try it on?'

I slammed the phone down. I was beside myself with rage, out of control, furious with everyone and everything: I had been left alone in the world, and, on top of that, I had to listen to something so vile from a woman who had abandoned me so early on. I was no longer that child, but a young man who'd grown up quickly because he had to, involved in the world of the bulls, and going round in the worst parts of a dangerous neighbourhood. I hadn't yet got self-confidence, but I did have the savagery of a wild animal, which my mother had set off with that phone call.

Some days later, when I got home from school, she was there when I opened my front door, inside with her two new kids. Pepita immediately introduced us.

'José, this is your mother and these are your brothers.'

I didn't want to see her. I threw down my bag, turned away and went to my room, shouting behind me, 'They're not my brothers, they're her brats!'

After I'd just been through the worst time of my life, that was a low blow. But perhaps feeling sorry about the row on the telephone, she was now more conciliatory. Pepita explained to her that she and my father had bought the apartment in half-shares between the two of them, and she accepted that. Her original thought was to take half of the inheritance because, although they were separated, they had never got a divorce, and legally she was still the wife of Bienvenido. Because there wasn't much in the pot, they had a talk together, and must have come to an agreement, while I stayed in my room, ready for the slightest excuse to rush out. In the end, nothing happened. My mother left, and I didn't see her again until many years later.

A WALK ON THE WILD SIDE

After the death of my father began the most difficult time of my life. With my situation and all the changes I suddenly had to deal with, for a long time I was on a razor's edge. On the brink of falling into an abyss from which I would never have been able to escape. With the passage of time, and looking back, I am certain that, if it hadn't been for the passion to become a torero, and for everything that I experienced and learnt in the Bullfighting School, I would've gone down for ever.

When I was just about thirteen, I was free to go wherever I pleased. Pepita was working, and she couldn't look after me anyway. Any free time she had was spent in the bingo hall. So I used to get up, make my breakfast and pack myself off to school, unless I was skipping class that day, and would hang out with the local comedians.

At midday, I would eat alone, either what I cooked myself, or what Pepita left for me, and then I would go to the School. Most of the time, I was free of any controls, and I began to develop my character and my own ways.

In the ring at Casa de Campo, I was one person, but in the street I was someone completely different. Dr Jekyll and Mr Hyde. In the morning, I would put on a black leather jacket which once belonged to my father, with my long hair, my coral choker tight around my neck... I got my share of the worst of everything.

Although things were really kicking off in those early years of the 1980s, with the famous *movida* of Madrid, like 'swinging London', but it had not yet reached La Guindalera. On the other side of the Avenida de America, in the district known as 'La Prospe' was a venue called Rock-Ola, where all the new bands played and where those who Mayor Tierno Galván baptised the 'beautiful people' met up. But that lot, who were really just rebellious rich kids, didn't mix with us. In La Guindalera, we were tough guys.

Our music was more flamenco-ish, or gypsy-ish, and that's what we listened to at home. My father always had the radio on with popular 'coplas', and, as a child, I was bored to death listening to the songs of *Marifé de Triana*, *Bambino*, Antonio Peñzuela and, of course, the great Manolo Caracol. Later, he moved on to *Los Chichos*, *Los Chunguitos* and *Los Calis* more than anyone else, because *Camarón de la Isla* wasn't yet on the scene.

That's the music I grew up with. But we boys had our own tastes. There were many favourites, but Boney M was big. Although what we really liked was what they called 'urban rock': Leño, Topo, Asfalto... And bigger bands like Obús, Barón Rojo, Iron Maiden, AC-DC. And the punk bands, the Sex Pistols and so on. That's what we listened to around the clock, loud and powerful – that's what they meant to us.

We liked films about juvenile delinquents too, like *Perros Callejeros*; *El Pico* and stories like *El Vaquilla*, about a real car thief, which was a model for all us lowlife 'bad boys'. It was true to life in La Guindalera, just like all those popular rumba songs about prison and drugs.

That was a critical time for me, when, as in the Lou Reed song, I took a walk on the wild side. I liked hanging out with the creme de la creme of the local small-time crooks. And to be accepted into that elite, you had to be more cool than them, more tough, more dangerous... We would steal watches from the kids who lived in the posh streets near our school. It wasn't hard. We'd surround them, scare them with a big, shiny blade, and they'd start crying and hand over their flashy wristwatches, which another mate would sell on for us, because he knew people who could fence them for us. We also stole car radio cassettes. We'd pick the car door lock with the key from a tin can. We'd put them on the metro lines so the wheels flattened them out, and they were so thin that they went into the lock of a Seat 127 as smooth as silk.

We didn't steal the cars, though, although we could have. I already knew how to drive because my father showed me how in the old Mercedes. We preferred to stick to watches and car radios, because they were easy to sell on, and didn't attract the attention of the police. Two boys, *El Pituco* and *El Pirvin*, looked after that side of things, and shared out the cash with us.

The others would celebrate our life of crime with sweet wine and brandy, or litre bottles of beer, and with smoking dope. But, because I was crazy about the bulls, I told them that I'd take my share in cash, and I'd buy myself a case for the mock sword, or a muleta stick... Sometimes, I would go to the district of Vallecas, to the house of the banderillero Girón, to ask his wife to repair my capes, because they were in such a state, so torn that there was nowhere to get hold of them by. At Bullfighting School, they called them 'the flags of the Red Cross' because they were so tattered. Girón, who was a bad-tempered sod, would get out of bed swearing at me whenever he saw me, because, although it was her living, his wife was a sweetie and hardly ever charged me for her work.

Our life as delinquents and junkies went from bad to worse, because, after a while, my mates started getting hold of amphetamines and *tripis*, those little acid tabs which made them speed like crazy. Then they got on to harder stuff. Luckily, I never got into all that, and I'm sure it's because I was already obsessed with becoming a torero, because otherwise... With time, many of my mates from the streets and from school became lifelong drug addicts, and these were normal kids, sons of working people from ordinary families.

When I went back there or met them by chance, I got to hear about their addiction and their problems. Many of them ended up in prison; some of the girls got into prostitution; and others just died from an overdose. All over Madrid in those years, heroin wiped out a whole generation. Late at night sometimes, I often think that I could so easily have been one of them too.

But, although I was running wild and spent my time robbing people, I never gave up school. By the end of the elementary EGB course, I'd become a useless student, because I was already obsessed with the bulls and getting screwed up inside – and elsewhere. I didn't care about anything else, but, as I've already said, I listened to what I was taught in class, and somehow I muddled through. In fits and starts.

It got worse when my father died. I lost touch with reality, and I turned up to school looking terrible: with the leather jacket which I even slept in; a pair of police Ray-Bans; drainpipe jeans, which was the fashion then; a white T-shirt; a check shirt worn outside my trousers; coral choker; casuals... I looked liked an over-the-top rocker.

That's how I looked when I started eighth grade. I sat in the last row, put my feet up on the desk, and sometimes would even light up a cigarette. I was heading downhill, completely adrift. I was coming up to thirteen, and I had seen almost everything in life. I didn't give a monkey's cuss for school, or for other people. I was a local hood, I was a torero, and I thought I was the business.

Because I was the number one, I had to show it all the time. Some days, I would walk out of the class halfway through, just because I bloody well felt like it. I opened the door, went down two flights of stairs, jumped over the fence, and went for a walk. After a while, I would come back and go into the classroom as if nothing had happened. My behaviour was like you see in those American movies about a school with problem students.

The English teacher was very straight, and one day I was behaving so badly that I made her cry. She bored me stiff. Another time in a practical class, we were supposed to work in groups, but I didn't want to know, and I went from table to table mucking about with the other kids. I wouldn't sit down, I would kneel on a chair, or climb on to a table, and one time the teacher came up behind me and gave me a slap. I reacted like a madman, grabbed the chair, and turned round to hit him with it. Luckily I stopped myself, and he stopped short too, otherwise it could've turned nasty.

The teachers in my state school in La Guindalera were very patient with me, and were always trying to help me out. I suppose they knew about my home situation, and held back. Especially Don Gervasio, who was my class tutor and maths teacher, my favourite subject, along with Spanish...which was taught by a young woman who wore a very short mini-skirt. Don Gervasio was a man with thinning hair, with light-coloured eyes, a vivid complexion and a forceful manner. I got on very well with him, because he taught me to see things how they should be.

And there was Don José too, the head, who covered up for me very often, because he was an aficionado. I had such bad attitude, that I was constantly being thrown out of the classroom, or sent to the head's office. Don José would sit me down and say with the patience of a saint, 'What, here again, Arroyo? You don't stop, do you. What's up? How are things at the Bullfighting School? Any practice lately? You can get close to the bulls all right, but when in school, do me a favour and behave yourself occasionally; I know you're a decent lad really and hard-working. I know that for a fact.'

Even so, two or three times he had no alternative but to suspend me.

With the exception of the caretaker, who couldn't stand the sight of me, the rest were very easy on me in that school. Above all, Don José, who always tried to play down the nuisance I created. He gave me a lot of confidence, because he understood me better than anyone. Anyone else would have walked away from my problems, but Don José and the other teachers tried to offer me guidance like my own father had failed to do. Bienve didn't put himself out for anything, me included.

I have lost contact with them all now. I went back to the school four or five years later, but they'd all left. The head must have retired; they told me that Don Gervasio had been transferred out of Madrid. I am sorry that I couldn't see them to thank them properly for the way in which they treated me in that difficult period of my life. I would have liked to invite Don José to a barrera, a ringside seat, because he was an aficionado, and I would have dedicated a bull to him. Perhaps he has seen me perform without my knowing because he didn't want to tell me he was there. Anyway, if they get to read these words, I want them to know that I will always be in their debt for their tremendous patience and the great understanding they showed me.

In Casa de Campo, I behaved very differently. I took things more seriously than in day school. Even in the bad months after my father's death, on arrival I would take off my choker, tidy my hair away under the shirt, and tried to lose my street swagger. Even so, the teachers knew that something was going on, probably because I was losing concentration and trying less hard. But what really gave it away was when I acted the fool and messed about in class with my best friend, Perea.

After I worked with the calves for the first time, I began to make good progress, and I'd earned some privileges in the School, like not waiting for my turn to go out to the heifers. But Martin Arranz saw what was going on and made me go down a level, and draw lots like the rest of them, or would stop me from working with the heifers, even when my turn came up.

I could handle that quite well, but, one day, he made me go out last, after all the new boys had had a go. That was too much, the biggest humiliation they could give me, to go out to the heifer after all those who hadn't got the slightest idea. And I thought of myself as the top dog. But it taught me a lesson. It taught me that, to become a torero, and to compete, you can't lose concentration for a second. And that friendships don't mean anything. Everyone has to look out for themselves, and you've got to go flat out to achieve anything.

The teachers at Bullfighting School were really like my second fathers. They are the ones who put some discipline into the wild kid that I was at the time, not Bienvenido, who was also strict with me...but only when he was home. It was them who kept me off the slippery slope that beckoned me in my neighbourhood, who saved me, whether they knew it or not, when I was living through the hardest time of my life.

Until then, my father's partner, Pepita, had been my lifeline. My life was tough, but she made it more bearable, especially at the beginning. When I was a child, although there was no blood connection, she looked after me like a mother. She did it well – or maybe not so well, because she wasn't capable of doing it any better – and she played an important part in my life. I even called her

'Mummy'. When my father died, she was my anchor. She wasn't very warm towards me, but she did stay by me. Then, as I began to grow up, things began to change, and I reached a point where I couldn't bear her any more.

Martín Arranz had offered financial help, because he knew about our situation even before Bienvenido died. When he noticed that I was arriving for lessons early, before the others, that I was at Bullfighting School at times when I should have been at day school, he asked me if anyone was looking after me at home. I told him how things were, that Pepita was at work and that my father was ill, and he decided to visit him in hospital.

When he arrived at his room, he confused Pepita with María Jesús, a nurse who'd been looking after Bienve, and who he had a fling with after leaving prison. My father must have already known he was on his way out, because he asked Enrique how my future prospects were shaping up. Enrique said it was impossible to say if I had a future as a torero or not, because the odds were against it, like with so many others. But he added that Bienve shouldn't worry about me, because he would take it upon himself to keep me on the straight and narrow. And he made a promise that he would do as much as he could for me.

Consequently, a few days after my father's funeral, Martín Arranz took me to have lunch in his home, and offered me his help; he said that I shouldn't hesitate to ask if we needed anything. Unfortunately, he said the same thing to Pepita. I respected him greatly: he was so strict and tough in the School that I was scared stiff if he even looked at me. So I didn't want to take advantage of his generous offer, and when I did ask for money, it was only for something urgent, for food or basic needs. Not for that woman who wanted to waste it all at bingo.

We had closed the baker's shop, and now she only had the job at the restaurant. She pinched food from work, and spent her wages on bingo cards. It drove me mad. Sometimes we were helped out by her friend, the policeman's wife, or by Pepita's sister, who earned good wages. But as soon as they lent her money, she blew it all on bingo in an afternoon. I could have killed her. She was so badly hooked, infected with the gambling bug, so that, if I saved up two hundred pesetas by walking to and from the School instead of paying for a metro ticket, she asked me for it to buy a couple of bingo cards. I gave her the money, because I had to keep on good terms with her. But we couldn't go on like that.

Things came to a head one day when she told me to ask Martín Arranz for money again, and I flat refused. As usual, she said that, if I wouldn't do it, she would ask him direct.

'Do what you like,' I answered, my mind made up not to give in, 'but I'm not going to ask him for money to pay for your habit.'

There were heifers in the School that day, and afterwards, with some holidays coming up (I can't remember if it was Christmas or Easter), Enrique offered to take some of us boys to train at his ranch at Colmenar del Arroyo, as we'd done before. When I got home, I told Pepita that I was going, but she didn't want to let me because I hadn't asked for her money. Her sister, brother-in-law and niece were there, but we had a terrible row, a screaming match, and I threw my things into a bag and went out the door.

On my way down the stairs, she came out and leant over the banisters and shouted insults after me. It was the last straw. I threw down my bag, climbed up the stairs four at a time, pushed her indoors, grabbed her by the scruff of the neck and threatened her with an anger that came from somewhere deep inside me, 'You're calling me names, you old cow, when all I've done wrong is refuse to ask for money because I'm ashamed by what you waste it on. I'll kill you!'

They all jumped on me.

'The kid is crazy!'

'Keep away, or I'll kill you too with my sword,' I cried through clenched teeth.

The row was off the scale, and I could see that Pepita was very shocked, which made me realise that I needed to calm down.

I went out the door and no one tried to stop me. When I got to the ranch, I swore that I would never go back to that house again.

3

A SUIT OF LIGHTS AND SHADOWS

Yiyo was my idol, and also the idol of all the boys at the Madrid School of Bullfighting. José Cubero Sánchez was the leader, our very life force. He was the most imaginative, the friendliest, the biggest rogue, the biggest joker. He had a special charisma. He was good-looking, a womaniser, above all – a great torero. He was like the hare that the pack of all us young greyhounds followed, as if his first successes as a novillero were ours. He was the first one to take the step up to full matador, to take the alternativa.

He was very fond of me, and although he was the one who gave me the name *Lentejita*, 'Little Lentil', I admired everything about him. One winter's day, towards dark, he came to visit us at the School when we were practising. He came down the corridor which led to the ring, backlit by a dim, dirty lightbulb. I couldn't recognise him at first, but as he came nearer he seemed to glow, shining in a glittering red tracksuit, much more classy than ours.

Yiyo had already been carried out on shoulders from Las Ventas in Madrid, he was a full matador de toros, and he had left the Casa de Campo only two years earlier. For the rest of us, he was nothing less than a myth. I had the clear impression that I was in the presence of an exceptional being, and that's what I felt as I saw him appear in this amazing lightshow. I already knew him well, and was used to seeing him on a daily basis, but that evening he inspired in me an even higher respect than before.

That image was the final boost which convinced me that I too could become a torero. He had come out of the district of Canalejas, and he was a kid from the streets, like me; he had been to the Madrid School of Bullfighting, the same as me; we had trained together, and there he was; he was a normal person, like me. So what could stop me from becoming an important torero like him? That's why, as I graduated from calves to novillos, all I wanted was to be like *Yiyo*. I even copied his body language.

In 1982, when the School had already been handed over to the Madrid local government, my number of events went up to almost forty becerradas, and I got to wear a suit of lights for the first time. This was on 15th August in Salas de los Infantes, in the province of Burgos. At the time, I didn't have my own suit of lights, nor the means to get one, the same as when I had my debut in Trujillo. On that occasion, the special trousers for a traje corto, the suit for informal bullfighting events, were lent by a friend from the School, Antonio Romero; the black jacket, which once belonged to *Yiyo*, was loaned by José Luis Bote. And my boots were bought for me by the hostesses and prostitutes working in the clip-joints in my district.

Later, I was able to order my own traje corto, which cost twenty thousand pesetas. When I picked it up, I gave the tailor half, but time went by and I couldn't pay the rest. So the tailor sent me a couple of reminders, and for the first time Martín Arranz had to lend me the money, as he had promised to my father. I never bought anything else from that tailor, because he wouldn't wait a bit longer. Not so much as a muleta.

The suit of lights for my debut was also borrowed; it was white and silver. It had originally belonged to Luis Francisco Esplá, and later one of the first to wear that second-hand suit was *Yiyo*. Enrique kept it in his house in Madrid. It was very worn, but when he opened the wardrobe and I saw that suit, embroidered with palm trees and with the stitching of the tassels done in silk thread, I was speechless.

And I remained so when I tried it on and saw that it fitted perfectly. What a dream.

The day I gave it an airing in Salas de los Infantes, *el Fundi* and I got dressed with our cuadrillas in a school building. I didn't know that, in order to put on the taleguilla, the trousers of the suit of lights, you had to remove your underwear, unlike the trousers in a traje corto, which you can put on over your underpants. I was horribly embarrassed, because I hadn't got a pair of tights to put on underneath, and a banderillo had to lend me some.

In the ring, the novillos were up for it and things went quite well. I felt I had grown as a torero, because putting on a suit of lights was the last step on the ladder. Other boys of my age had already fought in becerradas and had already worn a suit of lights, and when I saw publicity pictures of them dressed like that in taurine magazines, I felt they had overtaken me, as if they had attained a level of respect and status which I didn't have until that day of the Fiesta of the Virgin in August in the heart of Castile.

By this time, I was now completely obsessed and focussed on the bulls. In spite of that bad patch that I had gone through following the death of my father, I had made good progress. At the Bullfighting School, because they could see what each and every one of us had achieved on our own, they drew up a fixed group made up of the best of us, like the so-called Princes of Bullfighting of a few years earlier.

After giving it a lot of thought, they left some of the others out for a later time, and they decided to team up José Luis Bote with me and José Pedro Prados, *el Fundi,* and that was the order of billing. Bote, who was a friend and neighbour of the Cuberos in Canalejas, was two years older than me, and had been at the School since it opened. And *Fundi*, from Fuenlabrada, who was also three years older than me, began at the School in 1980, following in the footsteps of his brother Angel Luis, who was already a novillero.

Although he had already made the offer of accommodation several times, and I had asked him desperately to put me up after my last row with Pepita, Martín Arranz didn't want to have me living on his ranch until I'd finished my first level of the Baccalaureate at day school. Somehow or another, I'd managed to pass the exam at the end of eighth grade in Basic Education, but he said I had to sign up for the next level at the Institute.

Because I didn't want to continue, I desperately tried to avoid applying to the La Guindalera Institute, in the hope that no one would notice until it was too late to do anything about it. But Martín Arranz cottoned on to my little game, and he began to sort out a place for me.

The school of the Menesiano Brothers in the area wouldn't admit me because I had chosen Ethics over Religion in the last two years at school. I didn't want to have anything to do with the Church, but my choice wasn't an ideological one; it was just that the timing of the Ethics lessons coincided with classes at the Bullfighting School, and with the young Ethics teacher it was easier to skip off than with the priest. I preferred to be with the bulls rather than spend time doing my head in. But I didn't get away that easily, because, since 1982, the Bullfighting School had been taken over by Madrid's local government and Enrique spoke to someone there, who fixed me up in a Baccalaureate institute near Puente de los Franceses. I still lived in Calle Cartagena, but I spent more time in Colmenar del Arroyo, a village in the mountains to the west of Madrid, near the satellite tracking station at Fresnedillas. Martín Arranz was the tenant of a ranch there, where he raised a few toros bravos under his wife's name, Adela Amago.

I hardly ever saw Pepita. We led separate lives, and when we met accidentally during the week, before going off to the institute after training, our manner was cold, frosty even. From Friday to Monday, holiday weekends, bank holidays and other holidays, I lived in the country, in my own room in Martín Arranz's house. But at the beginning of 1983, I decided not to go back to Madrid, and to have nothing more to do with that woman. I didn't finish the course either, and never picked up a textbook. Instead, I read *Captain America* and *The Masked Avenger* comics; those were my favourites.

MY NEW FAMILY

Because we were appearing in becerradas more frequently, Enrique decided to bring my two fellow toreros to live at his ranch, Montes Claros; they had also finished studying. He didn't do that to distance us from the School, but to give us more time for dedicated training, as we were more advanced than the others; it was like an intensive training course. He had done the same earlier with *Yiyo*, Lucio Sandín and Julián Maestro, with excellent results.

When I moved in to live permanently at the ranch, once I'd settled in I suddenly had the feeling that *Fundi* and Bote would replace me in the affections of Enrique and Adela. I began to feel resentful towards those two guys who had moved into my room, who rode my horse, and so, as I thought, had displaced me in the hearts of the couple who had given me the warmth that I didn't have before. I went on the defensive, It was me against the rest of the world. All the problems I'd been keeping bottled up inside me for so long suddenly exploded.

I must have been very obnoxious to live with. I went through a patch when I was unbearable, constantly blowing hot and cold, and being downright out of order. I complained about everything: if they did something, it was because they had done it; if they hadn't done something, it was because they hadn't done it. As well as being long-faced and foul-mouthed, I was downright offensive, and no one wanted to know about 'that rude little bugger'. Everyone worried about me, but even that annoyed me. I was bitter and twisted, and kept myself to myself most of the time.

We spent our days in Montes Claros and in Los Valles, another ranch nearby which Martín Arranz also rented; there was a very big pond there for watering the land. One day, everyone went there for a swim, but I didn't want to go with them. I preferred to be alone, and not to join in the fun. I just didn't want to go along.

Enrique and Adela were like my parents, my new family, and *Fundi* and Bote were like my brothers, but they were always my fellow conspirators at home and in the bullring. We became very close, and were nearly always together, but there was always nevertheless something that made me hold back from sharing my secrets with them. I didn't feel happy telling them my innermost thoughts because I thought that would show up my weaknesses in what I thought of as a competition. I was outrageously jealous of them about everything: if they said something nice, if they had a triumph, if their families came to see them...

They called me the 'madman of the rock' because I would often walk off, alone with my thoughts, and climb a big rock near the house. I spent hours alone sitting there, going over my problems and the screw-ups in my head, revelling in my own mess. It was my way of getting noticed.

Dealing with me in those days was a constant battle. I have tremendous respect for Enrique and Adela because it was hard for them: taking on a thirteen-year-old kid, in mid-adolescence, and bringing him into your own home, and getting nothing but sulks and bolshie, disrespectful answers in return... I was a torrent of constant aggression. Added to that was the fact that life had taught me that all women were bad news, and that their only role was to foul up your life.

I was really screwed up, seriously. And there I was, suddenly pushed into a family setting, and with a pair of brothers like the ones I had never had. There was no constant arguing here, no exchange of mutual insults, this couple didn't hit one another, and lunch and dinner were always on the table on time. But instead of being a calming influence, this unsettled me even more.

A psychologist might find this normal, might say that I was looking for an explanation for all that unbearable stuff of my earlier days. But, at that time, I wasn't a psychologist, and I couldn't take in the sudden change in my life at thirteen or fourteen years of age. I had a hard time, and I made sure that everyone else had a hard time too.

Adela was the one who had the most patience with me. She treated me like her own son, and that boosted my confidence. She was someone I could confide in, a shoulder to cry on, because I told her everything, and unloaded my feelings. I stayed in her company as much as possible, and even helped her with the shopping and the cleaning.

Later on, after the others had left the ranch, we made an agreement: I would help her around the house, and in return she would help me with my training. Every day, for an hour, she would handle the carretón horns while I practised going in with the sword. She was also my harshest critic as a torero, because when I was bad, she balled me out and she didn't let me get away with anything. She was a mixture of mother and friend, but, like Enrique, she didn't hesitate to put me straight when necessary.

Adela played the important role of a no-messing mother during my adolescent years. She stood for affection, warmth and a normal home-life: meals were on time, clothes were laundered, and all those other little things which are more important to a child than is at first obvious.

I felt confident enough to call her by the familiar form of you, 'tú'. Not so with Enrique, who I continued to address by the more formal 'usted' until I was about twenty years old, because it didn't feel right doing otherwise; I had nothing but respect for that man. His wife found it all very funny, and said I was being ridiculous. Then, one day, I plucked up enough courage to call him 'tú' casually in conversation. Nothing happened, and he carried on speaking as before. It was like breaking through a barrier which I had imposed myself.

Anyway, of all the things that happened to me while staying in that house, the best of them was that, although I had all those crazy problems, I was kept away from bad influences, and was kept separate from the kids I grew up with in La Guindalera. My life in the country was a healthy one, living like a torero twenty-four hours a day. We three apprentices were certainly not on holiday.

We trained ceaselessly, or else we helped out on the farm. That way we felt we were doing something useful, and we also learnt the ways of the countryside. We hardly ever went off to Madrid, except for now and again when we would go to see our friends at the Bullfighting School.

The three of us fought among ourselves regularly – boys' stuff. When I was having a downer, the others put up with it, kept themselves to themselves, and left me alone. But the rest of the time, we got on like a house on fire. We enjoyed larking about, and if one of us didn't come up with something, another one would: one time we loaded up a Land Rover with cats, and pushed the farm's boxer dog inside with them, or we would tie a string of tin cans to the tails of the farm dogs, or whatever other daft idea came into our heads.

In reality, we didn't have much spare time to have a laugh. We got up at six or seven in the morning, in summer or winter, like in the army. We couldn't let up for a moment because Enrique was always on our backs. That's why we called him 'The Sheriff' or 'The Massa', like the slave gangmaster in the TV series *Roots*. If he caught us slacking, he gave us a terrible rollicking. We were more scared of him than of anything else.

We were as fit as a butcher's dog, because of the constant training, which was long and hard, and because of the farm work: this might be unloading a lorry-load of straw, or digging a three hundred metre long ditch, or moving a fence. We were kept busy all day long.

At daybreak, we would put on our tracksuits and run twenty kilometres, mostly across country. When we got back home, we would have breakfast, and then, at nine o'clock, we would walk the four or five kilometres to the small bullring in the next farm to do cape practice. At lunchtime, we went home walking or running backwards, which is a very good exercise for a torero. When we finished eating, we went back to the bullring, again on foot, to practise banderillas or sword-work with the carretón. When the sun went down, it was back to the house, running again. So we just ate our dinner and collapsed. We were already in bed by nine o'clock. And that was on a day when there was no work for us to do on the farm...

THE FORGE OF STEEL

That's how fit we were, and I've never been so fit again since. At fourteen or fifteen years old, we could pick up a bale of straw in each hand – hands which were covered in calluses by the way – and we would throw them up for stacking, as if they were cushions. We were pure fibre through and through. One time, I even wrestled one of the cows to the ground in open country, after running up behind it with the farm dogs.

We felt so confident with our intensive training that we were completely relaxed when appearing in the bullring, although we were short of some technical skills. The three of us trained together, and we didn't think too much about the bullfighting side of things. Enrique corrected our mistakes, but we mainly worked things out by ourselves, thinking only about going out into the ring and cutting ears by whatever means possible. It wasn't until much later, when I was already a full matador, that I began to give serious thought to the responsibilities of my position.

We grew up a lot on that ranch in the mountains, both as toreros and as men. But Martín Arranz didn't let us get too big for our boots. He kept a tight rein on us constantly, to stop us from easing up or getting too carried away. He didn't like people soft soaping us either. If he saw someone saying something nice about us or buttering us up, he would find an excuse to move us away. He wanted us to keep our noses to the grindstone and not lose sight of our targets. When we were alone, he would attack us remorselessly, and he called us terrible things. He really humiliated us. I remember one time when we were performing behind closed doors, and a bull caught Bote and ripped off his trousers. But Enrique was unmoved: he made Bote carry on like that in his underpants for a good while longer.

He wanted us to get used to the idea that bullfighting is a tough business involving a sacrifice on our side, that we needed to be as hard as steel, and to have the ability to battle through to the end. The reality was that it was not Enrique who was hard: in bullfighting, it is the toro which is the hardest. And above the bull, the public is the hardest of all.

I could talk about many of the psychological torments that the 'Massa' put us through, but I'll just give an example of the most significant one. It happened much later, when the three of us were already on the next step up, as novilleros with picadors.

We had made our first appearance in the Monumental bullring of Barcelona one Sunday, and had been contracted to reappear two weeks later. On that first appearance we were unlucky because the bulls weren't much good. I cut one ear, and overall we did okay, but not good enough to expect an enthusiastic crowd on our return. In the meantime, between engagements in Barcelona, we appeared in Barcarrota in the western province of Badajoz. And we had a great triumph. *El Fundi* went so far as to cut four ears and a tail, I cut three ears, and Bote, two. They carried us out on shoulders and through the streets of the town, with the public ecstatic after seeing us put on such an amazing show.

The next morning, back at the ranch, we were making hamburgers after our run. We were still excited, enthusiastically talking in the kitchen about what had happened in Barcarrota; Enrique arrived and slammed the door behind him. He was holding some papers in his hand.

'I have just been speaking to Balaña, the impresario of the Barcelona ring. See this? It's the contracts for next Sunday's corrida. You won't be going.'

And while tearing the papers into little bits, he continued speaking, 'You three are no more than a bunch of time-wasters who have no serious intention of becoming toreros. You, *Fundi* – better go back to Fuenlabrada and join your old man serving up beers in his bar. You, Bote, go back to your brother's garage, knocking dents out of wrecked cars. And you, José, go back to school, because you are a layabout. The three of you have no balls, and you're not toreros. You're just a pile of shit!'

And he left the room in the same angry way that he had come in. The hamburgers got burned and we stood there frozen to the spot. That unexpected attack was like a hand grenade lobbed in at our morale. We went to our room and cried our eyes out, except for Bote, who took it on the chin, said he didn't care what Enrique thought, that he was sticking with it because he was going to be a torero come what may.

I didn't feel the same, and decided to leave: I wasn't going to take any more from that little dictator. I packed my bag, walked down to the village and caught the first bus to Madrid, ready to go back to live with Pepita if I had to. After all, part of the place in Calle Cartagena still belonged to me.

But by the time I got to the Paseo de Moret, I got off the bus, and, without leaving the bus station, I waited for the return bus to Colmenar de Arroyo. Thinking it through, pulling myself together as I sat in the bus, I realised that I couldn't give up all I had struggled for so easily.

I spent the whole way back chewing things over, and I resolved never again to allow room for the slightest doubt, that no one would ever again think or say that I didn't have what it takes to become a torero. I would show my determination to make something important out of my life. And I started by working crazily close to the bulls in Barcelona, because Enrique hadn't actually cancelled the contract as he had threatened to do.

And that was how heartless Martín Arranz could be in order to make us strong mentally. Toying with our egos, making things always harder for us, bringing us up like Spartans. With the result that, in such an environment, José Pedro, José Luis and I became as close as blood brothers. We looked out for each other, we encouraged one another, and above all, we supported each other in that regime of hard-as-steel discipline.

We are still close. They are more than family for me. We have cried together, we have laughed together, we have been scared together, and we have had fun together, over days, weeks and months. We still have enormous emotional ties. Time can pass without us calling one another, but when we are back together, it's as if the years have not gone by. We enjoy the moment as if we were once more back in that time of our lives that was so tough, but so fantastic.

Now that I have at last achieved what he wanted for me, I must express my gratitude to Enrique Martín Arranz, a shed-load of thanks, for teaching me and shaping me as he did, even if it did seem so very harsh at times. Sometimes when I talk it through with Bote, who is now himself a teacher at the Madrid School of Bullfighting, both of us recognise that, although it seemed humiliating at the time, if it hadn't been like that, none of us would have achieved anything, not even as people.

SOMEONE CALLED DE LA LLANA

In 1983, the three of us appeared for the first time in a suit of lights in the bullring of Madrid. It was on 21st July. And we went back twice more that summer. I wasn't fazed by walking out in to that huge ring of Las Ventas. It was massive, but I felt quite at home, because I'd been there as a spectator so many times...even if I was only playing bottle-tops.

And I had already appeared in that ring once before, at the end of the previous year, in a sort of festival of young lads from all over Spain, organised by the impresario, Chopera. We three Madrid locals were the last ones out, and we cut the two ears from our calf. But what I remember most about that day was that we changed in the dressing-room of the areneros, who were responsible for looking after the sand, and I didn't have time to take a leak. Before our calf came out, after I had been standing in the callejón, the ringside passageway, for two hours, I sat down on the estribo, the small ledge on the fence; this was a very torero gesture, but my bladder was so squeezed that a few drops of pee came out. I felt awful.

But my first appearance there 'in lights' was easy. As I said, the Madrid bullring was nothing special for me. I had the feeling, which has never left me, that everything was familiar. I was so set on appearing in a real bullring with lots of space, instead of all those temporary rings and village squares that we had been in, and I was more impressed by the thought of all the triumphs great matadors had known in that very ring.

I had the same sensation when I appeared in Valencia, the first large-sized bullring I appeared in; to be able to take part, I had to forge my ID because I was only fourteen, two years less than the minimum age required to appear in a professional event.

I was helped in this by a policeman who was married to the friend of Pepita. He told me to take my original birth certificate and change the '9' in 1969 and make a photocopy to make it less obvious. For some days before going to ask for the ID, I even grew a skimpy moustache to look older, but the effect was exactly the opposite.

That's how I turned up at the police station: with the dodgy photocopy, my ridiculous moustache, and scared to death in case they sussed me. But the police didn't even ask me any questions. They gave me a receipt, and I went straight round to the offices of the toreros' union to take out a newcomer's card, which I needed to sign the contract for Valencia.

For that event, and for the three events in Madrid, I went on the posters under the name of Miguel de la Llana, using the second surname of Bienve instead of my own. I had my reasons. When I started, I needed written permission from my father. But when my father died, I had lots of problems without that written permission, because if anything happened to me in the ring there was no one responsible for me with the Social Security people. At that time, and still nowadays, that was considered very important.

El Boni, who is now a banderillero, knew about my situation, and went with his father to the ring and gave me away to the police, so that he could appear in my place. So I hid and came out at the last moment, already dressed for the event. If the police questioned me, I would say I was sixteen. If they found out, they would kill me. So, to throw them off the track, someone said I should change my name on the posters. But I was pissed off that the public and the new boys at the School would hear that a certain De la Llana had done well, but they wouldn't know that it was me. I'd always been known as 'Joselito', little José, since I joined there aged ten years. And, apart from that short period, I have always been known by that name on the posters, although a few purists criticised me for it.

In the beginning, because I was short and chubby, the name of José Arroyo seemed too serious, but I wasn't going to use the name that *Yiyo* gave me – *Lentejita*. And not '*El Choni*' either, which was the professional name that my father used for me when he signed me up for Bullfighting School. I may have lost the piece of paper now, but on it was written in very rounded, old-fashioned handwriting 'José Miguel Arroyo Delgado *el Choni*' – how about that!

The diminutive form, Joselito, was more natural. In the School I was known as Joselito this, or Joselito that, so when I appeared in public, I already knew what name I was going to use. In the School they had told us about Joselito *el Gallo*, the famous torero from the Golden Age, and I didn't mean to compare myself to him in the slightest, not for a second.

As a becerrista, working with calves and heifers, no one took things seriously, and no one mentioned the business of my name, didn't even question it. But on my debut in Seville with picadors, when they saw the name *Joselito* on the posters between Antonio Corbacho and *el Porteño*, it was, 'Who the bloody blue blazes!' and they laid into me. 'How does this young kid dare to use that name!' said the locals in the bars of Seville, and the odd Madrid voice joined in too, in the pages of the press. They thought it an act of sacrilege.

I didn't want to offend anyone or steal anyone's name. There have been other *Joselito*s in the history of the bulls, but few have made it big. What no one wanted to recognise at the time or since was that Joselito *el Gallo* never appeared under that name professionally: he was *Gallito* or *Gallito Chico*, after his father and brother, both called *el Gallo*. Joselito was an affectionate family name, and a name used by some aficionados from his beginnings as a bullfighter at a very early age. So gentlemen, let's see if you can get this into your heads: the only real Joselito is me! I am the real deal!

In 1983, I had even more contracts, some forty-odd novilladas. I took the step up to appear with picadors and bigger bulls in Lerma, in the province of Burgos, on 8th September. I appeared with two other novilleros, Sánchez Marcos and Marcos Valverde, not my usual companions. I don't know why Enrique arranged it that way. I wore a well-used turquoise and gold suit bought second-hand from Lucio Sandín, and my two novillos were very big, over four hundred kilos.

I didn't notice much difference between the three-year-old novillos and the two-year olds I'd fought previously. Except maybe they charged a little more slowly. I felt very comfortable, especially with the capote. But when I went in to the first one to deliver the coup de grâce with the descabello sword, and I saw close up that enormous head, those long horns and that huge morrillo, the neck muscle, I felt truly scared for the first time.

Fortunately, that didn't happen in subsequent novilladas, like the one in Fuenlabrada with el Fundi and Bote who appeared with picadors for the first time, and when we had to fight an enormous substitute bull almost in the dark. Then I went to Valencia for the final of a competition of bullfighting schools. Following the establishment of the Madrid School of Bullfighting, similar establishments had been set up all over Spain. The event was televised live, and José Luis Bote won, as he had done in Madrid, by cutting an ear, whereas I only won a circuit of the ring.

THE SPIRIT OF BELMONTE

It was because of things like that that I began to feel very depressed. For four years, I went around Spain with *Fundi* and Bote, but I didn't have any major triumphs. I was performing well enough, but I didn't click with the audience. I didn't reach out to the public, as we say in bullfighting circles. Because I was a bit dull, and didn't do well with the sword, I didn't cut many ears. And that was depressing.

Of the three of us, *Fundi* was the most artistic, he was strong, and animated. José Luis killed very well, and, because he had been longer at the School than either of us, he had more presence and showed confidence with the bulls, as well as being classy and brave. I was the ugly duckling. I would cut a solitary ear, win a circuit of the ring, maybe on a good day I would cut two ears, but the other two would cut tails and hooves every day. What I remember most about those times is that I never ever cut a hoof, not even as a becerrista.

That's when I began the practice of not taking a vuelta, a circuit of the ring, unless it was with an ear in my hand. A friend once said that I was like a steak on the barbecue, because, when he read the results of my novilladas in important rings, he saw 'vuelta y vuelta' which, in Spanish, means 'one side and then the other'. So from the day my friend made that joke, I gave up doing a 'vuelta' unless it was with a trophy. But I was even criticised for that in some quarters after I became established.

I got sick to the stomach living twenty-four hours a day with my two companions who were always coming out top. I was jealous and with my Madrid-bred big headedness, I still had a sort of street cockiness. But I got the tossings, and they got the ears. Seeing no immediate way out, I was so messed up, that I was on the verge of giving it all up three or four times.

I knew I had the potential to be better than them, but I just couldn't do it. Since I first began, I was haunted by that fear of making a fool of myself that I felt when I first caped a heifer. I was very shy in the ring, and I couldn't bring myself to give so much as a little smile and a wink to the public. So I tried desperately to do everything perfectly, for everything to come out exactly right. Even if I'd given four or five perfect passes, if these were followed by a slight snagging or some other mistake, I would stand in front of the bull staring down at the ground, ashamed. The teachers used to ask me if I had dropped something.

Fundi and Bote, on the other hand, had a special gift for getting through to people, and knew which buttons to press to get them to applaud, even if sometimes they were not doing very well. José Pedro was fantastic at that. Not only did he do well, he was also very cheeky and people warmed to him with his smiling face and childlike appearance...although he was actually three years older than me. He also had half of the population of Fuenlabrada supporting him, and he always had large numbers on his side in the ring; he wiped the floor with me, and I hated it.

But now that I can look back on it from a distance, I can see that it served to spur me on, and it made sure I didn't lower my guard. From the beginning, I was always aware of the painfulness of competition, the harshness of failure, the uncertainties of winning. In the professional world of the bulls, the law which rules is the law of the strongest, and you have to have a burning desire to succeed, and a capacity to make sacrifices in order to come first. As in life itself.

That is how I matured as a torero. But what I didn't understand then were the true secrets of the art, the reasons deep down for putting your life at risk to create emotion from what you are feeling. I realised that much later when I learnt about the great torero, Juan Belmonte.

That summer of 1983, the film director, Teo Escamilla, came to the School to make a film – a sort of documentary – about us weird boys who wanted to be toreros. He gave it the title *Tú Solo* ('You Alone'), and he succeeded very well in what he wanted to do, without the use of professional actors or complicated technical stuff.

The main protagonist among the students was Luis Miguel Calvo, who Escamilla later used in the well-known TV serial *Juncal*, but we were nearly all in the film. For reasons I don't understand, the director, who didn't know me at all, picked me out to play the part of a kid who was fascinated by Belmonte.

There is a scene where the students are resting on their bunk beds under the stands of the bullring one night. José Antonio Carretero, who today is a fabulous banderillero, is saying out loud that he misses his home and family, when he suddenly turns to me and asks me about my family.

With one of the few sentences that I have in the film, I answer him at once, 'You've no idea how much I envy you, Carretero. You don't know how lucky you are.' Very dejected, I get up from the bed and go out into the ring, and start to practise passes, but with my bare hands, lit only by a solitary light bulb.

Back in the dormitory, Pedro Vicente Roldán lays into Carretero, saying that my father has died, and that I haven't lived with my mother for years. Ashamed for putting his foot in it, Carretero follows me out into the ring, and, without saying anything, begins to charge at me as if wheeling the carretón, like he is asking for forgiveness.

It's a beautiful scene, very sad: two boys pretending to fight bulls at night, in the dark, and with a background of sorrowful flamenco guitar. As if bullfighting is the way to escape from any problem.

All through the film, there are references to the biography of Juan Belmonte written by Chaves Nogales in the 1930s; it's as if it was the Bible for those apprentice toreros. In the film, it was Carlos Neila who is seen reading the book, but I am the one who is most affected by the romantic dream which young people associate with the genius from Triana, and, just as he did when he was learning about the bulls, I encourage the others to come out to a ranch to cape bulls in open country, naked, by the light of the moon.

Those scenes, filmed with the special photographic effect 'la nuit americaine', day-for-night, in the ranch of Palomo *Linares* in Aranjuez, are some of the best scenes in the film. They reflect perfectly the innocence, the purity, and the sense of personal ambition of a group of boys who want to become something in life. It's me who takes the first steps to strip off and face up to a bull, while a surprised Neila says that the spirit of Belmonte must be somewhere around there. Then, slowly, everyone else copies me.

That scene of me with the bulls, naked before the cameras, was a very strange experience, and I found it very uncomfortable. It's amazing how much courage a millimetre of material can give you! It's a bit obvious to say so, but you are naked in front of a becerro, and you feel really naked, and more vulnerable than if you're wearing clothes. Can a pair of trousers really be much protection? Well, it feels so. And at the time, I'd already been working with the bulls for three years...

I agreed to do it because they gave me a suit of lights. One day, Enrique arrived at the ranch and told me that Escamilla wanted me to cape a bull for the film. The conversation went more or less as follows, with me climbing down gradually.

'A novillo? Fine.'

'Yes, but he wants you to do it naked,' added Martín Arranz.

'What? You're kidding! Not on your life!'

'Well they'll give you a suit of lights.'

'Completely naked, or just a bit?'

'Completely.'

'An old suit, or made to order?'

'Brand new.'

'Well tell him that's fine, then – he's got a deal.'

So I had to perform naked in order to get a better suit.

Although it's one of the key-points of the film, I still hadn't read the book about the life of Juan Belmonte, and didn't really know much about that man who changed bullfighting fundamentally, at a stroke. I didn't get to read it until I was already a full matador. I had heard about him in the School, in Molinero's classes, and even more so during the filming, but I didn't really understand it completely until much later. That marvellous book by Chaves Nogales made me realise that Belmonte was special because of his inner strength and his lifestyle. He turned bullfighting on its head by using his inner self rather than his less-than-perfect body. Using his willpower.

His life-story had such an effect on me that I identified with him completely, and I even came to the conclusion that we were similar in some ways. My childhood and adolescence had been hard too, and we had both been saved by the bulls. But I still can't understand how it was that Escamilla chose me out of twenty or thirty boys to play the one under the spell of Belmonte.

What did that film director see in me to link me with that unique character? Perhaps I know the answer now, because, if we ignore the distance in time, and the setting of both periods, during the time of my own adolescence my life resembled somewhat the beginnings of the extraordinary story of Belmonte.

The same passion and determination to escape from oblivion and express my feelings through the bulls were precisely the foundations of my own career. After several years with the bulls, I discovered that Belmonte had said that, to perform well, you have to do it with the feeling and the passion of someone in love. He also said that, when in front of a bull, you have to forget that you have a body. Those sentences made me very excited when I read them. I was surprised to find that he had the same understanding of the bulls as I did, although I had been unable to define it so well.

When I started, I wasn't interested in money. When you are young, you don't think of profit or material things. All I wanted to do was to make people feel what I felt that afternoon with Juan Mora, when I got hooked for ever. As I grew into the profession, I realised that I had many feelings inside that I wanted to express. I wanted to show my real self in the ring, which I couldn't show out in the street.

In normal life, I was a mass of complexes, and thought of myself as a pathetic creature who everything bad happened to. The past weighed heavily upon me, and I didn't feel I was on equal terms with the others. I envied my mates when I saw them with their fathers, their brothers and sisters, living a happy family life like normal people. I felt embarrassed to talk with anyone about my life. I was furtive, always holding back so as not to reveal my real self.

At the same time, I was very aware of everything going on around me. I saw through things at once, and was unsettled by any show of affection. Enrique said that he began to take notice of me because, when we went to Las Ventas, I would go straight up to the groups of aficionados talking about the bulls, but I didn't join in; I just enjoyed hanging out with them. And I sought out the friends of *el Fundi*, who followed him around everywhere, because I wanted them to follow me too, and give me their support.

This behaviour came out in my way with the bulls. The mixture of cheekiness and melancholy which I had picked up from the street became a sort of insolence in my personal way of performing with the bulls. A journalist, José Luis Carrabias, called me 'the torero with the sad face' and he was right, because I was living in my own little world of trials and tribulations. In the ring, as I gained confidence, all this translated into a personal style with a mainly positive attitude, as if I was making up for all my problems.

I think I was very transparent in the ring, not necessarily better or worse than anyone else, but at least classical and crystal clear. When I felt good, I could do anything in front of the bull, but when things changed direction in my head, I lost it. I was affected by the slightest distraction outside the ring.

The first time I went to perform with the bulls in Colombia, the image of all those urchins begging at traffic lights gave me a profound feeling of sadness which stayed with me for the rest of the day. So I used to take a crowd of the street urchins to lunch every day, telling them to bring along their brothers as well, because I felt like one of them.

I had never lived as badly as this, so short of so many things, but I blamed my detachment on a lack of normal family warmth. My father loved me, and even Pepita, but I lived on my own a lot, I saw everything that was going on around me, and I saw things which someone as young as me shouldn't see.

All these things screwed me up inside my head, until the bulls finally freed me. I wanted to be someone in life; I wanted to move forward and leave the past behind, to achieve something by my own efforts, and be worth something in the end. The lessons I had growing up at home were not exactly of the very best, and I wanted to forget it all as fast as possible.

That's why I took the step up to full matador so young, at sixteen years of age, so I would soon know if I was going to make it with the bulls or if I should be looking for another job. I had no time to lose. The prospect of living the life of a parasite after a few years was something that consumed me, and kept me in a constant state of anxiety.

BULLFIGHTING IS NOT A GAME

In March 1984, Bote, *Fundi* and I – and it's worth mentioning that I was the only one to cut an ear this time – appeared in Las Ventas in a charity event for the benefit of the School. It was our final event as students of the School where we became toreros. By this time, we were already *novilleros con picadores*, and they could no longer teach us.

We performed together on more than thirty occasions that year. Although there was still a connection, the Bullfighting School of Madrid didn't arrange any contracts, or put up a single peseta. The time for playing was over.

We went to Valencia, Bilbao, Barcelona – the two days when Enrique bawled us out – Zaragoza... Somehow or other, the three of us supported one another. Apart from the size of the novillos, there wasn't much difference from previous years. It became harder the following year, 1985, when we had to earn our own living separately, and we each got ourselves a different manager.

Martín Arranz was still in the background, but his exclusive responsibility was as head of the School, and he set me up with his friend Alfonso del Toro, who was an elderly ex-novillero from Murcia, who had been following our careers since we were becerristas. A good man.

I wasn't Enrique's favourite, but I was his protégé. It was more on a personal level than a professional one, because he'd made that promise to my father on his deathbed, and I was still living in his house like a son. Bote had gone back to Canillejas, and *el Fundi* was still on the farm, but, for some reason, he became unhappy, then went into some kind of depression, and after his presentation in Madrid as a novillero con picadores, he even gave up the bulls for several months. We tried to cheer him up, but he just withdrew inside himself, and kept himself apart. I wasn't the only 'madman of the rock'.

José Pedro's reaction was the reverse of what happened to me, because for me it was life on the farm, and bulls in a family setting, which got me over my madness. Once I began to take my career seriously, and began to see the world, and learnt that there were plenty of other people out there who had things happen to them similar to me, or even worse, I decided that I had to stop messing about, and to go for it.

Escaping from the house in Calle Cartagena was the first step to independence, and living in a proper family helped me to get my head straight. I came from a daily battle, a state of total chaos in a home which was anything but a home, but at last I was free, I was somewhere I wanted to be, doing what I wanted to do. And that's exactly why I loved the bulls, for the feeling of freedom it gave me when I was performing.

Now I had to fight to succeed in a world which was a lot harder and where the competition was much tougher than in the School. It was about then that the despicable practice began of having to pay to get contracts – an unfair contest which excludes many lads with more talent than those who get the work thanks to their 'godfathers' and 'mirlos blancos', literally 'white blackbirds' or a rare species. In the world of the bulls, we call them 'egg-layers'.

I wanted to maintain my artistic ideas, to express seriousness, purity and my innermost feelings, but the complicated circumstances obliged me to look for other ways to get success by the fast track, and as regularly as possible, to ensure that I didn't lose a single battle in that unjust war of hopefuls.

I was naturally shy and cold in the ring, but suddenly I was taking short cuts, hustling, and sometimes pushing my luck, placing my own banderillas in all my novillos, giving flashy cape passes on my knees, and performing the whole repertoire of what they had taught us in the School, preferably the most spectacular, the most impressive... Always in a great hurry to win a triumph, looking for applause and for ears, as if my life depended on it.

I made my debut in Las Ventas as a novillero con picadores during the San Isidro Fair in 1985, and nothing special happened. I was very down for a few days, but breathed again when I cut an ear in my next event the following Sunday. Then, because it's all there was, I entered the labyrinth known to us toreros as the 'Valley of Terror', which is a series of bullrings in the valley of the river Tiétar, infamous for the novilladas they put on with enormous animals, with gigantic horns, which are responsible for ending the careers of so many hopeful lads. It is an ordeal by fire which imposes character, because whoever survives it knows that he is ready for anything that the future can hold for him. I think I passed the test with enough professional pride to think of moving on to other more important things.

I was involved in this when, on 30th August and at dinner in the kitchen on the ranch, I heard that a bull had killed *Yiyo* in Colmenar Viejo. That it had broken his heart in two, literally. We had a phone call from Andrés Caballo, a fellow student from the School, who was a close friend of *Yiyo* and sometimes spent time in Montes Claros. Enrique was away travelling, and Adela answered the phone, and suddenly turned white.

'Don't joke about things like that, Andrés,' she said.

'It's true, I swear,' he answered.

She threw down the handset, and burst into tears. She was very fond of him. *Yiyo* was an institution in that house since the time he spent there before we arrived. I took over from him there when his career as a novillero took off and he left.

The death of *Paquirri* a year earlier had scarcely affected me. Really. I didn't know him, and he was a long way away. It made me sad, and it pulled me up short. After all, although I was only a novillero, I too had to stand in front of the horns. But I didn't really want to think too much about it. But *Yiyo*...

José Cubero was my friend and my mentor. I had lived alongside him, we laughed a lot together, we trained together... He had been carried out on shoulders in Madrid as a matador as well, and he was on the verge of being recognised as a top matador. Two months before Colmenar, we met up as spectators in Las Ventas. At the end of the corrida, he took me running to see his new car, a dark red BMW, and we went cruising in it for the rest of the night. Wherever we stopped, the girls crowded round. *Yiyo* was very happy, proud, excited. Me even more so, swanking it up with my friend and his car.

That's why his death seemed so wrong, inexplicable. Suddenly a terrible blow had robbed me of my idol. That larger-than-life youth was only twenty-one years old, in the prime of his life, just beginning to enjoy the fruits of his efforts and his sacrifices. However I tried to think about it, I could find no sense in these events. And yet, taken together with the death of *Paquirri*, it helped people to respect again the risks that we ran as toreros.

All of Spain was shocked to see his death on television, those grim images of how the bull took away the light from his eyes and drained the colour from his features. I couldn't bring myself to watch. Neither could I bear to go to the vigil they arranged that same night in his house in Canillejas, with *Yiyo* laid out in his favourite traje de luces, a beautiful Bordeaux-red and black suit, lying on the bed where he had dreamt of glory so many times.

I couldn't face seeing him dead, just as with my father three years earlier. It was hot, and that modest apartment was overflowing with people filled with a the morbid curiosity that the death of a young person attracts, hardly letting his grieving mother breathe. Her sorrow was total, and the family could scarcely hold themselves together.

I stayed outside in the street, talking with my colleagues from the Bullfighting School, trying to keep it together, and not to break down in tears of anger and of pain. I preferred to keep the image of José Cubero driving that car which he'd earned with his own work in the bullring. Almost thirty years have gone by, and I still miss him deeply.

4

BLOOD, SWEAT AND TEARS

One day after *Yiyo* was buried, I was supposed to appear in a novillada in Illescas. At first I thought of dropping out and not going. By the worst of coincidences, the novillos were from the ranch of the late *Paquirri*. But I thought better of it, and, in the end, I decided to go ahead and appear in that village, which is in the province of Toledo.

I was a torero, and, as such, I had to behave with responsibility and dignity, not get upset like a wimp. The fact is that I found it very difficult to get ready in my traje de luces; I couldn't get the tragic events of Colmenar Viejo out of my head, and I had a very bad day, unable to concentrate on what I was supposed to be doing.

For a long time, I was in a daze, miserable, with no wish to appear with the bulls. Obviously, I was thinking that the same could happen to me. You are aware of the possibilities from the moment you start thinking about the bulls, but it's better not to think about it too much and put such thoughts to one side, taking mental refuge in the idea that nothing like that could happen to you.

It's not until you see it from close up that death becomes a reality. But there's no sense in worrying about it. You have to beat it, to overcome the fears and think positively so that you can carry on taking the risk. In my case, I managed to deal with it early on, but the death of my friend, losing that reflected image of myself, confirmed to me in the most brutal manner possible that the bulls is a painful profession.

Scarcely a month later, in October 1985, I brought my time as novillero with picadors to an end by cutting three ears in the Pilar Fair in Zaragoza. When I was carried out of the ring on shoulders and was taken to the cuadrilla minibus, I saw things clearly at last, and I said to myself that the purgatory of the Valley of Terror was finished. My last year as a novillero had been tough, and what's worse, not very satisfactory, because I couldn't see any reward for my efforts, and I didn't feel comfortable in my work.

On the drive back home, with just the two of us alone in the car, I had a serious talk with Enrique. I told him that I was in a hurry to know if I had a future as a torero or not. That I didn't want to live the life of a hanger-on, and I didn't want to carry on living in his house on charity. I didn't like the idea of seeing myself at the age of twenty-five drifting around, with no respect or anything to show for it, like so many other lads who never made it. I wanted to take the alternativa, the step up to full matador, although I was only sixteen. If I didn't make the grade, there was still time for me to do something else.

Martín Arranz still couldn't be my manager directly, because, as head of the Bullfighting School, he wasn't allowed to. So he had the idea of getting in touch with José Luis Marca, an important person in the bull-world, who was then manager to two top-flight matadors, Paco Ojeda and José Maria *Manzanares*; his plan was to get Marca to take me on.

One day, he came home and this is what he said, 'José, I've sold you on. I've spoken to Marca, and you will have fourteen or fifteen contracts in the shadow of his toreros, to get the experience you need without being subjected to the high standards of Madrid. You won't see a single peseta out of it, but you will be toughened up.'

I didn't like the idea much. The thought of travelling here and there with a guy I didn't know from Adam, what with me being a bit strange and a bit shy, and without someone at my side who I trusted, like Enrique or Alfonso del Toro... Shortly after, Marca called and said that he was prepared to take me on, provided he saw me in the ring in Madrid; he couldn't arrange corridas for me without seeing me again in Las Ventas.

That wasn't what we wanted, so Martín Arranz had another think, and we decided to have a go at doing it by ourselves. We had to go for it. 'As Churchill said: blood, sweat and tears' – those were his exact words when he finally decided to leave the School to dedicate himself full-time to my career.

He sold up a lot of the livestock from his ranch to finance the costs of the preparations to make me a full matador. He made a supreme effort to ensure that I arrived at my alternativa with a bigger reputation than I really had. As a novillero, I was okay, but I didn't break any moulds. As they say in the world of the bulls, I was no more than a good torero.

That winter, there was a disaster in Colombia with the eruption of the volcano Nevado del Ruiz. There were twenty thousand dead, and everyone was very moved by newsreel footage of a little girl, trapped with the water up to her neck, saying goodbye to her mother. I think her name was Omayra. We had the idea of me offering to fight six bulls alone, without fees, for the benefit of the victims, with novillos from the famous and much-feared ranch of Miura: I don't know if that was to give the offer more impact, or if it was because when, as a child, I used to draw bullfight posters with my name on, I always put myself with those very demanding bulls – something which I never did in the whole of my career.

They didn't take up the offer, but they did put on a special corrida in Las Ventas for the same cause, and the organisers remembered me and offered me the place destined for a novillero in that festival. The top billing went to no less than *El Cordobés*, who was looking for something to kickstart his comeback from retirement. The day arrived, 5th April 1986, and everything was ready for another triumph from that great popular hero. The singer Julio Iglesias came all the way from Miami to sit in a ringside barrera seat to add a little colour to the event.

For Manuel Benítez *El Cordobés* they brought four carefully selected novillos from the prestigious ranch of Carlos Núñez. In the morning, they chose three, the one he would fight and two possible substitutes, and they let me have the other one, the ugliest one, which, as so often happens, in the end turned out to be the best.

When I found myself waiting in the passageway to make the parade, a little squirt alongside those other legendary matadors – *El Cordobés*, *Antoñete*, Palomo *Linares*... I felt totally insignificant. Certainly, without them even doing anything, I could feel myself shrink under the steely gaze of those superheroes.

When I arrived at the bullring, I was a bundle of nerves, but I gradually calmed down, standing in that rough tunnel leading to the ring, that fearful, brick funnel, where I would stand so many more times in the future. Either from boldness or ignorance, I didn't shrink into myself, and in no time I turned the tables and realised that I found myself on an important stage, surrounded by great heroes from the world of the bulls.

I was fed up with temporary bullrings, and I'd been fighting for a long time to earn a place in important bullrings like Las Ventas. In addition, the event was to be televised, so all my dreams were coming together on that day. I don't know where I got so much self-confidence from, but when the parade moved off, I was convinced that I was up to seizing the greatest opportunity in my life.

The novillos came out, and for *El Cordobés* things didn't turn out as he hoped, but *Antoñete* did well and cut two ears. They had seen the star acts, and because it was still raining, and the temperatures dropping, some of the public started to leave before I took my turn, waiting behind the fence for the novillo to appear which no one else had wanted. But none of that mattered to me.

It charged well from the beginning, and I moved in immediately. When they began to hear the cries of 'Olé!', those who were leaving turned round and came back to their places. I did everything right to that novillo with my left hand, and killed it with a single, powerful sword thrust. I cut the two ears as well, and for the first time in my life I was carried out of Las Ventas on shoulders. I was alone, because the superheroes from the past left on foot, and that went for *Antoñete* too because he didn't attach much importance to a triumph in a festival.

But it was important for me, being carried out on shoulders from the main gate of the most important bullring in the world. It was a marvellous moment, and unexpectedly I was suddenly surrounded by all my old childhood friends: Ángel, *Surjo*, *Carlitos*... those companions in adventures and mischief jumped into the ring to be at my side, thrilled to be sharing my moment of triumph. It was like achieving my dreams and going back to visit my childhood. In my ignorance, I thought that was all there was to it.

A SECOND-HAND SUIT FOR MY GRADUATION

That day finally convinced me that I could be successful in the world of bullfighting, and spurred Enrique to work even harder. He'd already organised my alternativa, my graduation from novillero to full matador, for 20th April in Malaga with José Luis Martín Berrocal, the impresario of the bullring. I would appear with bulls from the ranch of Carlos Núñez, alongside the two toreros who Martín Berrocal managed, Dámaso González and Juan Mora, who, on the day, would tell me that he was the same novillero who had fascinated me in Las Ventas on my tenth birthday.

Putting on the event required a great effort, in every possible sense. At the same time, following my success in Madrid, several important impresarios offered us some twenty novilladas for good money, and Manolo Chopera even offered us a de luxe alternativa in the Burgos Fair. This man from the Basque country dominated the business, and he wanted us to get out of the Malaga contract, although we finally decided to go ahead as planned. But Martín Arranz still managed to make an agreement with Chopera for two contracts during Madrid's San Isidro Fair.

That winter, thinking that the year would go better for me, I had ordered three new suits of lights. Pooling cash from here and there, I gave the tailor a deposit, planning to pay off the rest as the money came in from contracts. But when I went to pick up the white and gold suit that I wanted to wear in Malaga, he told me that unless I came up with the 'readies', he wouldn't let me have it.

I didn't have the money on me, so I got Enrique on the phone, who told him that he could send him a cheque. But that tailor didn't trust us two wiseguys, and he refused point blank to let me have the suit. So, on a day as important for any torero as the day of his alternativa, I had to take one of my least shabby ones, a red and gold one. I took my graduation in an old suit.

It was Easter Sunday in Malaga, and the bullring wasn't full. Barely one quarter of the tickets were sold, and a load of money 'went down the tubes'. For only the second time in my life, I flew in a plane. I only just made it because the workers of the oil company Campsa were on strike. When I finally arrived at the bullring, my head was spinning with doubts about whether or not I could take this step up in my career. But maestro Dámaso González calmed me down while we were waiting to go into the ring.

'How do you feel?' he said as I shook his hand.

'Nervous, maestro.'

'No, never. Don't worry because nothing's going to happen. Just take it like any other day, and enjoy it. You've got a future as a torero. I've been following you, and what I've seen, I like. Keep it up.'

Such words from a star matador who I admired so much were like a shot in the arm, and gave me a surge of self-confidence. I have tremendous respect for Dámaso, for his bravery, his way with the capes, and because he is a straight up and down bloke.

I cut an ear from the bull of the alternativa ceremony, which was called *Correrías* and weighed over five hundred kilos. I did well, but the kill was just okay. The second bull was dangerous, and hit me hard. Although it wasn't a great success, I felt good, made up at being a full matador at last. The step up from three-year-old novillos to four-year-old bulls wasn't so very different, because I'd been facing crazy monsters in the villages since I was fourteen.

What was very much different was the look of my new companions, stern faces like in the earlier event at Las Ventas.

As a novillero, I would find myself in the ring alongside boys of my age, or a little older, all a bit lightweight, like me. But now I was a matador, I would be among men hardened in a thousand battles, veterans with a chestful of medals who weren't going to give anything away, who would do me down if they could, and who wouldn't give me an inch. Looking at them, I began to realise that this side of bullfighting was a serious business.

After the corrida, back at the hotel were all my friends, some other followers, and a few colleagues from the Bullfighting School. They were all very excited. I was over the moon, bursting with pride that I'd been able to do well in my first corrida de toros, to know that I wasn't afraid to stand alongside those sly-faced old warriors.

The feeling of having passed the test was tremendous. Once again, my doubts had been overcome, the same doubts that I had every time I went up a step in my career: the first time I faced a heifer, the first time I took on a male calf, the first time I killed one, the first time I fought novillos with picadors...

I always had my doubts, always, but I never failed to come through. Now all I needed to know was if I was capable of competing at the highest level, and what would happen when I got my first serious cornada, a horn wound. What we toreros call a 'tobacco'.

There was no way back. I was now a full 'matador de toros', and, what's more, one of the youngest in history, because I was still under seventeen. As far as I know, only *Gallito*, Luis Miguel *Dominguín* and maybe one other took the alternativa at a younger age. I was starting out on a genuinely professional career which promised to be a big adventure, a leap into space.

Because, apart from the two corridas in San Isidro, I didn't have a single other contract lined up. We had received many offers, but for not much money. Enrique wouldn't shift from asking for a minimum of one million pesetas per corrida, and that was a lot of money in the mid-1980s. They said we were crazy, but I was growing in confidence all the time, and I was in no doubt that, if things didn't turn out as we wished, I would just do something else. I was ready and willing to take on the management of the bullrings face to face.

My greatest asset was the unflagging support of Enrique Martín Arranz, who staked everything on me without fearing the consequences. He had given up his all-important personal project of the Madrid School of Bullfighting, and spent a fortune on my preparation, because he had more faith in me than I did myself.

It was no longer a question of him fulfilling the promise he had made to my father, which had already been more than met, but this was a gamble to launch the career of an untried torero. I didn't have any obvious qualities to suggest to him that I would get to the top. Perhaps I wasn't that much different from dozens of others. But I wasn't a fool, I didn't get frightened easily, and could handle the capes reasonably well, although I didn't yet have star quality.

Enrique is usually so calculating, but it is possible that, on this occasion, the decision taken by Enrique may have been made for emotional reasons; it's possible that he was influenced by the fact that he liked me. But there's no room for sentiment in the daily struggle of the bullfighting business. Who knows if the case of *Yiyo* influenced his decision; did he think that he had perhaps not been as protective of such a promising individual in his business arrangements as he should have been, before that tragic day in Colmenar? He may have thought that he had done wrong in passing *Yiyo* over to someone who was not an expert in the business of the bulls, that he had left a lot of things to chance, and that was why such a promising torero had met such an end. Perhaps he feared that the same might happen to me and that's why he wanted to take over the reins himself.

He knew that I was volatile, that I was easily unsettled by problems, and so he made me develop a very positive attitude, and convinced me that any success in the world of the bulls would depend on my own efforts. He could manage things well enough, the bulls, the contracts, the money... But it was up to me, on my own in the ring; it was me who would give substance to his management. After all, he had nothing to lose.

After taking my alternativa, we paid to put on two village corridas with big bulls with big horns, to prepare me for what was awaiting for me in Las Ventas. I did okay, and went straight from there to Madrid, to the top-of-the-bill corrida of San Isidro. With no less than the legendary Curro Romero, and Paco Ojeda, the superstar of the moment. Fired up...and in a dream.

When you don't know anything, bullfighting is wonderful. I remember that on that day I dressed for the corrida in Enrique's apartment in Calle Santa Maria de la Cabeza, and a friend offered to drive me to the bullring in his Mercedes, which at the time seemed like the height of luxury to me.

But the friend, who was a tax inspector, got tied up at the office, and at a quarter past six I found myself waiting downstairs outside the front door, fully dressed in a torero outfit. Time was tight, so we had to stop a taxi to take us to Las Ventas, and when we got to the bridge over the M-30 highway, we hit the mother of all traffic jams.

It was now ten to seven, so, without thinking twice, I got out of the car and took off on foot for the rest of the way, I went in the wrong door of the bullring, and when I finally got to the tunnel, I found the two taurine legends folding their parade capes and giving me dirty looks for arriving late and making everyone nervous. But I was very cool. If the same had happened to me a few years later, I would have been a nervous wreck.

On top of that, maestro Curro Romero was annoyed with me because I was a bit cheeky in an interview with that day's *ABC* newspaper, 26th May, going so far as to say that I would wipe the floor with the two superstars in my alternativa confirmation in Madrid. So when he was presenting me with my cape in the confirmation ceremony, Curro said, 'Well, young man, what's this about how you're going to wipe the floor with me and this other gentleman?'

'Well, at least I'm going to try,' I answered chirpily.

And after making my dedication to the King, who was that day in a ringside barrera seat, I left the ring, *my* ring of Las Ventas, with a trophy of one ear in my hand. I passed the bull very close, I kept very still, and I felt I had arrived as an important torero for having won the day against those two established stars.

But I came back to earth when I arrived at the hotel and Enrique pointed out something that I already knew: this was just the beginning of a long, long road still to be covered. The best part was that, while we were having dinner, something happened which gave me even more motivation: the phone began to ring, and in no time we had eighteen contracts at the money we were asking for. Time had shown that we were right.

NO RESPECT AND NO GIRLFRIEND

After my second contracted corrida in Las Ventas, when I didn't cut any ears, I was invited to appear on the programme of Mercedes Milá on Spanish Television. I was on with *Antoñete*, who was planning a comeback, and he got annoyed with me because I said things without thinking first. I was just seventeen and on the way up, and I contradicted whatever he said without due respect, and since that day, the maestro and me fell out.

A lot of people saw the programme, and it was a good bit of PR for me. We didn't ask for it, but we were called by Teresa Doueil, a journalist working with Milá. She was the one who did the first long interview of my career, and because we got on well together, she was always very helpful and set up the TV appearance.

When I arrived, I was a bit taken aback, because I had never been in a television studio before, but I knew that I should take advantage of the chance to appear before an audience of millions. On the way there, Enrique asked me to speak purposefully so as to get across our message, but I asked him to let me speak as I felt, otherwise I would blow it all.

As it turned out, I wasn't at all nervous – quite the opposite. Before we went live, Mercedes Milá gave me a lot of confidence, and she made me feel relaxed. So I expressed myself very openly, and spoke very sincerely, which was my usual way then. I spoke very honestly about my situation, and I think that the image many people have of me – that I talk straight from the shoulder – comes from that TV programme in the spring of 1986.

All that apart, the best thing was that, thanks to the television, I finally got to meet up again with my brother, Roberto Carlos, who I hadn't seen since we were split up as kids, because they didn't even take him to our father's funeral.

At the end of the interview, I asked Milá if I could make an appeal. I explained that I had a brother who I didn't know. How, one time, I stopped at traffic lights, and a young boy was staring at me, and I thought that it might be him, but I didn't know because I didn't even know what he looked like. I spoke direct to the camera and it touched the audience.

'I want to know him and find out about his life. His name is Roberto Carlos and, if anyone knows his whereabouts, please ask him to get in touch.'

I didn't have to wait long, because someone immediately rang in to the programme, and a few days later, thanks to Fernando Utande, the President of the Caja Madrid bank, I got to see Roberto in Alcorcón. It was all very weird. We embraced, and then we didn't know what to do next, or what to say. Luckily, Enrique broke the ice, and we started talking to one another.

But it was obvious that we came from two different worlds: I was into the bulls one hundred per cent, and he, only fifteen years old, looked after the goats and chickens of the family he lived with. We didn't even look much alike, except for when we smiled; I don't look like my sister, Maribel, either, who is covered with freckles and has frizzy hair. We've got nothing in common, except we have the same mother. We couldn't talk about our parents either, because Roberto Carlos hadn't known them.

Later on, we saw more of one another. Roberto Carlos likes to work hard. He left school early to work on the land. They couldn't have treated him very well, though, because his only ambition was to get a little motorbike to go to work on, but his people wouldn't buy it; instead they hassled him to ask me for the money. But he wouldn't. When I found out, I told him that I would get the bike for him as a present, on condition that he take the school exam, the Graduado Escolar. And that's what he did.

He got a job in a chicken business and then he set up on his own. I offered to buy him a shop, and he could pay me back in instalments, but he turned me down again because he didn't want to take advantage of me. His business didn't do well, and he got a job in a firm cutting up and packaging chickens. He got married, but they broke up. He's now living with another girl, and they have two kids. He's happy at last. He's a really nice person. We don't see much of one another, and when we do, we talk about our other brothers and sisters, who are not the same ones, because they're from different parents.

In that year of 1986, I ended up with almost fifty corridas in nearly every one of the important Fairs. In the winter, I had another eleven in South America: Lima, Bogota, Caracas, Quito... I appeared with all the top matadors of the day, *Espartaco, Niño de la Capea, Manzanares*, Ortega Cano, *Antoñete*, Ojeda – people who were my gods.

So, to keep up to the high standards, I had no alternative but to go for it hard, setting aside my own ideas so I could cut some ears and not let the opportunities slip by without making an impression. But I wasn't comfortable, I didn't feel happy with myself. Suddenly, after so many doubts, everything was going too fast. My career took off like a rocket, and I barely had time to breathe, let alone to think.

I began the next year still much in demand, because I was a novelty. I started off well with the Castellón Fair. When I appeared for the first time as a full matador in the April Fair in Seville, I already had three corridas signed up for San Isidro, and that was just a few days before my eighteenth birthday.

A journalist friend suggested doing an article for the social pages to celebrate my 'coming of age'. We agreed, because the publicity was a good idea. So, after appearing in the bullring of la Maestranza de Sevilla, we went to the caseta of the press agency EFE in the Royal Fairground. I was introduced to the singer, Sylvia Pantoja, who they brought along to take photos of us together to make out that we were an item. This was typical stuff about the link between flamenco and the bulls.

When I was standing next to that girl, dazzling in a gypsy dress, my legs started to tremble, which had never happened to me when

I was facing the bulls. I lived a simple life in the country, naive and inexperienced, so the sight of such an Andalusian beauty – and I have always liked that look – sparked off a sort of hormone explosion. I couldn't speak. She was talking to me, softly, sexily, and I was looking away. It was one of the worst moments of my life. When I think back on it, I can only think what a prize wally I was. I missed out on a chance in a million.

Shortly after, they set up another photocall with her, this time on the farm. What a laugh! Sylvia wearing a flamenco dress again and me in a formal traje corto, on horseback. What some might call 'typical Spanish'. But I went along with it because we thought we needed to appeal to a different type of public, by showing my life outside of the bullring, and despite its shortcomings, everything was tastefully done, and respectful of the profession of torero.

They tried to sell it as a romance, but it just didn't work – mind you, I would have liked it to! I felt so uncomfortable that I swore to Enrique that I would never do anything like it again. Since that time, I've refused to have anything to do with the dangerous world of gossip magazines. Two or three years later, they invited me to the opening of a new disco, and they wanted me to go with Jose Toledo, which shows how little they understand about the world of the bulls.

'What, do you think I'm queer or something? How am I supposed to go with a bloke?' I said to the guy who phoned me.

And then when I saw just who that 'Jose' really was, a stunning looking girl, a model turned TV presenter, I wanted the earth to swallow me up. Anyway, I didn't go, with or without a partner. I didn't go in for all that, and I still don't. Not even when they called me to appear in that famous video with Madonna; I turned it down flat, despite the huge sum of money on offer. They gave it to another matador, Emilio Muñoz.

As for women around this time, it's not to say that there were only a few – there weren't any at all. I was stuck on the farm, obsessed with the bulls, which was the only thing on my mind. Not a nibble, not even in America where everyone was getting more than their share – except for me; unlike the rest, I trained like a mad thing over there, punishing myself so as not to lose my concentration. I had lots of offers, including a young dancer in Lima, who was a fantastic looker.

For a whole week, I saw her every day in the hotel, and she was a constant temptation. She must have noticed how shy I was because, in the end, she approached me. But because on the day of my debut in the bullring I had done really badly, I turned her down, saying that I had to shape up for the next Sunday. She didn't take no for an answer, and said why didn't we go to the beach together, or have dinner, or just go for a walk, but I said no. The fact is that, thanks to a supreme effort, I didn't do anything with her, but even so, I had another disastrous day in the ring. If only I had known that before...

My main responsibility was to keep my concentration on the job in hand, because the 1987 season was about to start, and that was the year when I had to get myself established. More than a big triumph, or the lack of it, my main worry was that I still hadn't had a serious horn wound, a cornada. Until then, it was like I was made of rubber. All I had were tossings, lots of tossings, the occasional minor injury, and several light wounds, needing only four or five stitches. Fortunately.

THE HORNS OF *LIMONERO* AND THE CIRCLING VULTURES

The previous year, the bulls used to catch me almost on a daily basis, sometimes two or three times a day, but none of them actually broke the skin. Some of those tossings were terrible, like the one in Bilbao. But I still hadn't had a serious cornada, and I didn't know if I was going to be able to bounce back from such a life-threatening experience; there is a saying that the bravery of toreros flows away through the wounds of their cornadas. I was almost hoping for the time to come.

Which, of course, is what happened. It was on 15th May, the saint day of San Isidro. It was my third corrida in Las Ventas, appearing alongside my idol, Curro Vázquez, with Pepín Jiménez.

My second bull, the sixth, was called *Limonero*, a huge toro bravo weighing no less than seven hundred kilos.

I stepped out to meet it with the capote as I would with any other bull, not put off by its colossal size, and I was suddenly up in the air. I don't know what happened because it was a sudden, short, sharp hit which I didn't see coming. There was a bit of wind and the capote must have lifted slightly, the bull caught it and, as it tossed its head upwards, it caught me, and because I weighed nothing, I went straight up in the air and so wasn't caught on the horns.

I lay on the ground semi-conscious until the others picked me up. I started to come round as they carried me to the infirmary, and I said to Jaro, the banderillero, to put me down because I was feeling better. As my feet touched the ground, I noticed that my arm was limp, and those who were carrying me saw that I was bleeding from the neck, so they wouldn't even let me speak, and went faster towards the operating theatre. I didn't stop them. My neck was ripped open from the throat to the ear, with all the veins exposed.

The bull had shattered my left collarbone. The bone stopped the horn from going any further and ripping my head off. I heard the doctors saying this, while I lay on the operating table still conscious of everything that was going on until the anaesthetic kicked in. Don Máximo García de la Torre, the bullring resident surgeon, seeing that I was only a youngster, set about calming me down before he started to work on me.

The medical bulletin stated that the horn had caused the destruction of muscles, and 'bruised and dissected the trachea, the thyroid, the carotid and jugular' in addition to the fracture. The next day, the doctor told me that I should consider myself lucky. He was surprised to find that, with such a serious wound, considering the point of entry, the horn hadn't cut those vital arteries: 'You've come back from the dead, young man.'

So the serious cornada that I had been expecting had finally arrived. I knew that when I woke up between the cold, faded walls of the old Loreto clinic. Now all I had to do was to worry about getting out of there as quickly as possible. Then it remained to be seen if I could pass the hardest test in my entire career: when I faced a bull again.

In the middle of all this, the same night that I got my cornada, Pepita turned up at the hospital. It had been a while since I had any news of her. My room had a sort of ante room with imitation leather armchairs for visitors, and that's where Enrique found her.

Under sedation, and feeling completely out of it, I didn't know what was going on. They told me later that, as soon as the door was opened, she threw herself at Enrique and scratched his face with both hands. Enrique said nothing and didn't react, letting her attack him and scream wildly like a mad woman, 'You're going to kill him! You're going to kill him!'

Luckily I was now eighteen years old, because, as soon as I began to earn some money, Pepita had been trying to get in touch, possibly hoping to hold on to custody of me. Even though I'd been sending her money, like Martín Arranz advised me to do.

'Look José,' he said, 'that woman, whatever has happened, was still the one who looked after you since you were a child, and she deserves to be recompensed for that now that you can afford it.'

I was still very angry about all the things that had gone on at home, and I didn't want to help her, but he made me see things clearly. In this, as in so many other things, Enrique is often right.

Once I took my alternativa, I paid for the apartment for Pepita, and I sent her money every month because she told me that she was out of work. Three or four years later, I found out that she had got another job, but hadn't told me. So instead of sending her money, I decided to pay all her food bills in the market of La Guindalera, whatever she wanted to eat, never mind the cost. I paid the bills at the end of the month, and that's why all the stall-keepers got to know me.

As far as I was concerned, Pepita never went short of anything. I had the apartment in the Calle Cartagena redecorated – it was in my name – and she kept on living there until the day she died just a few years ago.

She wasn't the only person who turned up at the clinic. My biological mother came the day after the cornada. I don't know if she had remarried or not, but she had a man with her who she lived with, and she had another son, my fifth sibling of sorts.

It annoyed me to see her. She wanted to be all loving, but her over-the-top show of affection at this point in the story turned my stomach. She was talking to me all lovey-dovey, and her man made cooing noises. There were other people in the room, and because I didn't want to make a scene, I resisted the urge to tell them what I wanted – which was for them to take a running jump! There I was, hurting like hell, and made filthy angry by seeing her, so I became very agitated. Thank God they didn't stay long.

But the next day, they were back with the same drooling crap, as if nothing had happened in the last fifteen years. As soon as we were alone, and as she got up to leave, I had the chance to say what was on my mind, 'Listen. Do me a favour. Since you say you love me so much, please do me a favour and don't come back. And tell that man with you to stop calling me "dear boy", and to stop patting my face, or I'll smash him over the head with the saline bottle. Get out now, and don't ever come back!'

She must have loved me a lot, because she never did come back.

But I saw her again the following year. She turned up at the hotel when I had a corrida in Alcalá de Henares, where she lived. She wanted to talk to me, but I made a quick escape. My own people knew the situation and covered for me. That day, I was a disaster in the bullring. I'd been having a great series of successes throughout the month of August, but, on that day, I couldn't do a thing right because I was so rattled by seeing her. I told Enrique to accept no more contracts for Alcalá. I didn't want to go there in case she showed up again.

I heard later from Roberto Carlos that this unpleasant woman won the lottery, but she didn't give him a penny, only to his sister, Maribel, who she was still in touch with. And then she called Roberto Carlos at a time when he was out of work, to offer him a job in her bar that she'd opened in Alcalá, but she didn't want to pay him anything. I think she went round the bend when she left us.

And in case you thought there was anyone missing, my sister Maribel also turned up to see me after my cornada in the neck.

That was one visit I enjoyed, because I always liked her a lot, just like I did Bienvenido. I hadn't seen her for five years, since the time our grandparents sent her to spend a few days with Pepita and me, soon after both of us were left orphans.

We were two kids together then, and we got on really well with each other. We didn't talk about our own lives or our parents, but we just enjoyed being with one another, and we were like best friends, walking down the street in a daze, looking in shop windows and buying sweets. We loved each other, but it was as if there was nothing to tie us together, we had nothing in common except our blood connection. But blood has no feelings. She went back to Leon and I stayed in Madrid. Things went back to normal. She went back to her stand-in parents, her real family, and that was it.

Maribel didn't stay long at the hospital that May afternoon, and I didn't hear from her again until a year later. She had got married and called me because she needed some money to buy a car.

I couldn't oblige, because I simply didn't have it at the time. I'd just made a down-payment on my first farm, at Monesterio in Extremadura, and I had bought a herd of toros bravos. I hadn't got a bean in actual cash, and my future earnings would go to paying off the investment I'd made. She got offended, we had a sort of row, and things went cold between us. Another time she came to see me when I was on at the bullring in León, with my grandmother, her husband and their son, but something had obviously changed between us.

A lot of water had gone under the bridge, and it seemed that she had made a break from that unhappy past we shared together and which had nearly destroyed me. I was now in new surroundings, I had sorted my life out, and there was little or nothing to connect me to my birth family and our genetic links. There was even less connection with my uncles and cousins who, following the chaotic day of Bienvenido's funeral, suddenly started to swarm around like flies round a honey-pot when I was beginning to become famous and earning serious money.

My father hardly saw anything of his family, so why should I? I was still feeling very bitter towards them because of the way they behaved on the day of the funeral, and because they hadn't taken any interest in me since then. I hadn't seen them since I left La Guindalera.

The only exception was my Uncle Pedro from Móstoles, who was an aficionado and turned up occasionally at my novilladas. But that's all. When I took the alternativa, he had the downright bloody cheek to write to me asking, among other things, if success had made me lose my memory, and I couldn't remember my family? I didn't even answer him. Then I saw him one day and told him that that, yes, I had lost my memory, and I had a case of severe amnesia, which was irreversible.

When I appeared on TV, a brother of my birth mother who lived in Burgos showed up. This was when I appeared there in the San Pedro Fair a few days after the programme with Mercedes Milá. I was carried out on shoulders that day, and while I was sitting in the car, a man tapped on the window and said he was related to me.

I ignored him, but he turned up again at the hotel. He came straight up to me in the reception and said that he was my Uncle Whatsit – I don't know his name.

'Okay,' I replied, 'and I am José Miguel Arroyo, but when I was here as a novillero two years ago, I didn't have an uncle, or a cousin, or a grandmother. You didn't look me up before or show any interest in me, so please close the door after you when you leave.'

The same year I went to Vitoria and something similar happened with my Aunt Janis – what kind of a name is Janis? She was godmother at my baptism, and my mother's sister. She came to the hotel to see me, and at first I tried to be polite to her, but I didn't pay much attention.

Even so, that woman came to see me whenever I went to that bullring. I didn't turn her away, I even went so far as to have lunch with her one time, but not even her, nor the rest of all those people, interest me in the slightest. It's not that they have done me any harm, but they haven't done me any good either. I don't feel that I owe them anything other than the basic politeness due to a stranger.

So, when I became twenty, I proposed to Enrique that he should adopt me legally as his son. Adela and him had just had a daughter,

Rocío, and at first he didn't want to go along with my idea. But I managed to convince him with a compelling argument.

'There are already a lot of vultures circling out there, and it's not impossible that one day a bull might finish me off, or that I might be killed in a traffic accident. The only ones who have helped me fight for what I have are you two, and you took a chance on me. I would be really pissed off if people I don't know in the slightest, and who have never done anything for me, could turn up and walk away with everything we have earned together. And anyway, for God's sake, you took me in when I was on the rocks, treated me like your own son, and made me feel like I belong here in your home. You are my real family.'

And so, in my birth certificate since 1989, I have new parents, although I have kept my original surnames, purposely turning down the idea of taking the names of Enrique and Adela. After all, there was no reason to confuse the public with a new name on the posters.

5

ARTIST AND WARRIOR

U ntil Enrique and Adela adopted me, three years after that first serious cornada, I went through a difficult period having to adapt to my new situation in the world of bullfighting. In order to get up there with the best of them, I had to keep having success after success, but that meant facing up to the tough side of the job, and at the same time as establishing my own identity, I had to be careful not to sacrifice my personal standards as an artist.

After *Limonero* opened up my neck, my return to the ring took longer than expected, because a bandage on the broken collarbone was tied too tight, and I lost strength and feeling in my left hand. But once I was fully recovered, I reappeared in the bullring of Teruel in the middle of July, less than two months later.

I was deliriously happy. I did well, and proved that, once more, I had overcome my doubts and fears. I had at last had the cornada I was expecting, and I had come back from it. One more obstacle overcome.

But in the following corridas I went downhill. I was a bit lost, and didn't know what was happening to me. I still faced an internal battle trying to feel like a real torero, and all this was making my head spin. But it got better. I forced myself to think positively, because now wasn't the time for self-doubt, or to take my foot off the accelerator.

It takes mental strength to deal with pain and fear, that's all. And overcoming the problem makes you feel proud of yourself. When I was a beginner, I learnt a lot about how other toreros deal with injuries. Some of these were especially instructive, like the case of David Silveti, when we appeared together in Guadalajara in Mexico in 1989.

A bonus bull, the last of the day, gored him in the thigh when he was using the muleta. But Silveti wouldn't allow himself to be taken to the infirmary, and he stayed playing the bull for a good while longer with his left hand, which is the side where he had been caught. He killed the bull with a single sword thrust, walked over to the fence and even washed his hands as if nothing had happened, although he was bleeding heavily from the horn wound, which had gone in one side and out the other. He held out until they gave him the maximum trophies of two ears and the tail, and then they lifted him up on shoulders. On his circuit of the ring, it was not until he was passing the infirmary that he asked to be let down, and he walked in on his own two feet to see the doctors. I thought, if that torero was capable of behaving like that, as long as my body held out, I would have to do the same.

I was very impressed by that show of macho bravery by Silveti, and it still gives me the shivers when I remember it. Some years later, he took his own life, when the doctors stopped him from appearing in the bullring because of a mental problem. He had almost forty operations on his knees. I'm not surprised that the man they called 'King David' is still a legendary figure for Mexicans.

Another torero who was a big influence on me was the Colombian, Pepe Cáceres, when I appeared with him in Manizales, a couple of years before he was killed by a bull in a local village bullring. That afternoon in 1987, he was caught by his second bull when he was working it with the capote, and it destroyed his thigh; it looked like a shotgun wound. Cáceres wouldn't leave the ring either, until he had cut the tail. He was over fifty at the time.

They couldn't have done much of a job on him in the infirmary, because when I went to find out about him after the corrida, they told me that he had already left for the hotel. When I got to his bedroom, he was lying on the bed, quietly smoking a cigar, while he waited for the doctor to arrive to close up the terrible wound, which was open to the bone.

These guys were made of something else, brought up a certain way and tough as nails, with the constitution of an ox. What I learnt from him made me think more about the meaning and philosophy behind bullfighting. Being a torero is a much more serious thing than people imagine. It's not just a question of making passes and cutting ears; it's how you carry yourself and behave in the bullring, and in life itself; it's like a cult of manliness, but not in the macho sense of the word. You must have overflowing qualities of integrity, poise and a capacity for self-sacrifice and for winning in the face of adversity.

A torero has to combine the sensitivity of a creative artist and the bravery of a warrior to overcome the pain and the fear. He has to pull together both these aspects of bullfighting, because the bulls are not pussycats, but wild tigers.

It's as Antonio Corbacho said: he was the manager responsible for the career of José Tomás, and he said that the mentality of a torero is very much like that of the samurai, who can keep going in a battle even when they are smashed up inside. You have to convince yourself that there is no such thing as pain, however great is the cornada.

Some years ago, a bull gave me a very bad tossing in a bullring in France. When I landed on the sand, I fell hard on my backside, my coccyx. When I stood up, I had no strength in my legs, which folded under me like a rag doll, and I thought I had been paralysed.

They carried me with my feet dragging on the ground over to the side of the ring, and I suddenly remembered that 'there is no such thing as pain', although the pain was immense, and I managed to stand up and get on with dealing with the bull. It was a long, painful walk to the infirmary, where they gave me some painkillers, and I went back to fight the second bull, as best I could. The worst part was later in the car, driving through the night all the way home.

This attitude, this capacity for putting up with whatever life throws at you, may seem out of place these days in a world where making an effort is frowned upon, but this is one of the great attributes of toreros. Since bullfighting began, it is gestures like this which provide the driving force. In the old days, the methods used for treating cornadas were unbearable. Before anaesthetics and penicillin, wounds were closed by binding them with yards and yards of gauze soaked in iodine for days on end: nothing else. Gangrene was a constant danger.

You had to have lot of guts to put up with this treatment, almost more than when you're facing a bull. Nowadays, after they get you to the infirmary, you hardly feel a thing; and if it hurts later, they give you painkillers.

What sometimes also takes place is what happened to me in Nîmes, when a bull smashed the top of my femur into three bits, and I saw ghosts in my bedroom at the hospital. The pain was so great that the doctors overdid the morphine, and, one night when I woke up, I had to dodge the dragons flying around the room.

Bullfighting is a very tough business. As I progressed in my profession, I found this more and more to be true, from what happened to my colleagues too. For example, when we were still kids, we were very affected by the terrible cornada given in Llodio to Ángel Luis Prados, the elder brother of *el Fundi*.

Enrique was with him, and he told us how he had to ride with Ángel Luis in the ambulance with his fist pushing into the wound, because the doctor at the bullring couldn't deal with it. She was a very young woman, very pregnant, and she fainted at the sight of the wound.

Losing litres of blood all the way, as happened to *Paquirri*, Ángel Luis was delirious. He was practically dead when he arrived at the hospital. Luckily, he still had a little blood pressure when they took him in to the surgeon, because otherwise he wouldn't have left the operating table alive.

The eldest of the *Fundi* brothers was lucky enough to be able to return to bullfighting, like Lucio Sandín after a novillo took out his eye the following year in the Sevilla Maestranza bullring. That generation of the Princes of Bullfighting were very unlucky, taking into account what happened to *Yiyo* too. We were very impressed by what happened to Lucio also, but we were growing used to this sort of thing. We went to see him in hospital nearly every day, but, as can be seen in the film *Tú solo*, Sandín himself talked about it in a very matter-of-fact way. He kept himself together, and put all of us at our ease, so we just took it as part of the job. An occupational hazard.

But after the tragedy of *Yiyo*, the other time I saw death up close was on 22nd May 1988, when *el Campeño* met his end. And I shat myself.

EL CAMPEÑO DID NOT DIE OF AIDS

That corrida in Las Ventas came after a couple of other low points. After we split up as novilleros, things hadn't gone too well for my friends, *Fundi* and Bote. José Luis left Enrique's ranch almost immediately, because he didn't feel at all comfortable in the countryside, and then a novillo gave him a very bad cornada in nearby San Martín de Valdeiglesias.

José Pedro became depressed and didn't fight for a few months, until he got his interest back while doing his military service, and he returned to novilladas, although without his previous enthusiasm. It was 1987, and while I was on the up, they were going nowhere.

One day that summer, they both came to see us to ask for help with taking their alternativas; they were a bit desperate, and trying to get their careers moving again. I was happy to agree, and we thought of the village of Villaviciosa de Odón as the place to do it, because it was close to Madrid and had been the scene of many of our earlier triumphs as becerristas.

The town hall liked the idea, we sorted out six decent bulls, and finally, on 22nd September, I had the honour of making my two best friends full matadors. On the face of it, this was a happy step, but their future wasn't bright, and so the atmosphere wasn't exactly cheerful.

Following on from that, we only managed one corrida together, in a different village. I was very happy to appear with them, but we couldn't keep helping them out forever. Our careers, our destinies and out interests were very different, and we each had to make our own way independently. Even so, I offered to try to get them a corrida during San Isidro, to confirm their alternativas in Las Ventas, and that was on the fateful day of 22nd May 1988.

After we went through the alternativa ceremonials, my second bull of the afternoon wasn't dealt with properly by the picador. It was still too strong, and it was a nasty sonofabitch when it was time for the banderillas. One of my banderilleros in the cuadrilla was Antonio González, el Campeño. When it was his turn to place banderillas, the bull went for him violently, and he couldn't place a single one. Out of professional pride and self-respect, he wanted to try again. I told him not to bother, to let the other banderillero have a go, but he ignored me. In a fraction of a second, that evil creature had plunged its horn into his neck.

I ran over from the other side of the ring to take the bull away, but I couldn't get there in time. Neither could those who were closer than me. Halfway across, as *Fundi* tried to lift him up off the sand, I saw that with every heartbeat a spurt of blood was pumping out and making a stain on el Campeño's shirt. And I saw death in his eyes.

I was frozen with fear, and in an act of pure cowardice I picked up a pair of banderillas from the ground and backed away; they were the ones that Antonio had been unable to place in the previous attempt. I gave a half-turn and went to the fence to take up my muleta and sword. If I had gone with him to the infirmary, I wouldn't have been able to kill the bull afterwards. I didn't dare to go to see Antonio because my heart was pounding like a drum. I still get the shivers just thinking about it.

I know perfectly well that I couldn't have done anything; the bull was determined to catch something, and as soon as Antonio decided to try again, a cornada was inevitable. But I still feel badly about not having reached him in time to be of help. *El Campeño* was with me from the time I was a becerrista, and out of friendship and genuine affection, I asked him to join the cuadrilla when I took my alternativa. His death affected me very strongly because I felt that

I'd let one of my own people down. And I suffered from that feeling for a long time.

That afternoon, the atmosphere in Las Ventas was extremely unpleasant, not just because of the cornada of Antonio. As happens so many times in Las Ventas – I don't know why – the crowd was against us from the beginning. There was one comedian waving an enormous cut-out of a saw from his seat, as if to say that the horns had been got at, and were harmless, because the tips had been sawn off.

Bote did well, but the crowd ignored this. He cut an ear, but they didn't care. *El Fundi* was terrific too, but in that atmosphere they even booed and whistled him. José Pedro was very affected by Antonio's cornada, and on his circuit of the ring, when he passed by the idiot with the saw in the crowd in the Tendido 7 section of the ring, he turned his back on them. They still haven't forgiven him for that.

My friends had shown that they were ready for major success as full matadors, which was the object of the exercise, but the tragedy had obliterated all the good things they did that day, and they still had a long uphill slog ahead of them.

And poor *Campeño*, although he was practically dead on arrival at the infirmary, the doctors didn't actually certify him dead until a week later. They kept him on a life-support machine, but in reality he lost his life on the horns of that bull. The worst part of it was that, while we were still trying to come to terms with it all, the same doctors pulled the dirty trick of telling the press that the man who lay dying had AIDS.

We knew this beforehand, because those who had carried Antonio into the infirmary, and had been in contact with the four litres of blood which he lost, were called by the resident doctor of Las Ventas, two or three days later; he wanted to make everyone take a blood test. Even so, the diagnosis was very dubious, because not all the tests they made on Antonio showed positive.

It looked most likely that the virus had got into his body from the blood transfusions he was given. Nevertheless, that scumbag director of the hospital opened his fat mouth and tarnished the image of a torero who had died a noble death in the ring. Enrique and I went to his office and told him what we thought of him. But he didn't withdraw a word, although he had trampled all over the feelings of a family shattered by grief.

At the time, they didn't really know much about AIDS. It was thought of as something like a curse, shameful, a sort of Biblical plague which spread through the slightest contact. Parents took their children out of school so they wouldn't be anywhere near Antonio's kids. There was one taurino, a really nasty piece of work, who went around saying that it didn't surprise him in the least, because *el Campeño* was always going with whores, when the truth was that he took good care of himself and lived like a monk, because he was nearing retirement and wanted to stay fit enough to do his job in the ring properly. It was totally unjustified, evil and despicable. That torero didn't die of AIDS. He was killed by a toro bravo in the Madrid bullring, in front of thousands of spectators.

It was a very tough time for me, too. I was so badly knocked back by it all that I was uptight and disturbed for a long time after. I couldn't help thinking that the cornada which had killed Antonio was in the same part of the neck as mine a year earlier. It was then, for the first time, I started to realise what could have happened on 15th May 1987, which I hadn't at the point when the surgeon spoke to me. With my fingers, I felt the scar which went from my throat to my ear, and it gave me the shivers.

MEDALLIONS, LUCKY CHARMS, QUIRKS AND SUPERSTITIONS

As well as bruises and broken bones, I have scars of fourteen cornadas all over my body. I feel I'm lucky because some of them could have been fatal, like, for example, the one in Madrid. Or like the other one at the beginning of April 1989 in Aguascalientes, in Mexico, where the horn went into one cheek of my backside and travelled along parallel to the rectum and damaged my intestines. Those doctors in Aguascalientes are the same ones who saved the life of José Tomás in 2010, and they are just unbelievable.

I had another cornada the following year which split my saphenous vein; it was in the same bullring of San Martín de Valdeiglesias where José Luis Bote had his 'tobacco'. But that wasn't the worst thing that happened that day, because as I was lying on the operating table waiting for the anaesthetic, they had to lift me off to deal with a woman who'd had a heart attack. It turned out that she was the same woman who brought up my brother, Roberto Carlos. They had come together from Alcorcón to see me, and because she had a weak heart, she died right there on the spot. I believe it was from the shock of seeing me caught by the bull.

For all these reasons – in search of something else out there to give us a hand, something to hold on to amid so much uncertainty – toreros go to pray before going into the ring. That's to say, all except for me. I didn't used to pray, either in the hotel or at the bullring, because it all seemed very selfish to me. Before a corrida, there are others who go into the chapel to ask for help and good fortune from the Christ or the Virgin there, but then afterwards, even if they don't go out on shoulders, none of them goes back to the chapel to give thanks.

In my opinion, that's not about faith, but a selfish use of religion when it suits in times of crisis. That didn't seem right to me, so I preferred not to go along with it. Although I did for a period in the mid-1990s, when I decided to pray like my colleagues, I wasn't happy about it, and I soon went back to my old ways.

Except for those few months, I never prayed before a bullfight, or afterwards. Not even during the time when I was convinced that I would be killed by a bull. I didn't feel like that while I was in the ring, because otherwise I wouldn't have been able to perform, but it did happen in the hours leading up to a corrida. Leaving a room thinking that I wasn't going to come back again was terrifying.

All through the months of one summer, I suffered from this, at the time when I was at my busiest, and it produced a terrible feeling of anxiety in me on a daily basis, when travelling, in the hotel, in restaurants. I breathed easy again once I left the bullring, but the next morning, the same suffocating sensation came back, and became an obsession when it was time for me to dress for the corrida, and while waiting in the patio of the bullring to go on. Right up to the moment that the bull came out into the ring – it was horrible.

Fortunately, because otherwise I would have had to retire, these gruesome thoughts went out of my head in the same way that they came in. I believe that all toreros go through similar experiences at some time in our careers. It's only human. Even then, I didn't call for divine protection. Except that after a corrida and when I was taking a shower, I might say the Lord's Prayer with the water running, to say thank you. I admit that it was more about selfishly feeling grateful to still be in one piece than about genuine belief.

I don't go to church much. I have never been one for relics and medallions, or carrying around those little religious packages that other toreros assemble in their rooms, with picture cards of saints, candles, crosses and rosaries. Some of them are so big that they look like a chapel in the Vatican.

Aficionados would give me hundreds of saint cards and medallions, and I accepted them all, because they were given with affection and in good faith, but I passed them on to other members of the cuadrilla. I didn't ever throw any of them away. Sometimes people would get angry with me if they gave me a medallion and I didn't put it on. Next to my heart I only wear what is dear to me personally: a dog tag with my blood group.

On the other hand, I have had lots of superstitions in my time. Too many by far. I was a bit quirky, and I paid attention to all those crazy things that pass through your head when you're stressed, stuff that you did when things turned out well, and so you do the same again next time, until such time that you realise that they're meaningless. Deep down, it's just a nervous way of controlling fear.

One year, I got it into my head that a pair of underpants with pictures of little elephants, which my adoptive mother gave me, brought me luck. The first day I wore them I had a triumph, so I put them on every day I had a corrida. I ended up with them falling to bits. If I had two corridas back-to-back, I would wash them out myself overnight in the hotel, so that I could wear them the next day until I changed into my suit of lights for the corrida.

On arrival at the bullring, unlike most people, I always took my first step with the left foot, and I also began the parade with my left foot, and my first pass of the bull with the capote had to be on the left side, even if it meant that the bull had to go round seventeen times before it came that way. If not, I wouldn't come out from behind the fence. My banderilleros knew this and did their best to make it happen, even though sometimes it was counterproductive, because some bulls just wouldn't go on the left, or turned away at the last minute. If time was being wasted, the crowd got angry with so much messing about.

In the end, I decided to do away with all this nonsense. It's madness to tie yourself down with so many ridiculous details which don't do anything; that's all they are – superstitions. But, to be honest, I must admit that I didn't give them all up.

I confess that I have never again placed my montera – the hat worn by a torero – on top of a bed, nor a brimmed hat or a cap. I don't know why, but it is one of the greatest taboos in bullfighting – a bad luck sign which cannot be reversed, a premonition of tragedy. And it's what made me begin to be superstitious.

Until I got the cornada in my neck, I wasn't like that and I didn't take the slightest notice of the warnings of others. The morning of that corrida in Madrid, my sword handler at the time, Rafael González, started to lay out my bullfighting clothes – what we call 'making the chair' – in the bedroom of the apartment in Santa María de la Cabeza. He left the montera on a chest of drawers, just as Adela passed by with her duster. Because it was in her way, my mother moved it and put it on top of the bedspread.

Rafael panicked, 'What are you doing? That's really bad luck!'

'Don't be so silly, it's nothing. José doesn't believe in such things.'

But the next day, when I was lying in bed at the hospital, Adela told me, very upset, what had happened with the hat a few hours before the cornada.

After that, it never happened again. But exactly one year later before a corrida in Valladolid, Rafa and Adela were together in my room, like on the day of the incident. I lost my temper, picked up the montera and put it down on the bed. I was fed up with the whole business, which was getting on my nerves. I thought that, by doing this with the same people as before, I could break the curse. Adela and Rafa got very nervous:

'What are you doing? Are you mad?'

'Nothing's going to happen, it's stupid. I'm fed up with this nonsense and I'm doing this so that you will see that nothing is going to happen. We'll have a good laugh about it tonight.'

Even so, when I went to the bullring I was a bit tense, like them. But everything went very well, the bulls didn't touch me and I managed to cut ears. When we got back to the room, the three of us breathed easy again, although we had been uncomfortable thinking about the jinx.

'Do you see? Nothing happened,' I told them. 'Before, it was just a coincidence. That's all there is to it.'

The phone rang. Someone was on the phone telling us that Doctor Ochoa, who was a good friend, had just committed suicide.

I never played silly games like that again. It was like a warning from on high not to leave the montera on the bed under any circumstances, and it's the only superstition I respect. The rest were just hang-ups. For example, I don't like having people in my room before a bullfight. Only the sword handler and Enrique are allowed.

I used to let friends in, and maybe a fan or two, until I decided one day in Bilbao to put an end to these visits. At one time, I had as many as fourteen or fifteen people together in that tiny space. They were all known to me, but I suddenly saw them there, all laughing, smoking, drinking, while I was stuck in a corner, cold and unhappy, because I was going through a bad patch and I knew that I had to do something special that afternoon, or else. I was edgy because I knew that I had to take risks, no question about it. So I cleared them all out. I told them that things would be different from that moment on, and if they wanted to have a bit of a laugh, they would have to come after the corrida, provided there was a good reason for it.

As well as those worries about doing everything on the left, I had a lot of other quirks in the bullring. I didn't like having hugs or squeezes, or people patting my face while waiting in the patio. Even less, something which became common at one time, when banderilleros used to give me a little slap on the backside to wish me luck. That silly custom annoyed me so much that one day I actually turned on someone who did it to me.

At times like that, when fear builds up the tension, it's best to keep your distance and let others deal with it as best they can. Only minutes before a corrida, when your mouth is dry and nerves are raw, everything gets on your nerves, especially offensive gestures.

I was the same on alternativa days, because I have never liked giving hugs or taking off my montera in the ceremony. All that sort of thing isn't necessary between men: it's enough to speak the usual few words, wish them good luck, and shake hands with the new matador. And then get on with it.

As for the colours of torero suits, I have always preferred dark ones. When I was a novillero, I had a few lighter ones, because they were cheaper. But the first one I had made to my own specifications, the one they gave me for appearing naked in the documentary film, was dark blue. Since then, my favourite colours were: navy blue, dark red, Bordeaux red, bottle green, purple... Always with lots of gold trimmings.

I ordered six suits every year, plus another half-dozen capotes and muletas, and I never managed to use all of them. I would use them in seventy-something events in Spain and America every year, plus the ones I used for training in the country, and I always had some left over. I think I still have some unused ones somewhere. Other colleagues use many more – some even take out a new capote and a muleta every afternoon – but the tailors didn't get rich out of me.

It wasn't because I was mean, but ever since I was a kid, I got used to making the same capes last a long time. My first capote which Bienvenido bought me, the one that was so ragged, lasted me for more than four years, and in the end it was like a hand-towel. I was so used to those soft capotes that, when I got hold of a new one, I found it very hard and stiff, and I couldn't make it move properly. That's how I began using capotes with the reverse side in purple.

People thought that there was a special reason for that, maybe just to be different, but the real reason was simply that I wanted to use a softer material than the usual yellow one, and all I could find that fitted the bill was only made in the colours of blue, green or purple. *Rafael de Paula* already used a blue one, so...

Until I found that material, I used to spend days trying to make my capotes softer, spraying them with water, scraping them with a knife, screwing them up, giving them to others to wear in – even driving a car over them, because I needed them to be more responsive to my touch.

As for the other accessories, as a dressmaker would say, I wore the same castañeta for many years, that's the false pigtail worn by all toreros; it was given to me by José de la Cal, my teacher from the Madrid School of Bullfighting. On the occasion when I dedicated a bull to him in Madrid as a becerrista, he gave me an old pair of cufflinks with brands of bull ranches on them, and the castañeta, which was made out of his own real hair. I wore it until it fell apart from old age.

I have only ever had four monteras. The first one was made of braid, and was given to me by Iluminado Menés, the banderillero who became the caretaker at the Bullfighting School. Then I bought a beautiful one with silk knots from another banderillero, Antonio Briceño. But it was too flat, and the ties were so big that I couldn't keep it on my head, so I had to buy another one. And then I had a new one made for the first time I faced six bulls alone in Madrid in 1993, and that was the one I used right up to the end.

JOAQUÍN RAMOS, MY LOYAL SUPPORT

The montera is the most sacred item of a torero's clothing. One year in Bilbao, they stole mine. I was carried out on shoulders, and gave it to Joaquín Ramos, my sword handler, who put it on his lap with the parade cape when he got into the cuadrilla minibus. He was giving out photos of me through the open window to the crowd milling round the car, and someone reached in and stole the montera.

We didn't realise until later.

We were supposed to leave that same night to drive the length of the country down to Malaga, but I said we weren't going anywhere until the montera was returned. Joaquín moved heaven and earth to get it back: he spoke to all the ticket touts, who always seem to be in the know about these things, and he even put an ad in the local paper *El Correo* saying that we were offering a reward to whoever found it. At two in the morning, two French lads turned up at the hotel with the montera, saying they'd found it thrown away in the street. We didn't believe them, but we gave them a few banknotes and at last we could set off on our long drive south.

Joaquín Ramos was the sword handler who stayed with me the longest. It's very important to have someone with you who is completely on top of the job, because he is truly your right-hand man. There's a saying that no torero is brave in the eyes of his sword handler, because he sees you in your worst moments, in those difficult hours before a corrida. I didn't need someone unusually special, just a good professional. But most importantly, he needed to know how to handle me in tricky circumstances, when to be there for me, and when to keep out of the way.

My first sword handler was Antonio Martín Arranz, Enrique's brother, who was as well-read as he was strange. He wanted to be an actor, and he left me because he had a Spanish language degree and wanted to teach in Germany. I have a lot of time for him, because he taught me a great deal.

After him, I took on Antonio and Rafael, the two sons of my banderillero, José Luis González from Bilbao. They were a couple of nice boys, but they were completely crazy, incapable of taking on the responsibility of working for an important torero.

The year they came with me to the Bilbao Fair, their hometown, they cocked up big time. When I arrived at the hotel, I saw that they hadn't laid out my clothes – 'made the chair' – although they knew perfectly well that I liked it to be done in the morning. The time came for me to get dressed, and they were still nowhere to be seen; then, an hour and a half before the corrida, they came into the room, smoking a large joint, and pissed as newts, because they'd been out on the booze with some mates they hadn't seen for a long time.

A few months later in Jaén, after getting paid off by the impresario, they went out boozing with some local tearaways who ended up taking all the money off them. They were great guys, but I just had to get rid of them.

When I appeared in America, I didn't take my own sword handler at first, and I always signed up Franklin Gutiérrez, a Colombian, so I asked him to come back to Spain with me. He worked for me for two or three years, and then he left to join Enrique Ponce. He was really good at looking after all my outfits, and that's not an easy job.

I had two or three others, who probably didn't last more than a few months between them, until I finally found Joaquín Ramos. I saw him working with his brother, José Luis, also a matador, when we were on together in a festival in Salamanca, their hometown. I was so impressed by the way he worked that I offered him the job on the spot.

He will tell you that the first day he arrived at the ranch was awful; I seemed unbelievably rude, and a bit of an unpleasant bastard. I think I was in a bad mood because one of my horses had picked up an injury, and then I sat down on the arm of a sofa and lectured him, laying down the law about how I liked things to be done. He even thought of leaving there and then, but he soon came round when he realised that I wasn't so bad after all.

He stayed with me until 1999, when I retired for a while, and then, when I came back, Antonio Pedrosa took his place. Joaquín is a personal friend rather than just an assistant, the kind of friend who is closer to you than your own brother.

We are about the same age and we've grown up together; we met and fell in love with our wives at the same time; and we've done everything together. Because we lived in the same house, we were in one another's company twenty-four hours a day. He has been my closest friend, and has protected me from so many things which were best kept from me, and pulled me out of so many scrapes, both inside and outside the bullring. I still keep in touch with all the members of my cuadrilla, but much more with him, because he decided to settle down near to me in Talavera.

I have a special affection for Joaquín. Alongside Enrique, he is the best friend I have ever had. He has put up with all my moanings and groanings, as well as the highs. And all my bad moods too. Because I trust him completely, and because he's always to hand, he was always on the receiving end. He has known me with all my defences down, probably more so than my wife. He has been sword handler, friend, secretary, companion, whipping-boy, and chief press officer, because, even before public relations became fashionable, he was fantastic at dealing with the press. He is an extremely likeable guy.

He made rapid progress in the job, and as he grew into it, he became a respected figure in the bullfighting world. He learnt much from Enrique, because he was like a sponge, and my father taught him everything he knows. He is very intelligent, and a good aficionado too, so he knows about everything: how best to deal with impresarios, the toro bravo in the countryside, and the torero in the bullring. He is one of the best professionals that a torero could have at his side, and that's why he is now working with José Tomás.

When he was with me as my sword handler, he knew extremely well all the customs I liked to follow on the day of a corrida. In the morning, if I had arrived early, I would go for a walk around the town. I didn't use to get up very early, around nine o'clock or so, have breakfast and go for a walk. On my return to the hotel, I would have a snack, lie down on the bed, read a little, and take a short siesta until it was time to go through the very precise ritual of dressing for the corrida.

Two hours before the start of the corrida, Joaquín came into the room, drew back the curtains – I was neurotic about the wind, and I thought that, if I drew the curtains, it would be windy – I then went to the bathroom and washed my face, I took off my pyjamas and we began the business of dressing, always in the same sequence: first the stockings and garters, always below the knee, and then the long body stocking; next I put on the taleguilla or trousers, and attached the braces, then I tied the laces that kept the trousers tight over my calves, next the shoes; I fixed the castañeta in place, put on the shirt; and finally, the tie and cummerbund, and the chaleco or waistcoat. Then I would sit and wait a while, because we always had an hour and a quarter or so in hand. If I felt like it, I would chat to the sword handler. If not, we sat in dead silence until it was time to put on the chaquetilla or jacket, and we set off for the bullring.

With this procedure, which I never varied, it was said I always showed myself to be a creature of habit. But in important things, like the way I performed in the ring, I was sometimes inconsistent in my early years. And full of doubts, because I still wasn't sure what I wanted to do as an artist. In reality, it was not until the cornada from *Limonero* that my ideas changed. Or rather, that's when I came back to the ideas I had as a child. In that respect too, there was a 'before' and 'after' of 15th May 1987.

CURRO VÁZQUEZ OR *ESPARTACO*?

My broken collarbone was lucky for me, not just because it stopped the horn from going through my neck, but also because it gave me a period of almost forty days of enforced inactivity, which gave me a lot of time for reflection. I went for very long walks alone in the countryside, speaking to no one, and doing some hard thinking.

I was already up there with the big boys, about to join them, but I didn't feel comfortable with myself. I didn't like what I was doing, how I was expressing myself in the face of the bull. That energetic, restless kid who did so much lightweight stuff in the ring in the pursuit of a fistful of ears by whatever means – that wasn't really me.

That sort of performance had got me up to where I was, but I couldn't help thinking that there was no future in following that route. I couldn't betray the ideas of integrity which I had talked about endlessly with my friend Perea when we were kids, when we discovered the magic of bullfighting for the first time.

I had to give the problem a lot of thought, because when I returned to the ring, if I was less 'courageous', people would think that I'd lost my nerve. I thought about it a lot, whether to carry on as before, or whether this was a chance for me to begin to get more enjoyment out of what I was doing; the choice was between carrying on making good money or feeling fulfilled within myself.

Then one day, *el Fundi* came to Colmenar el Arroyo to cape some heifers. He had a really good one, number 614. I can still remember it perfectly. They had just removed my bandages, and I was watching from the top of the seating, and suddenly, as I watched the little heifer charging, I had a terrible urge to cape it myself. I asked *Fundi* for his muleta, and I gave four or five extraordinary passes with my right hand. They were so good that they confirmed what I had been thinking. This was what I truly liked, and what I wanted to be doing in future. At last I was going to be true to my own feelings, and people could think what they liked.

Changing my style took a long time; it didn't happen overnight, because I had to take into account the adult bull, which is more complicated than a novillo. When I reappeared in Teruel, things turned out the way I wanted, more because I was enjoying it than because I had put in the work beforehand. But from that day on, I had to work a bit harder. I had got over the cornada, now I had to get back on top, and to do all this with a style of bullfighting that was different from what I had grown used to.

Some older toreros warned me that I was trying too hard, and that I should back off a little, if I wanted to continue to appear in a large number of corridas. José María *Manzanares* told me that the effort I had put in with a bull in Valencia, and from which I didn't even cut an ear, was enough to last him for a whole season. But I couldn't do things any other way.

Around that time, my father and my banderilleros, Juan Cubero and Antonio Romero, began to have a go at me during training, saying that I needed to find ways that were less risky. They would keep on at me day after day: do this; hold the muleta like that; look what *Espartaco* does and he's made a fortune... They got to me with all that stuff, and I even began to doubt myself, because their remarks undermined what I was trying to do.

That was the situation when we went to an event in a village in La Mancha. I cut three ears doing it their way: 'wham, bam, thank you Ma'am' – like they were telling me – but it didn't seem right. I was carried out on shoulders, and when we were back in the minibus, they started in on me.

'Great stuff, José! That's the way to do it. Do you see? You still cut ears with half the effort, fantastic!'

They got my goat, and I snapped, 'I was good then, yes? I cut ears, they made me the hero of the feria and next year they'll be asking me back. But listen to this: all of it sucks! Today I was a clown, I was ashamed of myself doing that stuff, and I felt ridiculous. If people don't understand me, or if I get it all wrong with a bull, I don't feel right, and performing like that and cutting ears makes me feel sick. What sort of a torero am I, dancing around like that?'

I hadn't finished yet.

'Listen, if I have to keep performing like that, I'll hang up my magic wand and go home. All sodding day long you're breaking my balls with how *Espartaco* does it, and I'm fed up to the back teeth with it, because his ideas are not what I want. I want to be a torero like Curro Vázquez, use my capes like he does, and be as free as he is to express what I feel inside. Get this for once and for all: I have nothing but admiration for both of them, but I would prefer a thousand times more the dignity of Curro Vázquez rather than to be rich like *Espartaco*. You won't change me.'

And I felt great.

I began to want to be a torero in the first place because I was turned on by something I saw of beauty in the ring, not for money or profit. I was impressed by good bullfighting, pure, honest art, not the millions earned by some of my contemporaries, who, as good as they were and as successful as they were, just didn't move me.

I can remember the performance of a novillero, Jaime Malaver, in Madrid. He didn't come to anything later, but I have his performance engraved in my memory next to indestructible images of performances of Curro Vázquez. Those are my icons. I could have chosen a more commercial style, one which is easier to develop, and which, by the way, would have meant less exposure to danger. But that wouldn't have been me, it would have been some shadow of myself, a working torero, not an artist.

I have never worked at developing a broad technique, and that shows a weakness in my abilities; as a result I have sometimes missed out on an opportunity for success with a good bull which needed to have a few problems solved. But that's not the way I felt. If I had gone down that path, I wouldn't have been happy, and I wouldn't have the feeling of satisfaction that I have now.

THE MYSTERY OF THE BULLS

One of the great truths in bullfighting is that sentence of Juan Belmonte which says, 'Se torea como se es' – 'You fight the bull the way you feel inside'. If you are true to yourself, you won't let yourself down in the face of the bull. As far as I was concerned, it left a bitter taste if I had to express myself differently from the way I felt.

Enrique, my father, insisted that a good artist is one who can bring out the best in himself in public, even when he is falling apart inside. I always gave him the same answer: that I must be very bad then, because I can't help showing it on the outside when I'm falling apart inside. People can either enjoy my performance or not, depending on how I am feeling. I can't show them something I don't feel.

Bullfighting is the expression of intimate, deep emotions. At least, that's how I see it. And because of this – like all art – it can move the feelings of a spectator. A performance with a bull, a faena, is like a painting, a sculpture, a symphony... If something you see gets to you and moves you, it's art. And only an artist can do that.

The matador Rafael *el Gallo* said that bullfighting is about having a mystery to tell, and then telling it. I had that mystery, and a background of hard knocks which could be seen in everything I did in the ring. I am not saying I was better or worse, just different. My difference came from exactly that – all the pain and incomprehension

*Aged three, together with my brother,
Roberto Carlos.*

*My natural father,
Bienvenido Arroyo.*

This is me aged seven.

*My father, who was very keen on
cars, soon showed me how to drive.*

This Bullfighting School photo shows the difficulties I experienced the first time I faced a bull.

In my early appearances, I was billed as Miguel de la Llana, using my father's second surname.

The first prize I won as a becerrista, in 1981, was awarded to me (left) by the matador Paco Camino in the presence of bull-breeder Victorino Martín (with muleta and sword).

The Madrid Bullfighting School's three becerristas – (l-r) el Fundi, José Luis Bote and me.

With my father at one of my first public appearances

Giving a chest pass to a calf in Villaviciosa de Odón's main square.

With Enrique Martín Arranz, much more than a maestro, the day of my debut in a suit of lights at Madrid's Las Ventas.

Life as a novillero was tougher than in the School; suddenly I was taking short cuts and pushing my luck, placing my own banderillas and giving flashy cape passes on my knees.

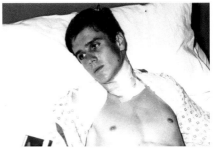

The horn-wound that Limonero gave me – my first really bad one – not only left a scar on my body, but marked a turning point in my approach to bullfighting.

Las Ventas, 22nd May, 1988: Together again as matadors – I confirm José Luis Bote's alternativa while el Fundi looks on.

What I enjoyed more than anything was giving the verónica pass.

There was a time when I was dissatisfied with my appearances with the top bullfighters and the way I expressed myself in front of the bull.

In barrera seats with my adoptive parents, Enrique and Adela.

Giving a media verónica: performing with the capote calls on excellent hand co-ordination.

*Juan Belmonte said, to perform extraordinarily well,
you have to forget you have a body.*

Appearing in 'my' bullring, Madrid's Las Ventas. Despite its having the biggest bulls and the most demanding spectators, I always wanted to perform there and secured several triumphs.

*My best hand was the left – but I also liked to hold the muleta
without the sword in my right hand and guide the bull past
with the folds of the cloth.*

*When I added purple cloth to
my capes, the press attacked
me for republicanism!*

*Seville's La Maestranza,
26th September 1998:
Telling Enrique in the
arena that I was dedicating
my last bull to him.*

Achieving success at Mexico City's Plaza Mexico became an obsession for me.

With Adela, the woman of my life, and our daughters – my joy and my preoccupation.

Zaragoza, 13th October, 2003: Only a few spectators knew this was to be the last afternoon of my career as a matador.

King Juan Carlos presents me with Spain's Fine Arts Gold Medal in November, 2011.

José Miguel Arroyo Delgado now, farmer and bull-breeder.

in me since I was left an orphan burst out when I was able to express myself in the face of the bull.

I had such a bad time that, when I fell under the magic spell of the bulls, I showed all the feelings of satisfaction which it produced inside me. I had a lot that I wanted to say with my capes, and that is what spoke to the public. For me, it was a marvellous relief, a dangerous but wonderful way of expressing my innermost feelings, and a means of proving myself as a person.

When you are bullfighting, your feelings come out through the tips of your fingers, which are very sensitive. At the same time, you have to be very strong mentally, to deal with the fear. It is a strange art, because you have to be right at the limit to be able to create, even putting your life in danger. Paradoxically, I am a very frightened and apprehensive person.

Rather than courage, what I had was a great passion for bull-fighting. That passion made me overcome my fears, and when I was enjoying performing well, I found it easy to work close to the bull, because I enjoyed so much making my dreams come true. Probably I'm not right in the head. In reality, I know quite well that I am to-tally mad, and that I more or less adjust to the system because I have to remain a member of society. But, by definition, a real artist is an emotionally unbalanced individual. A torero, even more so.

I can see it in others, and I understand the reasons behind their genius. I see it in artists in another field, like Edith Piaf, who I love. A funny-looking, oddly shaped woman like that, the perfect image of post-war misery, how can she capture so many hearts? It's because she could express all that sadness in her voice. When a person creates something as deep as that, it's because they're putting so much of themselves and their experience into what they are doing. That's when art transmits feelings and gets to you.

The more you live life, and grow richer with life's experiences, the more – and the better – you express yourself. I used to talk about that a lot with Enrique in long conversations about human existence and spiritual powers, philosophising about the bulls and life. On those long drives between bullrings, I also talked a lot with the members of the cuadrilla, especially about the old-time toreros, and what we could learn from them.

I loved talking about the culture of the bulls, and I was lucky enough to have as picador Juan Mari García, who had worked with great matadors like Antonio Ordóñez and *Paquirri*. And Juan Cubero, who told me so much about his brother, *Yiyo*. They taught me a lot, because they made me wiser and reconfirmed my beliefs about the bulls.

All this improved my performance in the bullring, but let's not forget the hours on end that I spent training my body in 'toreo de salón', rehearsing and perfecting the moves I would make with my capes in the bullring. This is fundamental in a torero's training, and it's not just about practising empty passes in mid-air; it's about everything, a daily obsession like the pianist who is tied to his keyboard day in day out. The daily life of a torero has to be just like that.

Someone seeing me when I was training might think that I had lost my marbles, because I would spend hours looking for the right posture to call the bull, improving the way I positioned my feet and my body to give the pass more depth, repeating over and over again fluid movements or contrived ones, but always trying to avoid distortion. Like a ballet dancer virtuoso who repeats the same tiniest detail a thousand times over.

I have been fortunate, or unfortunate, to be a perfectionist in life, and that's why I could put up with repeatedly banging away until it hurt in training. And if I did take a rest, Enrique was there prodding me on, to stop me from easing off. Even after my best faenas, or performances, he always had a comment to make. If you set yourself a target, there's no such thing as a break.

'Toreo de salón' is a way of refining your mind and body for the bull. When you give yourself over to the movements and the feel of the capes, you need only a minimum of courage for the performance to become as natural as breathing, and you can concentrate on your feelings. What we call 'perder el sitio,' or losing one's place, is really losing your sense of touch, the natural bond you have with the capote and the muleta, which become like an extension to your hands, like the tail of a mermaid. That is something which is very difficult to achieve, and easy to forget unless you give up a lot of your time to it.

Bullfighting has to come from the heart, flow down your arms, become smoothed out in the wrists, and emerge into the daylight through the tips of your fingers. You have to forget that you have a body, as Belmonte said. Thanks to all that training – both physical and mental – it comes naturally, without thinking, even at a time of great tension like when your back's against the wall. The only problem there should ever be in the ring is the bull itself, and that's all you should be thinking about, never about problems in yourself.

A shortage of skills can get in the way of feelings, especially in toreros who are just setting out, who will need to pile on passes and keep on top of the bull, rather than going in for self-expression. But that's not bullfighting, which is about giving your soul free rein in the face of the bull. It's about offering up your vital organs, sticking out your chest and following the direction of the charge of the bull with a swing of your waist. Your heart only comes into it when you get completely involved, when you stop thinking about the possibility of a cornada.

It's as if the bull understands this, because you encourage it to want to join in. You either beat it, or you win it over with your mind and determination. It's a contest on a psychological level between man and beast. If you gain control over your mind and control of the capes, then you control the bull. It's only if you have internal doubts or fears that the bull takes over.

My great paradox is that I was able to perform as I did despite the fragile and unstable state of my mind. That's why I was so variable as a torero. If I wasn't focused, I didn't know how to perform. Even if the bull was as good as gold.

Maybe that's why they said my style was pure and honest. I'm not sure how to define the purity of bullfighting, but maybe it's something like the rejoneador Ángel Peralta said: it's to deceive the bull with the truth, without lying to it. That truth is essential in your coming together, always to give the animal the choice between charging the cloth or charging your body. That's what purity must mean, standing in front of the bull, between the horns, and saying, 'Here I am, and this is my muleta; the choice is yours.' If you take steps back and forth, if you go in for little tricks of the trade, if you use technique to hide behind, and show less of yourself, you are quite simply lying. Purity is the height of engagement, an honest dialogue with the bull.

That's why I identify three ways of bullfighting: use of the legs to avoid the charge; use of the head, employing technique to make passes; and use of the heart, giving yourself up to your feelings. That was behind the greatness of *Rafael de Paula*, who lacked physical ability and technical resources, but went along with his creativity and his emotions. When that happens, no one notices if the torero has done it according to the rules, just that he has poured out his soul. When you think, the public thinks also; when you feel, the public feels too.

Morante de la Puebla and José Tomás, for example, both have great technique, but the public doesn't see it. One of them puts his talent to the service of art, and the other to that of emotion. Magicians never let you see how they do the trick. How they do what they do is about uncertainty, surprise, presentation and expression. They are unpredictable.

There are other toreros who also put their life on the line, but they look as if they are fireproof in front of the bull, because they don't let go. The public may not be able to explain what they see in the ring, but they know what they feel. So they only follow great toreros, the most pure, wherever they appear.

Truth is a question of the difference of only a few centimetres in the short distance to the horns. As the great taurine writer Pepe Alameda wrote, 'One step forward and the torero may die; one step back and art may die.' That marks the difference between the sublime and the vulgar.

6

THE WAR OF INDEPENDENCE

In this new state of mind, and at the point of rediscovering my early artistic ideals, I had a great success on 1st June 1989 in Madrid. I cut two ears from a bull from the ranch of Atanasio Fernández called *Cordobán*. The faena was quite close to what I was aiming for. The public enjoyed what I did, and I went out of Las Ventas on shoulders for the second time, from the bullring which had launched my career three years earlier, and which once again proved decisive in confirming my place among the elite.

This time, my exit by the Puerta Grande, the main gate, had tremendous repercussions, because it happened on the day of the most highly regarded event in the San Isidro Fair, which, in its turn, is the most important fair of the year anywhere; I was appearing with the two great stars of the time, Ortega Cano and *Espartaco*, the matador they kept putting up to me as an example I should follow. I was on cloud nine.

My fame and my fees went through the roof. The phone was red hot. All the impresarios from Spain, France and America were on the line. They offered us a choice of dates, who we appeared with, which bulls we wanted, whatever money we asked for... At last I was up at the top; for the first time in my career, I could make my own decisions. In the world of the bulls, that is known as 'being in charge'.

But the reality is that the success did me a lot of damage. I thought that I had arrived, and I took my foot off the accelerator. After that day, I began to train less, I took things easy, I lost concentration. If I had a bad day, instead of thinking how to get over it or improve things, I paid it no attention. 'I'll put things right tomorrow,' I said to myself. That's what happened day after day, and in the end, I had a poor season.

By the middle of September, I was but a shadow of the torero who had triumphed in Las Ventas. In Nîmes, in the Roman amphitheatre where the French hold corridas, I had a bull which was really quite good, but I was incapable of dealing with it in the way I should have. I gave it a lot of passes, some of them not too bad, but I didn't give it the faena it deserved. The public seemed to like what I did, but I felt frustrated by my performance.

Mentally, I was in a sorry state. When I arrived back at the hotel, I told Enrique to cancel all contracts for the rest of the season. If I was incapable of doing the right thing with a good bull, it was time to stop and recharge my batteries. I went into the countryside for a couple of weeks to recover my spirits, and I emerged in much better shape. I was a different person when I reappeared in Úbeda and cut four ears and a tail, from bulls which were not half as good as the one in Nîmes.

That exit on shoulders in Madrid in May was one of the great moments in my career, but it also caused me the most trouble. I couldn't shake off an arrogance which lingered in my head for three or four months. Fortunately, it didn't finish me off as a matador, and I got over it when I realised that, if I slowed down, I was in danger of throwing it all overboard. It's not true to say that you only learn from your mistakes.

In those early years as a matador, my emotions were barely just below the surface, and my mind was fragile and unstable. The slightest thing disturbed me, and put me on edge. On the day of my confirmation in Colombia, something really silly happened. In the morning, as usual, I went for a stroll around the town, I ate a light meal, and went to my room. I wasn't sleepy, so I put the TV on. Going through the channels, I stopped on a channel with a black-and-white movie which looked interesting, even though it was in English. The actors were very good, and their expressions told the story even though I couldn't understand what they were saying. I later found out that it was *Romeo and Juliet*.

I watched it all the way through, and when it finished, I was left feeling really miserable, and quite depressed by what is a very painful love story. As I got dressed, I kept thinking about this classic tragedy, which really got through to my romantic side. Enrique said I didn't look well, but I told him that the food hadn't agreed with me, which wasn't true, but I didn't want him to say I was an idiot.

We made our way to the bullring, but I couldn't get *Romeo and Juliet* out of my head. In the parade, instead of the pasodoble played by the band, I kept hearing the music from the film. When my bull came into the ring, I was still behind the fence thinking about the two tragic lovers. The long and the short of it was that I blew out big time – a disaster. The bulls, Bogota, the crowd, nothing was of the slightest importance to me. All I could think of was Shakespeare's tale of woe.

That wasn't the only time it happened. On another occasion, as we were arriving for a corrida in San Sebastián de los Reyes, I saw a car run over a dog, and I was terrible all afternoon, thinking about the poor animal. Sometimes I would get a song into my head, and I would be humming it to myself all through the corrida, doing everything to the rhythm of the song, and unable to get it out of my head. I don't know if it's caused by nerves or stress, or because I am some kind of an obsessive lunatic, but it's something worthy of psychoanalysis.

And then there were the times when the problem was a real one, either because I had had a serious argument with someone, or because something really important had happened. At such times, I would lose it completely – I behaved like a total idiot in front of the bull, or I reacted very badly with the crowd. Everything got twisted round.

Sometimes I would use my state of mind like a blunt instrument, waiting for someone in the crowd to say something, and I would turn round and let them have it, just to get rid of all that built-up anger and aggression. The doctors said I had a stomach complaint because I didn't eat properly, but I think it was because of the nerves eating away at my insides.

If it's true that I have had big successes, it's also true that I have had major flops, and been booed to the rafters. One of the first ones was in Logroño, and it was quite something. They nearly killed me. In 1986, I was signed up for two corridas in their San Mateo Fair, but I couldn't go to the first one because I had food poisoning. Although I was feeling only a little better, I made it to the next one, with Julio Robles and Ortega Cano, who had a great time, cutting three ears each. I couldn't do a thing with my first bull, because it was 'manso', it wouldn't charge, and 'distraido', just wandering around. And I did even less with my second one.

I should have made an effort that day, because it was my debut in Logroño; because it was late in the season; and because it was the local ring of a personal friend, Pedro Ochoa, the doctor who later killed himself. He was always singing my praises, and I needed to put on a good show for him in his hometown. But I didn't like the second bull, and it didn't give me any options. So I cut things short, gave it four flaps with the muleta, and killed it in under two minutes.

The public got really angry. In the middle of the furore, while I was washing my hands, I went back to my roots and I swore very violently at a man who was shouting out insults at me from his seat. He reacted like a wild animal, and started throwing things, and those sitting around him did likewise. I was really scared.

I had to move to the centre of the ring, because there was a hail of drink cans and heavy cushions being thrown at me from all around the ring. The police had to come and escort me out of the ring using their riot shields. Even so, when I got to the minibus, some jerk grabbed me by the arm and gave me a huge bruise. I got the hell out of there, leaving the cuadrilla behind. When we went back for them, we had to take the stickers off the car first, so that the mob still waiting outside wouldn't know it was us. Since then, my minibuses don't have my name on the side like those of most other toreros do. Just in case.

Even the best toreros can get a bad reception, a bronca, from time to time. Today's toreros are easily unsettled by this, but it has always been a part of the job. Someone calling himself an artist must be made up of sharp contrasts, black and white. Half-tones have no place; they don't describe you either one way or another. Obviously, you have to stand up for yourself to be able to put up with it.

I was very impressed by the attitude of Curro Romero when a nutcase jumped into the ring in Las Ventas and pushed him against the fence. Curro still had the descabello sword in his hand, but he got to his feet as if nothing had happened, and remained perfectly calm and under control. If that had happened to me, I am sure I would have stabbed the man in the neck with the sword.

Curro showed great courage in that moment, because it takes a lot of nerve to suffer a bronca quietly and with dignity, amid a storm of cushions or sometimes glass bottles, like they threw at me one year in Medellín when I wanted to call off a corrida because the ring was flooded.

In Pamplona, they throw things for the sake of it. It doesn't matter what is happening in the ring. It doesn't matter how well you do with the bull, the people in the Sol section throw things at the toreros anyway. The only time I ever appeared in that bullring, they threw a chunk of melon at me first. I thought it must have just been just bad luck, that it wasn't done on purpose, but then I got hit on the head with a piece of stale bread. I have never gone back. I can't stand the racket there either.

Even apart from unusual cases like that one, most great toreros have suffered a serious bronca at one time or another. The one and only Paco Camino, one of my idols, had a huge number of triumphs, but also other days in which the public set about him. It must be because they expected so much of him.

I get very annoyed when someone takes pity on a torero and says something like, 'Poor thing, he was so good and they didn't notice.' Poor thing? Certainly not. Let them call him foul names if they want, but you can't take pity on a torero because that would be disrespecting la fiesta. You can be fantastic or rubbish, but never a 'poor thing'. A man who puts on a suit of lights and risks his life, especially if he is a top matador, can't be pitied, not even if he has been a disaster or been injured. He's not to be judged on the basis of a 'one-off', or as someone who 'did their best' and then makes excuses when there's nothing that can be done with a particular bull. If someone said I had 'done my best,' that would be the worst insult anyone could say to me. I don't like being called a 'professional' either. As *Rafael de Paula* says, a professional is someone who comes to your house to repair the washing machine. A torero has to live like one, and show it, with passion.

ARM WRESTLING FOR POWER

Although I went downhill in the three months following my triumph in Madrid, I still managed to stay at the top. I was one of the most popular toreros with the aficionados, and was still considered a draw at the box office. But things didn't go easy for us. The way things worked in the business world of bullfighting, where power was in the hands of a few individuals and had nothing to do with the toreros, meant that Enrique and I had to break down a lot of barriers in order to protect our independence and our self-respect.

We had experienced problems the previous year with one of the big bosses, the Basque impresario, Manolo Chopera, who ran a good many bullrings, including Madrid, and he pretty much controlled things across the board.

It started when we wanted him to put *Fundi* and Bote on in San Isidro, to confirm their alternativas. I wanted three appearances during the Feria, including this one. Chopera accepted this, but with the condition that I fight in a corrida that no one else wanted. But by using the argument that we were reducing my fees as a favour to my two friends, we convinced him to drop his demands.

Even so, it must be that he didn't like not having his way, because he offered me the same bulls in the Bilbao Fair. This time we said, 'Of course!' – provided he put on *Litri* and Rafi Camino alongside me; they had just taken their alternativas, and hadn't yet done enough to deserve the quality corridas which Chopera had put them in, in preference to me.

He was the most powerful impresario of the day. He had the last word in about twenty very important bullrings, and what he was really up to was trying us out to get the measure of our strength, so he could have an idea how far he could push us in future negotiations. We didn't accept his offer, and we didn't get any invitations to appear in any of his other ferias: Bilbao, Vitoria, Logroño, Salamanca, Bayonne, Almeria... This meant that we lost a lot of money, but we didn't mind. 'We've already got enough on our plate,' said my father.

That challenge to the impresario's power might seem suicidal, but I saw very clearly that, if I was going to be a torero, I would only do it as an independent, without bowing down to anyone. Although I might be hungry, I was still in charge. In 1987, I turned down an exclusive offer from Manolo González, who at the time was the manager of *Espartaco* and *Manzanares*, in which he offered me one hundred and fifty million of the old pesetas for fifty corridas, at a time when I was earning just over one million pesetas a time. But thinking about my independence and not being at the beck and call of someone solely for money, I turned it down. I would earn less, but I would keep my freedom.

Bearing that in mind, how could I not face up to the all-powerful Manolo Chopera? Living on your knees is not nice, and I wasn't going to do it. If my work in front of the bulls had earned me some privileges by my efforts and sheer guts, I wasn't about to sell myself down the river.

As on the ball as ever, Enrique immediately got in touch with Teodoro Matilla, who also ran a large number of second-class bullrings, to help us out. Teodoro was terrific, and although I got a bit fed up with appearing in the provinces all the time, at least I wasn't left high and dry that year.

The next year, everything was sorted out. I did very well in America that winter, and the Spanish public was still keen to see me, so the self-same Manolo Chopera sought us out in the Castellón Fair in March. In the crush of the patio at the bullring while I was preparing my cape for the parade, he came up to me himself. I saw his enormous hand appearing between the surrounding heads, and heard his rough voice wishing me well. 'Many thanks, don Manuel,' I said, as much surprised as I was pleased. After seeing me cut four ears, that very same night he told Enrique that we could rely on appearing in all his bullrings in the year ahead.

He was a proud man, and a tough nut to crack, but that well-respected impresario knew how to accept defeat. Once you got over the inevitable cut and thrust of a negotiation, and reached an agreement with him, he stuck by it. He always kept his word. After that first tussle, he always got on very well with my father. He had been trying us out just to see how tough we were, but, once he saw that we didn't back down, and that I had my say with my performance in the ring, that was that. Enrique admired him very much, and held him in great respect.

Shortly after coming to an understanding with Chopera, as soon as the decade of the 1990s began, we had to confront the new bosses at Las Ventas, the Lozano brothers. Martín Arranz and *Joselito* were up against the people with all the clout again. These new guys didn't arm wrestle with us, they straightaway tried to disrespect me in the bullring I had already made my own, Las Ventas, where I must have earned more than enough merit points to justify having first pick. But this band of brothers from Toledo screamed blue murder if you hurt them in their pockets.

They never accepted what we asked for or opened discussions with enough time realistically to put together the programme of events for Madrid. They offered the best deals to others before they even spoke to us, so our talks always started with some dates already set in stone. That's why I was left out of San Isidro for two or three years.

The worst wasn't that we didn't reach an understanding, or that they did their utmost to screw things up. The nastiest thing was that they also set about spreading untrue stories and fairy tales in the press about Enrique and me. Their favourite line was that *Joselito* was tight about money and insisted on small bulls: he was not a real star. Just to give them a punch on the nose, in 1993 I decided to kill six bulls on my own in the Corrida de Beneficencia, which is outside their control. This would be in Madrid, with bulls appropriate for Madrid, that is to say the biggest you will see anywhere in the world; and I would appear without a fee, to show everyone that money didn't matter to me. I have never been tight, it's just that I have always asked to be paid what I thought was my fair share of what I pulled in at the box office.

It wasn't just power that we were facing up to, but injustice. My father in business negotiations, and me in the ring, we both defended our positions with a similar attitude. And when we felt that someone was taking liberties, we leapt as one at whoever was against us, and they just happened to be, more often than not, the most powerful impresarios. But with the little guys from village bullrings, we were always generous. Some even took us for a ride.

I have appeared in a lot of charity corridas for friends who came straight up to us and asked for a favour. Enrique, unlike other managers, was only hard on the big impresarios. But once he had signed on the dotted line, he would even go so far as to help them sort out any problems arising from the organisation of the event.

BLIND CONFIDENCE

Even so, some wagging tongues began to create a very unpopular image of him, telling the world that Martín Arranz was a tyrant and a skinflint. They tried all sorts of ways to get at us, and wanted to bury us for ever. But they couldn't sweep us under the carpet, and my father was just unbelievably patient, doggedly waiting for them to come back and offer us a booking – because, although bad-tempered and grudgingly, they had no alternative but to come back to us. And we made sure that they paid for bad-mouthing us and for their nasty campaigns to undermine us.

I admit that the team of Enrique and me was a fly in the ointment for the impresarios on the business side of the bulls; before we'd sign a contract, unlike the majority of my fellow matadors, we insisted on knowing who else would be on the bill with us, which bulls we would be facing, and the money we'd be paid – all this before they could publish any official announcements. We were certainly a pain in the arse.

Some of them thought of us as a couple of starving deadbeats who had just arrived on the scene, a snotty-nosed new boy with an upstart manager who had the bare-faced cheek and such a total lack of respect for the system as to think they could play by their own rules. They tried to put a stop to us. We were very lucky, and we managed to win nearly all of the fights they had with us. They spread the word that we were crafty. My father believed in me very strongly, and I felt the same about him. He always believed in being very straight about what he wanted, just as I was straight in the ring. If it hadn't been so, they would have said that we were out of our minds. In fact, we had nothing to lose. We were like kamikaze pilots attacking an aircraft carrier, except we didn't crash out.

Enrique learnt his way through the jungle of the offices of the business side of the bulls, because he is very clever and gifted with great common sense. He had one tremendous asset in particular: like the great apoderados of the past, he didn't work on commission. He never closed a deal thinking about the commission he would get out of my fees, but instead he always put my interests first, and he thought of them as the same as his.

Only once did he sign me up for a corrida purely for the money; it was in Jaén, and I really didn't want to do it. He told me to think about it some more, because they were prepared to give us whatever we asked for. I felt very bad about it while waiting at the bullring to make the parade. I was badly knocked about from a tossing that a bull had given me in Zaragoza, and I felt sickened by the fact that I was only there for the money. I would happily have given the money back and gone home with a clear conscience.

Like so many other things in life, the price of independence is very high. It cost me, as I have already said, being kept out of 'my' fair – San Isidro. While the negotiations for Madrid were going on, I had a terrible time, because – although not at any price – I always wanted to appear in Madrid, which was the bullring where I felt most at home. My father went backwards and forwards, day after day, to talk to the Lozanos, but without success. I would ask him anxiously every night about any progress, until at last he'd tell me that the negotiations were broken off, and my heart sank. I was a wreck for more than a month after that.

So much so that, one year when he gave me the bad news and he saw me looking so miserable, he returned to Madrid the next day without telling me, and went back on everything he'd been trying to get for me for months just to try to clinch me a deal for Las Ventas. He did it to stop my morale from going over a cliff. Like most managers, an apoderado needs to be a psychologist for his torero. He has to be able to read his state of mind, his weaknesses, his strong points, as well as organising his season. And because he knew how fragile I could be, he knew how important it was to keep my spirits up to carry on fighting.

Enrique understood me very well. He could sense what I wanted and what I needed at any moment in time, when he needed to put on the screws and when to let go of the reins. He left room for me to make my own mistakes. He never said any of this in the bullring when I was waiting to go on and put myself on the line. If necessary, he might suggest something two or three times when things were not going well. Before the bull came into the ring, he would come up to the fence and would say very carefully, 'José, we need a special effort here. If you can, and you see a chance, go for it. If not, the sun will still come up tomorrow and we'll see what's to be done to sort things out.'

All the struggles with the establishment put me on the spot to deliver the goods, and I was very aware that I had a responsibility to build up a string of new successes to help our cause. All that put a tremendous strain on me. That's what Enrique meant by 'blood, sweat and tears' when he decided to act as my apoderado without any outside help. Because being independent, and with your own fixed ideas about the bulls, you only need one slip and it's the firing squad.

I had to be constantly on my toes, and to continue to have successes in important bullrings, because everything is a bit more difficult there, and successes in top rings carry more weight. We had to stay up there in the ratings despite the efforts of others.

It's a hard road to be a torero, but no one ever said it would be easy. I was never tempted by the apparent carefree life enjoyed by other matadors, who were guaranteed a good number of corridas under the protection of the big organisations, because, if I didn't have my freedom, I would have lost my drive. I felt totally free with Enrique. We could say yes or no as we pleased, never having to think too much about the money, although they go hand in hand. And I was soon in the big time.

In 1987, I took out a loan and bought a herd of fighting bulls. The following year, I bought Los Barrancos, a ranch in Monesterio, Badajoz. In 1990, I bought Prado del Arca, the ranch in Talavera de la Reina where – by pure coincidence – the bull *Bailaor* grazed before killing *Joselito el Gallo* in the ring of Talavera in 1920. That's my home now, although I have bought other ranches since then.

For that sort of thing, material things, money can prove to be a stimulant for a torero, but the truth is that I never wanted to know anything about fees, payments, mortgages or banks.

My father ran all that, and I never opposed any decision he took on that side of things, and I never wanted to. During the years when I was active as a matador, I allowed myself the luxury of only worrying about my capote and my muleta. I had no idea if I had money or not, or how much I earned or turned down. Enrique had my total confidence, and if he had wanted to rob me, he could have done so. But he didn't: everything my adopted father did was always with my interests in mind.

As I say, I have properties and ranches, but money was never the reason I became a torero. Mainly because I have always been very conscious of my origins, where I come from and my situation when I began. I've been lucky enough to be a torero, to be successful and to have made a lot of money, but I don't think I'm better than anyone else. I've thought many times that the day after tomorrow I could be in a hostel for the homeless or queuing up at a soup kitchen. And I don't care.

I know that I come from a microscopic attic room with a miserable shared lavatory, and then from a 'mansion' of thirty-two square metres. I am what I am now, but I am also what I was before. I am the same person. Obviously, I have no wish to go back to living as I did in those days, but, if they did come back, I believe I would still be the same person.

It's easy to say that, now that things are going well for me. But I know what I'm saying, and I mean it. I'm not frightened to think about it all going wrong, because I know that I would adapt to the new situation. I would find a job, I would earn a living, and I would still be José Miguel Arroyo, *el Moreno*.

I have the soul and the feelings of someone from the working classes. I do not flash my money around or show off. I have seen how other matadors immediately went out and bought themselves a Mercedes, and then the next year the bank took it back. I got my Mercedes too, but not until I had enough money to pay for it and its upkeep. Otherwise I would use an ordinary car, because strutting around and showing off are not my style.

I am happy living in the country, going horse-riding, having fried eggs and chorizo for lunch. Everything else is superfluous, because I'm not worried what people think. When I was eighteen and the big boys wanted to take me on board, I was already satisfied, because I had been able to afford to buy a sofa, and I didn't need much else. The only thing against it is that life can be a struggle, as it was for Enrique and me. If you have nothing, you can't lose it. You can only win.

To be so little concerned about material things is what helped me artistically, because I lived for my feelings. It was my father who worried about the financial side and success. That's the job of a true apoderado: getting the best return for his client for the minimum effort, given that the bull business is a hard game.

The apoderado of a torero has to be a bookkeeper, a psychologist, even a sociologist. As I said, he must be a psychologist to understand and look after the artistic side of his torero, but also a sociologist to understand his surroundings and to defend the interests of his torero, without overdoing it or being too ambitious. And he must look out the best bulls, from the best ranches, so that his torero can develop his own ideas about bullfighting.

A RED, REPUBLICAN AND ANTI-CHURCH

This kind of thinking is why they put me down as a rebel. If defending your own interests is being a rebel, then I was. And I meant it. I suppose that, because I didn't follow the rules, they would also have called me a red as an insult, something to be ashamed of.

The way things are now, I don't know if I am or not. Probably yes, given that my biological father was one of eight children and was born in poverty, where the only way out of hunger was with your fists, and sometimes it was the Civil Guards who served out the beatings. Such suffering would probably have inclined him towards being a bit on the red side, and the same for my adopted father. I don't understand anything about politics, but from what I have heard spoken around me at home, and coming from where I come from, it would be very strange if I'd turned out to be a fascist sympathiser.

As you get older, you begin to realise that on both sides there are some good arguments, and good and bad people too. The sensible line must be somewhere in the middle ground. But I suppose it's fair to say that, if anything, I am a bit of a leftie, rather like my best hand with the bulls, which is the left one. I get very annoyed by injustice and the abuse of power, like you get with typical rich kids, or the well-off who throw their weight around. I have seen this a lot in Spain, especially down south in Andalusia, although it's on the decline. But you still come across it a lot, especially in South America, and I hate it.

I've always been careful to avoid the company of this kind of person when I'm over there, the oligarchs and land-barons who own ranches of fighting bulls and have tried to be friends with me because of my reputation with the bulls; I couldn't stand them because of the way they treated the people who worked for them, and also they were always surrounded by armed bodyguards. I have seen scenes of bloodshed over there, social differences and terrible economic crisis; I could never understand why the people didn't rise up against it. As far as I'm concerned, I would rather keep company with the local urchins, the street kids.

I've never liked abusing my fame. Out on the streets, I like to be unobtrusive. In supermarkets, restaurants, and cinemas, I like to pass unnoticed. I don't even like being treated differently, and not because I'm modest, because false modesty can hide a lot of other problems.

In life, you have to be honest with yourself, and never think of yourself as superior. I like equality provided it's been worked for, if it's been achieved by actually making an effort. I can sit down to eat with a government minister or a shoeshine boy, because I believe in the individual, and their personal self-respect. The truth is that I have always preferred the company of the lower classes, especially those underworld characters who hang around on the fringe of the world of the bulls. They have taught me a lot.

Maybe it's a legacy from my years in La Guindalera, but the fact is that I am attracted to people living on the margins. That neighbourhood is inside my head and my heart, the way I live, and when I'm with people like that, it's a way of going back to where I started from. My mother, Adela, who is a bit dramatic, used to say to me that I only really enjoyed the company of muggers and drug-dealers. But that's how it is.

I surprised my cuadrilla one day when our corrida in Madrid was suspended after the third bull because of the rain. We left the bullring early, at eight o'clock, and the driver, who was a bit useless, had forgotten to fill up with petrol, and was running on reserve. There wasn't even enough to get us to the hotel. So because we couldn't go far from Las Ventas, I told him to go up the Avenida de los Toreros and drive through my old streets, to Calle Cartagena where I remembered there used to be a petrol station. And it was still there.

While we were filling up, a minibus full of men dressed up in torero suits, a bloke went by with long, greasy hair and dressed in leathers, like a rocker. I recognised him immediately, because he was a friend from my schooldays.

And because he recognised me as well, he came right over to the car window and spoke in the slow heavy drawl of a seriously laid-back dude, 'Hey blockhead, what's happening? I know you're José *el Moreno*, but what are you doing dressed up like that for, man?'

'See for yourself. I've just been to a fancy dress ball, haven't I?'

'Don't give me that, I heard something about you being a torero...'

In a flash, a bunch of locals surrounded the car all saying they remembered me, while the cuadrilla were in the back, busting their sides laughing about the friends I had. For a long time after that day, they kept calling me 'blockhead'.

Some people may think that I am a millionaire who wants to be thought of as 'red' and 'alternative', and that's my problem in a nutshell: right-wingers won't accept me because of my political views, and left-wingers because I've got money. And as always, I just can't win, so I'm better off being not one or the other. But I want to be clear about one thing: money hasn't made me change my ideas. It hasn't changed my critics either, just because one day I didn't dedicate a bull to the King.

But on the day of my confirmation, I did, and I told Don Juan Carlos on that occasion that I felt proud that he was present in the bullring that day, but, like everyone else involved with the bulls, we would like to see his son there more often too. On the day when I didn't dedicate the bull to the King, I had various personal reasons for not doing so.

A few days earlier, José Luis Bote had received a cornada in the spine. That same morning, I'd been to see him in hospital, and although it didn't happen in the end, the doctor told me that José would be ending up in a wheelchair. That knocked me sideways, to think that, at twenty-something years old, in the flower of his youth, my friend would be left a paraplegic.

That afternoon, with that thought weighing heavily on my mind,

I took advantage of the fact that the corrida was being televised to dedicate the first bull to Bote, and to send him a cheer-up message from the television cameras. Protocol meant that I was under no obligation to dedicate to the King – because he was sitting in a ringside seat, not in the Royal Box – and I could still remember His Majesty with a dedication on my second bull.

But, looking around, I saw *el Fundi* sitting further up, with his arm in a sling because of another accident, and I decided to cheer him up too. The long and short of it was that they were two good friends who were having a bad time, while the King was there like any other spectator. There were some people who took that incident really badly, and they wrote that what I did was provocative and an insult to the monarchy, and that I was using politics just to make publicity for myself.

The truth is that, although I recognise the King's contribution to democracy, I suppose that, yes, I am a bit of a republican, but what I did was about friendship, not politics. They kept having a go at me about it – so much so that I started to use banderillas with the colours of the republican flag, just to annoy them, more that anything else. If they were going to give me a hard time, let it be for a good reason. I had to change them for white banderillas pretty quickly, though, because a real scandal kicked off and they gave me a serious going over in the press.

Then they accused me of using a muleta with the republican colours. I started using a muleta with the yellow side changed to the same purple that I had on the capote, and the idiots said fanatically that it was like the republican flag and was meant as an insult. They kept on having a go at me about it, especially in the monarchist newspaper, *ABC*.

They were so crazy about my supposed republicanism that they even said that the King had refused to go to the Beneficencia charity corrida, as he usually did, because I was on the bill. What rubbish people can stir up.

In his place, probably because Don Juan Carlos must have had a more important engagement, his daughter the Infanta Elena went, and I dedicated a bull to her. Afterwards, as is the custom, she met the toreros in the Royal Box. As I was making my way up there, I asked her people what was the correct protocol on how I should address her. But I was in such a bad mood because of the corrida, in the end I didn't call her 'Señora' or anything else: I gave her two pecks on the cheek and left it at that. The Madrid politicians held their heads in their hands, but she took it perfectly naturally and was actually very friendly towards me.

Years later, the King's son, the Prince of Asturias, held a reception in the Palace of the Zarzuela for celebrities who'd been born in the 1970s. They included: Alaska, Almudena Grandes, Miguel Bosé, Perico Delgado, Zubizarreta... I hardly spoke to Prince Felipe, because I was talking to the actor Jorge Sanz for most of the time. He's a working-class boy like me, and I had more in common with him than the rest of them. Now I suddenly remember, and as my last word on the subject, I want to say to all those ultra-monarchists out there that I have been given several presents by the Royal House, thanking me for some of the dedications I have made: a cigarette case, a silver ball-pen and a key ring with the King's personal coat of arms. Just those three little things. Maybe I was expecting something more splendid: a watch, a gold pen...

I've never got on very well with authority or the Church. I always say that I suppose I must be a Catholic, because I'm Spanish, I have grown up in a Catholic culture, I was baptised...but like the great majority, I don't go to church. I've never believed much in priests, because of the bad experiences I've had with them since I was little. Later on, I met some others, like Father Antonio and Don Jorge from Talavera, who I think are great guys.

My first clash with the clergy was when I went to take my first communion. After doing my catechism in the local church, San Cayetano, the next step was when the parish priest said that our parents had to go to see him, on a certain date, at a certain time. I told Bienvenido, but he said for some reason or other that he couldn't go that day, and he told me ask for a different appointment, but the priest said no.

I was running backwards and forwards between my father and the priest, who wouldn't budge. And he was so pig-headed that I snapped, my nostrils flared, and I told him that, in that case, I would refuse to take my first communion. Bienve thought that was fine. I wanted to do it because of all the presents, but that's all. It wasn't going to be something I would regret, in that unusual family set-up of mine, where no one attached much importance to religion.

The next skirmish was when my biological father died, when Pepita asked for a mass for the dead in the parish church. After receiving the condolences of our neighbours, she took me into the sacristy and I saw her give an envelope to the priest. Back in the street, I asked her if what she had given him was money.

'Yes, of course. Five thousand pesetas.'

'And the sonofabitch took it, knowing that we haven't got two coins to rub together?'

I wanted to go back and go through his pockets to get the money back. That incident was the last straw that broke the camel's back of my childhood dislike of the church; remember, by that time I was already nicely set up in my career as a local petty thief in La Guindalera.

After they turned me down for the Menesianos Institute because I chose Ethics rather than Religion, I didn't have any more dealings with the Church. Until I was getting married in 1999, when I asked my wife – who's called Adela, the same as my adopted mother, who's her aunt – what sort of a ceremony she would like, because I didn't mind either a church or a civil wedding. She felt the same.

But in the end, we decided against a religious ceremony to keep the lid on things as we didn't want to make a lot of noise about it. We wanted our wedding to be a quiet affair, and I knew that, with all the preparations, all the paperwork, the rehearsals and such, the news would be bound to leak out. I was afraid that on the big day it would be like Lola Flores when her daughter Lolita got married – in the end the bride said to her, 'If you really love me, please leave!' – with the church full of onlookers and the press.

So we had a civil ceremony, and that was another adventure. Because of the way I'd been moving house all the time, for some reason I wasn't registered anywhere. Not in La Guindalera, not in Santa Maria de la Cabeza, not in Talavera de la Reina.

After going backwards and forwards between different offices, a friend said she knew someone in one of the courts of Fuenlabrada, who could probably sort it out for me. So it proved, because that gentleman not only registered me there very quickly, but he also arranged the documents for me to get married. But I didn't get married in the designated official suite, but in the McDonald's over the road.

We made our way there doing our best to avoid the press, and I still don't know what had happened in Fuenlabrada that day, but the courts were full of cameras and reporters. If we'd gone in through the main door, we would have been caught *in flagrante*, and been on all the TV news channels. Fortunately, the judge was on the ball, and told us that it would be best to wait in the burger bar opposite until he was free. So that's how it came to pass that, sitting at a table in McDonald's, with some Coca-Colas and a plate of chips, Adela and I signed our marriage deeds, with my friend Julia and her husband as witnesses.

A few days later, we had a more formal ceremony in the registry office of Tarancón, where the friend worked, although we had to wait for them to shut, so no one could see us. And two days later, we held a proper ceremony at my ranch, in a symbolic act with a few guests, the way I wanted.

When Alba, my first daughter, was born, there was no problem in having her baptised. But a few years later, she said that she wanted to take her first communion. She wanted to see her parents take communion with her on the same day, and because it didn't seem right for me to hold my tongue and take communion in bad faith, I made the arrangements to take my own first communion. And then to have a church wedding as well.

Running short of time, I started to get the papers together only a few days before. I went to Alcorcón to ask for the baptism certificate, but the church where I was baptised no longer existed and they sent me to Getafe, but they couldn't find anything. And because I wasn't getting anywhere, and time was running out, in desperation I went personally to the archives of the Archbishop of Madrid.

Luckily it was there that, as I was going up the stairs, I came face to face with Father Lezama, the well-known priest who, as well as being a great aficionado, also owns a chain of restaurants, where he employs boys who want to be toreros as waiters, as he did one day with no less than Enrique Martín Arranz. I explained the urgency of the matter, and, by leap-frogging several intermediate stages, he offered to give me communion the next day. But he still couldn't find my baptism certificate.

While all this was going on, my wife called asking me to come back to Talavera immediately, because the priest from the school, Don Jorge, had decided to give me the sacraments that very afternoon at four o'clock. I rushed home, put on a business suit, called some friends to be witnesses in secret, and at thirty-nine years of age, I was baptised, took first communion and got married in church, all in one go.

A strange story altogether, because I don't know of any other couple like Adela and me who have been married four times and in places as different as we did: in a McDonald's, in the Tarancón registry office, at home, and in the parish church of Talavera. Original – or what?

ON THE RUN FROM NATO

For one reason or another, I've always been a bit of an anarchist, and never got on well with official documents. Something similar happened to me with my military national service.

Known as the 'mili', it was compulsory, and hardly anyone remembers it now, but it was a big pain in the arse for young people, especially if they'd already started out on their professional career. When it was my turn in 1989, I was already hard at work, so I needed to look for a way out. Antonio, my sword handler at the time, advised me to sign up for a correspondence course and then ask for a dispensation to study. This worked fine the first time, but because I forgot, I missed the deadline for the next call-up. Even so, someone told me not to worry because that year there was going to be a big surplus, and they'd only take around thirty to forty per cent, because, in my age group, there were still a large number from the baby boom of the 1960s. So I wasn't worried.

It seems that, because Spain had gone into NATO, or some such story, things didn't turn out the way I'd been told and I was put into the draw for the intake. I remember seeing it on television as I was getting dressed for the baptism of Rocío, the daughter of Enrique and Adela, and that's when I realised that I could be sent to Ceuta in North Africa for twelve months. The army was going to interrupt my career at a very important time.

Although I was leaving it late, I began to take the steps that I should have started long before. With the help of a friend, I went to see Colonel Mimoso – a strange name for a soldier – to ask if he could arrange for the sort of dispensation that they gave top athletes when the time came for them to 'serve their country'. The conversation went more or less like this:

'Please understand, Colonel, that I want to serve my King and country...'

'Pleased to hear it. That's what I want to hear, a man prepared to meet his obligations. What's more, a torero! As brave as they come!'

'But what I am asking for is that I want be based in Madrid so that I can continue with the bulls.'

'Impossible!'

'I was told that for sportsmen...'

'But you're not a sportsman.'

'No, but what I do is something similar, and the army is going to stop that.'

'Well, let me see what can be done.'

And he did something all right. I was sent to Madrid, but to the San Pedro Base, the tough training centre for recruits at Colmenar Viejo.

Three days before I was due to report, I got the cornada in San Martín de Valdeiglesias, and I couldn't report to the barracks. I didn't tell them, as I thought that, because I was a torero, they would already know what had happened and that I was convalescing. But a week later, an army sergeant I knew called me to say that, if I didn't show up within twenty-four hours, I would miss this intake and would need to go in the next one. In other words, if I didn't go to 'take the oath' by the middle of November, I wasn't going to be able to fulfil my contracts in America.

So, with the wound still open, I went to the base, the Centre for the Instruction of Recruits (known as the CIR), picked up my kit, and checked into the bunkroom with three hundred other rookies.

In the evening, the captain called me to say he was very surprised that I was there in 'the worst barracks in Spain', because my time doing the 'mili' there was going to be miserable, 'Because of who you are, they should have sent you to Headquarters, like they do with the recruits who've got the right connections, so you wouldn't have guard duties, and you could get on with your own business. It's not going to be much fun for you here.'

He painted a grim picture. But I was lucky, because, after taking the oath, I was attached to the junior officers' mess and I managed to get permission for time off to go to America.

I was already in Bogota, and convinced that I had escaped the worst of it, but then the Gulf War broke out, and they recalled all soldiers to return to their barracks. They called me from mine and said I had to be back the next day. I was due to appear on the Sunday in the Colombia capital, I hadn't got a plane ticket...there was no way I could get there on time.

'Sort yourself out, because, if the balloon goes up and you're not here, they'll post me to Mahon,' the Colonel said later.

I tried to get the Spanish Consul to help, but there was no way he could. So I got on a plane by myself, and reported to Colmenar on the Wednesday, thinking that I could go back to Bogota at the weekend. But on the Friday, they posted Private Arroyo to guard duty and to be on standby for Saturday and Sunday. I couldn't go back to America and I spent the whole winter shut up in the barracks, and frustrated too, because, on top of everything else, there was a lieutenant, one of the first women soldiers, who kept annoying me for weeks. At least they didn't send me to Iraq.

The 1991 season was about to start, but the war was still going on, and there was a rumour about a threat to poison the reservoirs in the mountains around Madrid, so they wouldn't let me out. The occasional weekend leave I had was hardly enough time to train with some heifers in the country. Seeing that this was going to go on for a long time, Enrique went higher up, until finally an assistant to Nárcis Serra, the Minister of Defence at the time, managed to arrange for me to be transferred to Telecommunications.

I arrived at my new post and presented myself to the captain, who was already half-cut, even though it was early morning. He was very surprised to see me there, because he didn't know what I was talking about, but he still took my papers to admit me.

When he read them, he jumped out of his skin, 'You say you are from the High Command staff, but in your photo you are wearing the uniform of the Medical Corps!' he shouted, spluttering great gobs of saliva.

'It's what they gave me, sir.'

'Go back to your barracks, get a photo taken with the correct uniform, and come back here tomorrow.'

'Certainly, sir. Do I have your permission to leave, sir?'

'Granted.'

And because I realised that he hadn't written anything down, and that he didn't even know my name, I went home and told everyone that I'd been given three months' leave. I never set foot in a barracks again. By a stroke of luck, I had been transferred out of Colmenar, and they hadn't admitted me at Telecommunications. I was in limbo, and neither one nor the other ever recalled me.

I heard nothing more from the army until, a while later, when I was appearing in Talavera, I received a call from a friend I had known in the CIR base, who was downstairs in the reception of the hotel where I was being dressed.

'Arroyo, I am here with the lady lieutenant who has brought your "blanca" (the military paybook stamped with your discharge).

She's in the bar waiting for me, having a beer.'

'What? You haven't found me, for chrissake. Don't tell her anything.'

I was so taken aback that I imagined that they'd come looking for me as a deserter, but probably all they wanted was a couple of tickets for the corrida.

'Listen, I don't want it.'

'But I've got it right here; I'll bring it up.'

'No, for chrissake. If you give it to me they'll know where I am. Forget it! Tell the lieutenant that you couldn't speak to me and take it away.'

After the corrida, I wouldn't go back to the hotel. I went straight home to get changed in case they were waiting for me at the hotel. That's the last I heard from the army from which I was a deserter before and after my military service, my 'mili'. Ever since I forged my birth certificate to appear in the bullring, my relationship with official papers has been a bit special.

But, as time went by, I became more and more fond of reading the other kind of papers, the ones you find in books. Although I left school early, and didn't touch a book in those years while I was living in the countryside, after I became a matador, I began reading and started to think about teaching myself a few things.

INDEBTED TO GABRIEL GARCÍA MÁRQUEZ

Antonio Martín Arranz, the sword handler, was the one who got me interested in books. He had studied Spanish literature, was very cultured, and spoke with a rich vocabulary, which impressed me. By this time, I had already realised that I needed more education.

Around that time, in the course of the presentation of a book which had just been written about me, a fellow matador, Luis Francisco Esplá, used the word 'chaotic', and I felt very embarrassed because I didn't know what it meant. There were many things I didn't know, and it worried me that I couldn't express myself like other people. I didn't really have much of a vocabulary because I was used to the street-talk of La Guindalera and the argot of the world of the bulls.

Antonio, brother of Enrique, was a strange type, half punk rocker. He was a sight to see, at the side of the ring with his sticking-up hair and punky platform shoes. During a corrida, you would suddenly notice him sprawled among the sword cases, reading a book while someone else was working their bull out there in the ring, because he said that the only one who concerned him was me. That strange-looking but so well-educated individual was the one who began to open my horizons.

When I began to read, my style in the ring improved, because I was more self-confident. Until that point, I found it very difficult to connect with the public, both inside and outside the ring. I was withdrawn because I was very aware of my limitations and my lack of culture.

Going to any public event, a discussion, an awards presentation, was very difficult for me. I didn't know what to say, or how to behave, and I was always afraid that someone would bring up a subject which I knew nothing about; I only knew about the countryside and about the bulls. But thanks to my reading, I began to use a dictionary more, I knew more words, and I could talk about other things. With the increase in self-belief, I became stronger as a person, both inside and outside the bullring.

Reading gave me peace of mind. I always read a book before appearing in the ring, and it helped me through difficult moments. If I was interested in a book, I would carry on reading right up to the time to dress for the corrida, and sometimes even up to the time I left for the ring.

The first book I began was *Memoirs of Hadrian* by Marguerite Yourcenar, but I found it so difficult that I couldn't finish it. I was seventeen, and had never even opened a book before. But the next one I read right through to the end. *One Hundred Years of Solitude* by Gabriel García Márquez really got me hooked on reading.

Nowadays, I read all sorts. I like Vargas Llosa very much, and he's the only person I've ever asked for his autograph. I like realism and historical novels, because they're entertaining and I learn a lot. At one time, I used to read philosophy books. I found it hard to take in, but it made me think and go over many aspects of life. It taught me to think carefully about things, that nothing is like it is just because they say so, but that there is a reason for everything.

I have been lucky enough to meet very interesting people from all walks of life. I have attended receptions, special events, lunches and dinners with top people in the world of culture, politics and art. But they were only brief meetings, from which I drew no clear impressions.

However, there have been others I have known better, who have been to my home, and I have learned quite a lot more about culture from them. For instance, there were two writers, María José García and Lola Crespo, who wrote books about me. María José is a very unaffected person, and she introduced me to her academic world. Lola is a marvellous woman, a bit bohemian, and through her I met very cultured people who are more from my level; I felt more at home with them, and we had some marvellous times together.

I was very flattered that they should write books about me, because I was still very new, just four years or so after taking the alternativa. Unless I am mistaken, between 1990 and 1999 six books in total were published about me: those by Lola and María José, two by Mariano Tomás, another by Joaquín Jesús Gordillo, and another one by someone who self-published a book off his own bat.

I couldn't understand it, I didn't see how I could give rise to such thoughts in the short time that I had been in bullfighting, and while there was still a lot left for them to find something interesting to say about me. But even so, I was very flattered, obviously.

It's very important for an artist to be able to provide subject matter for writers in their work, to give rise to thoughts and analysis, to inspire literary texts. That alone made all the trouble and heartache worthwhile.

What's more, nearly all of them understood me well, and I was happy with what they wrote about me. They were people I didn't know from Adam, but they understood exactly what I wanted to express with my work in the ring. For example, Lola Crespo, one day when I had a corrida in Guadalajara, went to the hotel and left a pile of papers for me, even before she'd thought of publishing it as a book. I'd never met her before, but what she'd written was very close to what I am and what I felt. I must have been very transparent.

I would be lying if I said that those books didn't pump up my ego, and they fed my artistic side too, because unconsciously it was what I needed, to communicate with my bullfighting. Mariano Tomás is a magistrate, and, as I said, he wrote two books, including the first to be published at the beginning of the 1990s. I met him for the first time on the day of the book's presentation, and I'd never spoken to him before. He was a lawyer in Valencia and he struck me as very reserved. So, because I was very withdrawn in those days, we hardly exchanged two or three sentences in a rather awkward conversation.

But, little by little, a great friendship began to take root. For three or four years, he would travel with us whenever he could. He gave Enrique a quick course in what he called 'Vatican diplomacy' designed to make his dealings with the impresarios easier.

I learnt an enormous amount from Mariano. Spending so much time in the company of someone so cultured made me look at life in a new way. Because we are so different, we used to have a lot of arguments, but always as good friends. I think that the contrast between his life and mine has been enriching for both of us. That's why, among all the friends who have helped me to progress, I will put Mariano Tomás as number one on the podium. He has proved to be a cornerstone in my life.

Certainly, reading and culture changed me. Because I was so engrossed with the bulls, it took me a long time to understand the importance of knowledge in my day-to-day existence as a person and as an artist. But I think I got there just in time, thanks to the magic spell of *One Hundred Years of Solitude*.

One fine day, unexpectedly, I had the opportunity to thank Gabriel García Márquez personally, and what would be the best way for me to do that? By dedicating a bull to him in Las Ventas. When I finished the parade, they told me that he was sitting at the ringside, and I became very excited. By now I had already read several of his books, and I admired him enormously. I let my first bull go by, because it wasn't much good, but when I saw possibilities in the next one, I began to think of dedicating it to the Nobel Prize winner.

When the clarins sounded for the third act, I went straight over to him with my sword and muleta to tell him I was dedicating the death of this bull to *One Hundred Years of Solitude*, because, thanks to his book, I had become an avid reader, and also because I was delighted to see him there, uniting two great arts: literature and bullfighting.

And, although it wasn't easy, I made a special effort to give that animal one of my best-ever faenas. I was obliged to because of the dedication. I cut both ears and went out by the main gate of Las Ventas on shoulders once again. It was 15th May 1996, nine years to the day after *Limonero* spared my life in that same ring. It was the highpoint of my career.

7

FAME AND SUFFERING

The charity corrida of Beneficencia in Madrid in 1993 marked the start of my best period, five very satisfying years. I had matured both as a man and as a torero, and I enjoyed a period which was full of great faenas and overwhelming triumphs. These were my best years artistically.

However, at the start of the 1993 season, things didn't go easy for me. We still had problems with the new management at Las Ventas, and in the preceding winter, Enrique and I already knew that I was going to be left out of San Isidro, and if we didn't have a success in Madrid to build on, the rest of the season would be all uphill.

During another visit to Bogota, while I was dozing in my room – most of my best ideas come to me in bed – I began to think about the forthcoming season, and what the Lozano brothers would be up to in their nasty little schemes to smear my reputation, saying stuff like I was money-grabbing and mechanical. Thinking of ways to hit them where it hurts, I remembered the great day of my hero Paco Camino in the charity corrida of Beneficencia in 1970, when he took on seven bulls on his own and cut seven ears, and I thought that perhaps I could do something similar.

I had never appeared solo in a corrida of six bulls, but I had the crazy idea to do it in Madrid in the same Beneficencia event, and I would refuse any fees, like the toreros used to do in the old days. The point was that the organisation of this corrida was out of the hands of the usual Lozano management, but was the responsibility of the Madrid Community, the regional government, as the owners of the bullring; so I was certain there wouldn't be any problem with our offer.

I woke up Enrique, who was sleeping in the other bed, and told him my idea. But he was unimpressed and said, 'Don't be daft, go back to sleep. You've had a nightmare.'

But the next morning, I explained the idea to him again, and he had no choice but to call Madrid and put the proposal to the Community politicians, and they thought it was a great idea and accepted. We told them to keep it a secret in case the Lozanos tried to scupper the project.

As we'd expected, we couldn't come to an agreement with the Lozanos for San Isidro, but nevertheless, I still got to appear in the most important corrida in Las Ventas that year.

The image that the public has of me as a torero who uses a great variety of passes in his performance dates from that day, because that's how I decided to play it when I began thinking about how to handle taking on six bulls on my own. Enrique warned me of the risks involved, because I would be the sole focus of attention in the spectacle for the whole two hours; physically, I would need to be strong enough for the task, and also to be very concentrated on what I was doing, to avoid any blank periods or monotonous repetition. My mother, who is more outspoken in giving her opinions than most, said that, because I am made the way I am, she was sure I would bore the hind legs off a donkey.

I made my preparations to make sure that didn't happen, and for months I was recalling and putting into practice all those traditional passes that I'd been taught in the Madrid School of Bullfighting, when Molinero used to give twenty-five pesetas to whoever gave the most different passes. At first I thought it wasn't possible to use passes like that with the modern bulls I was working with, but I was wrong.

On that 17th June 1993, I demonstrated a wide selection of different passes, including some that I hadn't even tried out in practice with the heifers. Without really meaning to, by reviving all those old passes, I had made it fashionable again to employ a wide variety of passes with the capote. Throughout the corrida, I had to keep an open mind and approach each bull with a different performance, adapting to the individual circumstances without boring the public, and without repeating myself. This is a basic requirement for anyone who takes on six bulls by himself.

At the end of the corrida, I was carried out on shoulders for the third time from what was, after all, my local bullring. I only cut two ears, but more important than the number of ears was the sum of my complete performance. The corrida was televised, so all of Spain could see for themselves that I'd grown up, and once and for all they could see my abilities as a torero. Just as we hoped, that Beneficencia corrida established me at the top of my profession.

After that, I took on a corrida of six bulls solo several times – eleven altogether. If we include an earlier one in Alicante, when I had to kill all six because it was a mano a mano with *Litri*, who had a cornada in his first bull, that makes thirteen in total. Nearly all of them were successful, and were highlights in my career, because that's where I was able to develop my personal style and its richness.

Because of my work with the capote, from that time on, aficionados have considered me a torero capable of showing great variety in what I do. The truth is that I've always found the capote easy to use, which allowed me to give more passes than others. But what I enjoyed more than anything was performing the 'verónica' pass, the most basic of all the passes with the capote. In a verónica, dropping my hands smoothly at the same speed as the bull, I think that maybe I was not too bad at all...

With the smaller muleta cape, as I said earlier, I've always tried to be faithful to my ideals: not to crowd the bull, but working close, and keeping up a slow rhythm whenever possible. What we call 'temple', the most important quality to be found in the art of bullfighting, is not simply to move the cape slowly, but to impose a rhythm on everything you do, and everything you make the bull do. Before, during and after every pass.

My best hand was the left one, giving what we call passes 'al natural' – literally, naturally. I felt more comfortable than with the right hand, because then you have to hold the sword as well. That's why sometimes, when I was doing well with a bull, I would throw away the sword, and move the muleta with the right hand in the same way as with the left, with just the cloth of the muleta.

I also had a reputation for being good with the sword – some said I was the best from the latter part of the twentieth century – but the truth is that I was never a conventional swordsman. Yes, I was reliable, because I always entered for the kill in a straight line and without hesitation, but not necessarily following the established traditional conventions.

The sword thrust, the so-called 'moment of truth', is a very tense moment, and the pressure is on. You are aware that the ideal outcome is to drop the bull with the first attempt. If the rest of your performance has been good, this is to ensure that you don't lose any trophies; and if it was bad, to get it over with as quickly as possible. If the bull has been a good one, it is also because the bull itself deserves a dignified death; if it was bad or dangerous, it is so you don't have to put yourself at risk any more than is necessary.

It is unlike anything else, because, up to that point, you've been moving fluidly to counteract the violence of the bull, but suddenly it's your turn to be aggressive. In a matter of seconds, the roles have reversed, and you have to adapt to this at a critical moment, because, for a fraction of a second, you lose sight of the bull and you don't know what its horns are doing.

I soon learnt the important thing is to be icy-calm at this time, and I could then enter for the kill very effectively. But I have also had the good fortune that a bull has never caught me in the 'moment of truth'. If it had ever happened, I don't know how I would have reacted afterwards.

In the Beneficencia corrida in 1993, I gave a very rounded performance. I was close to becoming fully developed as a torero.

As a human being, I had done away with all the crazy thoughts in my head. In their place, there was common sense, and I was ready to reach maturity with a more consistent approach to life. That success gave me the self-belief and peace of mind that I was missing before, and it helped me to take control of my career the way I wanted to. With all the goings-on behind closed office doors, and the struggles with the management of the bullrings, the pressure of it all, I hadn't had time to think about my own way of working with the bulls. But now I was able to concentrate on what I always wanted: as Belmonte said, bullfighting should be done 'with the feelings and passion of someone in love'. And I was.

WITH A LOVER'S PASSION

When it comes to women, there are certain things that a gentleman should not talk about, even if he doesn't have much to say on the subject. I am sorry to disappoint those who are reading this book in the hope of discovering tales of torrid romances with famous actresses, or stories of endless, passionate love affairs.

I'm not just saying this to dodge the issue, but the truth is that, in the course of my life, I've been in love with many things, not just women. If not 'in love', at least crazy about many things. Because I had my dreams, I was able to achieve whatever I wanted. I would get excited about the tiniest detail, a goal to be reached, whether it was getting a girl to go out with me, an artistic ambition, something I wanted desperately to buy... If I had a target, my way was clear, and I could give one hundred per cent in the ring. That was what I loved doing.

I don't hold back, but I've never really been obsessed with women. When the season was in full flow, it wasn't easy for me to have even casual relationships. I was very shy, and guys like me need time to build up a relationship. In periods when I was working, time was exactly what I didn't have.

I didn't have time in the winter either, because I shut myself away in the countryside, going round and round in my head, correcting weaknesses and as much as possible making improvements. I was thinking and living exclusively for the bulls. I didn't even ride a horse, in case I had a fall; I didn't play football in case I picked up an injury which stopped me from working.

My family and friends kept telling me that, in the months that I didn't have corridas, I should try to keep myself entertained, I should travel, I should take it easy. But concentrating on my performance was enough to keep me in good spirits. I had to be on top of things to keep myself together and to be able to keep up the struggle. So, quite honestly, it wasn't worth taking time off.

Most relationships are not based on true love, but just sexual attraction. True love happens very few times in a lifetime. I didn't fall in love in between that kiss with Patri in La Guindalera and a brief affair I had with a girl in Colombia many years later. That didn't last very long though – too short a time by far.

I went out with other girls – not many – but there was hardly ever time to get involved. I even had a fling with one of the daughters of the owner of the famous Pablo Romero ranch, just as Joselito *el Gallo* did with another girl, an ancestor of that same family. As well as the cultural differences – *Gallito*'s affair was truly passionate – her parents were not happy about one of their daughters taking up with a torero.

It was different with Adela, the love of my life, probably because she was around for a long time without me noticing her. I first knew her when she was a child, and we travelled in the same car together to Enrique's ranch one time. She was going to spend a few days in the country with her uncle and aunt, because she is the niece of the other Adela, my adopted mother. I must have been thirteen and she was nine, and we were both very shy and spent the journey staring out of different windows without looking at one another.

In the few days that Adelita spent on the ranch, it wasn't me but *Fundi* and Bote who played with her, because I was going through my most unsociable period, and I didn't even look at her. When her aunt told me to look after her, I remember that I was rather unkind to her.

Later, I used to see her every year at family get-togethers or at Christmas. We were already quite grown up when I began to take an interest and, at last, I felt like showing my feelings towards her. It was one night in February in 1994, after a festival in which she'd come to see me perform. During dinner, I couldn't stop thinking about how I should take the first step, because I didn't want to just come out with it, and I thought it could give rise to lots of problems. After all, Adela was family, and people might start thinking all sorts of things.

Imagine the state I was in, because, after the restaurant, we were going down the street, and I walked straight into a traffic sign. I just didn't see it. Mariano Tomás, who was with us and knows me very well, said, 'What's up with you, José? You're not with it, you're somewhere else tonight.'

But no, I was there all right, in the same hotel as her. It was the right place at the right time. When everyone else went to bed, I phoned her and asked her if she would like us to watch a film together that was showing on TV. She said okay, so I went along to her room in my pyjamas; in the corridor, I met a drunk from a wedding who mistook me for a waiter and asked me to bring him a bottle of champagne.

We sat there on the edge of the bed like two good little children, watching the box until two in the morning, without me daring to say a word. I was in danger of missing my chance, or as toreros say, 'the bull was going to be returned to the corral alive'. Then, at the last minute, summoning up more courage than I ever had in the ring, out on the hotel balcony, with the sound of the waves and the light of a full moon shining on the water, I poured out to Adela everything that I felt for her. Just like a romantic scene in the movies. She told me that she had loved me since that first ride in the car together in Colmenar del Arroyo.

Overcome with happiness, the next day I caped a bull in a private ring out in the countryside; that performance has rarely been bettered since. That bull later became one of the best seed-bulls in the herd of my friend Daniel Martínez. With its offspring, I have enriched my own herd of toros bravos. As the song says, 'Love is strange'.

Later, we quarrelled and broke off our short engagement. I took up with a lovely girl from Madrid called Cristina, and I went out with her for a while, until I finally realised that the only one I really loved was that dark-haired girl who was always around. I made my heart see reason, and in 1999 I married Adela in the strange circumstances I've already described.

As I feared, some of the twisted minds in the world of the bulls started to say that my marriage was yet another trick of the Machiavellian Enrique Martín Arranz, so that my fortune would stay in the family. And that he had waved Adela in front of me every day to keep his claws in me.

What no one knows is that the first person to blow his top when he found out about us was none other than my father: 'Are you telling me you couldn't find someone else, José?'

Knowing what I was like, he was afraid that one day we would have a row, and it would have repercussions on everyone in the household.

But Adela is the love of my life. In my active years and since my retirement from the ring, she has shown immense patience with me and has been much more patient than I have with her. In the reverse of what happens in most marriages, in my case, it had to be the woman who did what the man wanted, because in our home everything revolved around me.

If I had a good afternoon, she stayed in the background while I dealt with other people; but if I had a bad day, she had to put up with all my bad moods and ravings. My constant unpredictability was a dead weight on our relationship. When we were engaged, there was never a problem, because we weren't together all the time. But it's different when you have to put up with someone like me, day and night...

On top of this, Adela had to learn to deal with the typical worries of the wife of a torero, waiting every evening for the phone call that everything had gone okay and there were no accidents. That's why she preferred to go to the bullring. She suffered a lot watching me with the bull, but she still felt better than staying at home, when every time the telephone rang in the two hours from the start of the corrida until the finish, it made her heart leap.

I recognise that things were not at all easy for her then – she couldn't even have a social life, because I hate all that stuff. I've always tried to avoid being out and about in the public eye, in case people or the press start talking about me. That's why we didn't go out much, and when we did, we made sure we kept out of sight. So much so that some friends said they were surprised when they heard I'd got married because they didn't even know I had a girlfriend.

When they did find out, some of them wanted to know who Adela was and what did she do in life. When I told them that she worked in a dress shop, the smartest among them thought that, because I was who I was, she must be working in Loewe, Prada or some other high-class establishment, but they were shocked to discover that she worked in a shop called Euronido in the unfashionable district of Moratalaz.

Adela's origins are as humble as mine, and because she is instinctively very bright, she knows how to adapt to any situation. She even succeeded in domesticating me in the house. It's also true that I've changed a lot since those days, and even in the most difficult times, I've fought my utmost to keep my marriage alive. The traumatic experiences of my childhood, the unhappy relationship of Bienvenido and Pepita – these are the best possible lessons for me to know what I want to do with my own life. I wouldn't want to be the slightest bit like my biological father for anything in the world.

LIGHTNING ALWAYS STRIKES AT THE HIGHEST POINT

That preference for keeping out of the limelight led to some of the gossip-mongers to make up their own stories about me. They invented fairy tales about Enrique and me in our professional life, but they made up some terrible lies about my personal life, especially after they heard that Adela was the niece of my adopted father. The reality was exactly the opposite of the rubbish they spread around, but that gang of muck-stirrers preferred their own wicked stories. Some of them were unbelievably disgusting, twisted and libellous.

As for the money, they said that Enrique kept everything I earned by using a chain of companies that he controlled. The truth is that this was a legal formula that we used to avoid paying the extortionate tax rate of fifty-six per cent of my earnings, more than half of what I received.

Nowadays, all my colleagues do the same, but as I was the first torero to put his revenue through a limited company, the charming guys out there who loved us so much were taken aback by the new arrangement, and as ever they thought that Enrique was up to what they called his usual tricks. But my father has always been scrupulously honest in his affairs. I'm sure it's more likely that I've been guilty of using his money more than he ever did mine, because he never kept back as much as a five peseta coin that belonged to me.

All those nasty stories about me and my family affected me a lot at first, but they became so outrageous that, in the end, I decided not to take any notice. I had to get on with my life, and to stop worrying about what those people who just wanted to do us down were saying.

There was no point in rising to their bait. I am quite confident about who I am and who my parents are, and how they've treated me, and of everything they've done for me. All I have for them is my heartfelt thanks, and my most profound respect and admiration. So who cares what the gossips out there say?

Enrique Martín Arranz is a mirror image of myself. He is thought of as a tough nut, a hard man in the world of the bulls, but he is actually the most straightforward and honest individual I've ever met, a good man who was obliged to act tough to avoid being eaten alive by the circling sharks. He is my real father, although I don't have his genes, and we have no blood connection, which doesn't really mean anything at all. Enrique is honest and straight as a die, and has taught me how to conduct myself in life. Of the many good pieces of advice he has given me, since he told me that one about the hammers and the nails, the most important one is as follows,

'If you are with someone who is more important than you, be yourself. And if they are less important, be yourself also. Don't play humble pie with the one, or pump yourself up with the other. Don't show off when you have a success, or be all doom and gloom with a defeat. Always hold your head high, but not with arrogance. Never imagine yourself either bigger or smaller than you are.'

If it wasn't for him, I wouldn't have lasted for five minutes in the bull business. I would have got swollen-headed immediately, and it would all have collapsed before I got halfway down the road. I've gone so far as to think that, when my biological father died, that was lucky for me, because if he'd been at my side, he would have been a terrible influence in my career, as has happened with some other matadors. I can just imagine how Bienve would have reacted when he saw his son beginning to earn serious money, and on all those trips to America, and it just doesn't bear thinking about.

I was very lucky to find Enrique. It was through him that I achieved everything I did. After that triumph with six bulls in Madrid in 1993, many of my most important faenas followed on from that. Among others, I recall the one of the same year with *Flamenco*, a bull from the Buendía herd, in Santander. And another, even better one a few days later with an Osborne bull in Benidorm.

I was up there, right at the top, and I could afford to make gestures by taking on six bulls solo. The one in Zaragoza in 1994 was a demonstration of determination and commitment, because I had to go twice to the infirmary. Even more so was the one the following year in Nîmes, when I held on to finish the last two bulls off after receiving an eighteen-centimetre cornada in the leg from the fourth bull. On a different note, the one in Valladolid in 1995 was a complete anthology of my repertoire of passes.

I realised that the public was completely receptive to what I was doing; they got my message, responded, and took to me. The press was behind me, and I noticed that I was less moody as a person. I was happy and in love, and going through the best patch I've ever had. I still had a few ups and downs, because I was never able to keep my instability under control, but from those low points there always emerged my most successful afternoons. I had the very good fortune that, at key moments, I had a good bull to make a triumph possible.

The peaks and troughs which defined my career were essential to keep me going. If I'd experienced triumphs on a regular basis, I would have found it very boring, and I wouldn't have moved on to better things. I needed contrasts to feed on, like the one I experienced most memorably in the bullring of Mexico City, the biggest in the whole world.

I still remembered the film of *Manolete* in that same ring, which I'd seen in the Bullfighting School in Madrid, and I imagined myself creating the same frenzy as he did with the Mexican public. The Plaza Mexico became an obsession for me, more than any other bullring in America. I had been there several times before and had even cut a few ears, but I hadn't really left my mark there yet.

Things weren't turning out well on that day, 25th February 1996, because my first bull pulled up short almost immediately, 'gripping the sand', and I couldn't do anything with it. I killed it quickly, and as I walked across the ring to salute the president, I was convinced that my dreams of a triumph in Mexico were over; my chances of seeing the Mexican public screaming for more were simply not going to happen.

I resigned myself to an inevitable failure, and quietly accepted that there was nothing else for it, because I expected my next bull to be a case of me going through the motions. But out came *Valeroso* from the ranch of Garfias, and by the fourth capote pass the public was already starting to jump about. The forty thousand-odd spectators in that giant funnel-shaped bullring started roaring with delight when they saw how I worked the bull, and they did so with a passion which I'd seen nowhere else in my life.

At the end of every series of passes, the trumpets played the reveille, and the sand was filled with sombreros and jackets thrown by the wildest members of the crowd. It was the same as I'd seen in the old film, but this time it wasn't *Manolete*, but me that set them off. They say that what they like over there are long faenas of over fifteen minutes, but I cut the tail of that bull in just five, with only four series of passes. I was thrilled.

Let's not forget the bit about being carried out on shoulders, first climbing up the tunnel which spirals upwards behind the seating before reaching the exit to the street. And it didn't end there, because, as we tried to leave for the hotel, people swarmed round and began shaking the cuadrilla minibus so we couldn't leave.

'Matador, come down off your high horse!' they shouted. They wanted me to get out of the car so they could carry me on shoulders again, this time through the streets of the city. I was scared, but they more or less forced me to get out of the car, and they carried me around in the main street, Paseo de Reforma, for two hours, stopping the traffic, until finally I had to beg them to put me down, because I wanted to call home to tell them I was okay.

I remember that day in Mexico as one of the best in my life, because of the massive contrast I lived through in scarcely an hour: from abject despair, to being on cloud nine. Like in my own life, no half tones.

THE HIGHPOINT OF 2ND MAY

1996 was my most satisfying year, when I gathered in all that I had sown, especially in Las Ventas. On that great day in Mexico, I already knew that I was going to face six bulls in Madrid again. This time, we chose the date of 2nd May, which is the day of the Fiesta of the Madrid Community, because this event was also organised by the Madrid politicians, not the Lozanos, who, again, would have done their utmost to stop it happening.

Even so, we had problems. Enrique chose good bulls from good ranches, but when they got to the corrals of Las Ventas, as if working under orders, the vets and the president decided to reject everything we offered up, no matter what they looked like. Several lorries called by and delivered animals, and in the end they finally approved a bunch of bulls which were not nearly as good as the ones we'd chosen at first. They were not at all promising. My father was tearing his hair out.

Someone wanted to put the mockers on the event, by whatever

means, but we decided to go ahead anyway. The challenge had been made, and we weren't going to back down at the last moment. I was so enthusiastic about the event that I would have fought the mythical giant bull of Saint Mark if they had offered it. Enrique knew this, and the build-up had created a lot of interest, so I had no choice but to accept the rubbish they had left me with.

Fortunately, I didn't know about all the goings-on that had taken place in the morning until the last moment, because it would have upset me. What I did know about was the wind and the rain that I saw when I woke up that morning in Talavera. It was no better when I got to Madrid. I didn't want to think about anything. I went with my mother to the Alemana bar in the square of Santa Ana, I had a glass of wine and a croquette, and then I went to my room in the nearby Hotel Victoria.

I didn't even open the curtains to get dressed in case the sight of bad weather got me down. When I left for the bullring, a heavy downpour started, which made me wonder why I allowed myself to get into a situation like this. Then I thought better of it and relaxed, thinking that, if the weather continued like that, the corrida would have to be suspended anyway. By the time I arrived at the tunnel where the cuadrillas wait in Las Ventas, I was wearing a grin from ear to ear, and there I met up with many of my old friends from the Bullfighting School who were going to act as banderilleros for me that day.

The skies cleared, the wind dropped and the corrida went ahead. Maybe it was because I was already calm and relaxed that it went on to be one of the most important days of my career. The bulls didn't make it easy for me, but I was still able to demonstrate the variety of my performance, and I went on to cut six ears without stopping. My cup was running over.

There was one marvellous moment during the fourth bull: I finished a series of passes and realised that everyone was on their feet; I looked upwards from that impressive viewpoint in the ring at all the rows of seating, up to the balconies and right on up to the boxes of the Las Ventas bullring. It was like a pressure cooker about to explode with the yelling of twenty thousand people crying out to me, 'Torero! Torero!' It was fantastic to realise then that I was responsible for creating the collective madness of the most critical bullring public in the world, and that my performance had touched the hearts of so many thousands of spectators.

After that uproar, they carried me out of Las Ventas on shoulders as if I were a god. They tell me that, afterwards, the people from the corrida were going round the local bars all night, unbelievably happy. Everywhere they were talking in glowing terms about the corrida, drinking, laughing, and having a great time.

A number of aficionados have told me that the corrida of 2nd May is one of the best memories of their life, and some others have said that, after seeing it, that night they plucked up courage to go out on a date with the woman who later became their wife. That sort of enthusiasm, of positive vitality, is what a corrida can spark off when it's as good as it was that day.

But as for myself, I didn't do anything special. I went back to the hotel and for almost three hours I entertained my fans and friends who were all so excited with my success. After I left them at about midnight, I went out for dinner with my girlfriend, my parents and Mariano Tomás to the only local restaurant which would serve us food at that late hour.

I remember that, when we were sitting down, eating our pasta, the background music started playing 'La Vie en Rose' by Edith Piaf, and I had a wonderful feeling of inner peace. No big party celebration, no drunken booze-up, even though I am very partial to a good red wine. I just wanted to take things quietly. I enjoyed my triumph without going crazy, because I already knew what the possible consequences of a success like that could be, like what happened after the exit on shoulders of 1989, which messed with my head for such a long time.

That day was something else, something fantastic, and the effect was very out of the ordinary, but I had to carry on as before. I went home to Talavera to sleep, and the next day when I got up, I was immediately back in my training routine, as if nothing had happened.

Maybe that's why I was able to return to Las Ventas two weeks later, once again leaving on shoulders, the day of my dedication to García Márquez.

That period of four excellent seasons, above all in the season of 1996, is when my real personality took off, my best qualities came out. And that's what the public wanted to see. Don José de la Cal told me so much about the legendary toreros of his time that I always wanted to be like them – artists, but tough guys, magnificent and awe-inspiring with the bulls and in the company of their colleagues. Like César Girón from Venezuela, who Enrique spoke of constantly, or *Miguelín*, who Bienvenido was always going on about. For me, they were like gods come down from Mount Olympus. They were under my skin, and I wanted to be like them in practice.

Maybe I was less outgoing than those fighting cocks, but one thing I did have was the ability to 'fill the bullring' as toreros say, to dominate in the ring, and hold the attention of the public. I was shown the way to do it some years earlier in Colombia, in a long round-table discussion – a 'tertulia' – with the journalist Curro Fetén and Hernando Santos, the editor of the newspaper *El Tiempo*, and uncle of the current President of the Republic.

Santos was a close friend of the famous matador Luis Miguel *Dominguín*, and he later became a fan of mine, because he said we were both Madrid 'Cockneys'. He told me that, although *Dominguín* was a great character, he was probably not the best torero, but he was Number One because he caught the eye of both women and men. Everyone was waiting to see what he would do next in the ring, even when it was the turn of someone else to work the bull.

That's when I understood the importance of charisma for an artist. Without pushing it, because you can't do it if you haven't got it inside you, I decided to go for it. How? I don't know, maybe just by doing my job in the ring with a sense of it being a dignified occasion.

I now had self-belief, and staring down at the ground was long behind me, or maybe it was because my fragility made them anxious, but I now knew that the public related to me. Not for my looks, because I don't think of myself as good-looking, but something in me caught their eye and it came naturally to me. When I dressed up as a torero, I became someone you couldn't ignore.

As Hernando Santos said, maybe it could also be because of my air of being a Madrid 'Cockney', born and bred but not too cocky with it. And I didn't disguise it. It is something which is fundamental to the way I am, it marks me as coming from the working-class background of La Guindalera and the Madrid School of Bullfighting. That upbringing shaped my character, and gave me the confidence to face up to life.

For whatever reason, nearly all the toreros from the Madrid School of Bullfighting have a similar stamp. I think that Madrid people have special characteristics in our conduct and approach to the world of the bulls. There's a lot of talk about the Seville School, but in my hometown, there have been a long line of toreros who are excellent, courageous and don't go in for meaningless showing off. Take, for example, Manolo Escudero, the *Dominguín* family, Felix Merino, Luis Alfonso Garcés, *Antoñete*, Luis Segura, Ángel Teruel, *Tinín*...they all have that mix of arrogance and free spirit, but with tremendous class in the face of danger. And I belong in that list too.

Another factor which comes into the personality of a torero is his outward appearance. As well as being a torero, you have to look like one. I have always tried to dress in well-made clothes of high quality. My trajes de luces are of the best quality, with lots of gold trimmings. I am the same with my business suits, so much so that, one time in Bogota, a man worked out that I must be a torero by the way I dressed and the way I walked down the street; that made me feel very proud.

From the beginning, when I had money and even when I didn't, I have always worn the best torero clothing that I could afford. Not necessarily the most expensive or flashy, but the best, in traditional good taste, and from the best tailors. What I wore in the ring was also an important part of what made me different from the rest.

I already said that I favoured dark silks, lots of gold trimmings, and the design of embroidery they called 'traditional', because I felt that such details were part of my 'look'. The traje de luces is your second skin when you are facing danger, like the army uniform of a warrior, and that's why you must treat it with care and respect when you get measured up. You shouldn't think only of a comfortable fit, or leave off bits which might seem unnecessary; if you're going to do that, you might as well put on a tracksuit to go out into the ring.

Even when testing the calves in my ranch, I always dress correctly in 'traje corto', the traditional Andalusian style of clothing; I don't approve of some of my colleagues who do their testing wearing jeans and trainers. And that goes for the kids who are learning too.

The best way a torero can show respect for his profession is to show respect for himself as well. That was the way of the old-time maestros who influenced me so much, and they showed it in their deeds and in their behaviour. Men like that were toreros even in the bathroom. Like Ángel Luis *Bienvenida*, who, at the age of eighty, wore a suit and tie and looked the part of a torero. I admired him tremendously and said to him that, when I grew up, I would like to be like him. Or Rafael Ortega, who, when he came to the Bullfighting School to give us a master class, appeared perfectly dressed in his traje corto and leather chaps.

It's not about artificial posturing, but a natural masculine elegance, looking distinguished and rejecting bad taste or the idea of trying to draw attention to oneself. It's about being a torero and looking like one. Even in unguarded moments.

Some may find these thoughts snobbish and superficial, but they are not. A torero has to be faithful to all aspects of what is effectively a creed, the way of life which is the art of bullfighting. It is important to maintain your composure at all times, whether in or out of the ring.

KNICKERS IN THE RING

I've always been a defender of the traditions associated with the corrida, and I have always observed them, from the moment I dressed in a traje de luces until the moment I walked out of the bullring. I am proud to consider it a commitment which was taught to me since childhood.

As a grubby little thirteen-year-old, I once tore a strip off a veteran torero who told me that I wasn't in the right place when placing banderillas, because he was the one who was standing in the wrong place. Even in those days, I didn't miss the tiniest detail in the ring, because I was already quite familiar with what was expected of me regarding traditions and conduct.

Enrique says that, the day that bullfighting loses its traditions, it will be finished, because that's what gives it its magic, the fabric which gives importance to what is important. To respect tradition is to respect your profession, and to reveal the shallowness of others. A priest doesn't give out the sacramental wafers like playing cards; he conducts the Eucharist with the solemnity that the act demands. If you think about it, they are really nothing more than little biscuits which can be bought in a pastry shop by the kilo. But the ceremony gives it a religious significance. The same thing happens in bullfighting, and even in life itself. Without tradition, any spiritual thing becomes mundane and loses its magical appeal.

This is what was happening in the bulls in the mid-1990s, when some toreros started lowering the tone and they brought about a loss of respect for the set of values which lie behind the spectacle.

With the arrival of *Jesulín de Ubrique*, vulgarity took over, not because of his style of handling the bulls, so much as his silly behaviour outside the ring. He reduced it to the level of a mass entertainment. Suddenly, the only thing that mattered was the numbers – quantity, not quality. His kind of torero believed that what was important for them was to fit in a large number of corridas in the year, break records, as if bullfighting was a sports competition and the torero was just an individual of no importance, something to be used and then discarded by the bullfight promoters as much as by the gossip magazines.

Television was everywhere. Independent channels got in on the act, not for the good of bullfighting, but just chasing popular taste to bump up their audiences. And so they repeated, day after day, the ugly, cheapskate image of this caricature of bullfighting, with women forgetting themselves and throwing their knickers and bras into the ring. In that madness, it was just anything goes! And it was made to look as if just about anyone could put themselves in front of a bull.

When tradition went by the board, the damage was done, and the image of the bulls was seriously harmed. But the ones who were really damaged were the toreros who played this silly game. Not just *Jesulín*. They were just showing off; they lost respect for their profession and they ended up losing their own self-respect.

A key moment in that story, the thing that brought it to an end, perhaps, was another TV programme with the famous Mercedes Milá again, when *Jesulín* dropped his trousers in front of the cameras to show the scars of the cornadas on his backside. It wasn't as spontaneous as they would like us to believe, because it actually wasn't the first time it had happened. *Jesulín* had done it once before in public, and, on that occasion, he did it because he was asked if bullfighting was all for show, and the one who put the question was a waiter in Bar Donald, that well-known taurine bar in Seville.

I was also appearing on that same TV programme with José María *Manzanares*. Our hearts sank. I have always tried to deny the image popular in some circles that all toreros are idiots. On primetime television that day, I was quite pleased with how the interview had been going, because *Manzanares* and I were handling ourselves very well. During an advertising break, I even commented that, for once, we were coming across as very normal people.

But then, bloody hell! When we came back live, that clown did his thing and we were blown out of the water. In the video which was going round at the time you can see my face perfectly; it says it all. I could have choked him on the spot. If it was about showing off scars, I could have done it without going down to my underpants. Having scars is the side of our profession which is hard to take, but there are better ways to show it.

That bit of nonsense was great for *Jesulín*, though, because the next day the whole of Spain was talking about him, as happened to me ten years earlier, but for different reasons. He and the other toreros who followed him got bored with bullfighting after two or three seasons. They were celebrities. But they put themselves down there with the lowest of the low, and they are still paying for it.

I didn't want to be one of them in all that mess. I was completely the opposite, and I couldn't even imagine that a torero could get out of the cuadrilla minibus and step into the bullring unless he was carrying his montera hat and special parade cape in his hands, unlike those who walked into the bullring giving hugs and being hugged back by all and sundry, arriving like a country bumpkin straight off the farm. Some of them looked like anything other than how they should be.

That lack of respect for the most revered elements of bullfighting is like a kick in the stomach for me. I couldn't stand it, but it made me stronger in my convictions. I benefited from the contrast. If it hadn't been for people like that, I wouldn't have been the torero that I became, and I have nothing but respect for aficionados.

Even so, it wasn't easy for me to maintain my standards and to oppose that river of vulgarity which carried all before it, while other colleagues took to clowning around without thinking of the consequences, although they were never that way before. Once again, I had to fight alone against the elements.

Soon, however, I learnt how to use this difference to my best advantage. They handed it to me on a plate, really, because all I had to do was to be myself and to maintain my position, which was exactly the opposite of theirs. Before then, I was just one more star performer among the others in the first rank, but suddenly I had become the model for a classic approach, either in an older, classic style or perhaps in a way of thinking and a discipline for which the troop of clowns hadn't the slightest respect. Even less so in important things like the way they treated their cuadrillas, or how they should look after their own interests professionally in the offices of the promoters. For most members of that crazy gang, the most important thing was to get lots of corridas, by whatever means, which meant handing themselves over lock, stock and barrel to the bosses, without retaining a shred of dignity.

So I set about quite consciously doing exactly the opposite. If the current done thing was to have a hundred or so corridas a year,

I would do even fewer than previous years. Maybe I wasn't capable of more, but, in reality, it wasn't worth me doing more than that without running the risk of being thought of as vulgar.

It didn't occur to me to go to the places which a top matador shouldn't appear in. As *el Gallo* said, if you go to towns with a tram system, they are the important places which make demands on you and put your qualities to the test, but you can't also go to the lesser places on the novillero circuit, favoured by second-rate toreros.

A star should always try to ensure that his appearances create expectation, whatever happens later. My reference in this respect was always Curro Romero, who stayed at the top for many years, although he generally had only ten or twelve corridas a year, but for good or bad, they were always met with great anticipation.

If you do too much, you get stale and lose the capacity to surprise, and your self-belief suffers. It's not possible to do something fresh if you are appearing day after day without a break. That approach finishes you off in the short term, and I was in it for the long run, not for a sprint lasting only four or five years, squandering money...and ruining your health too.

That's why I didn't want too much exposure on television either, to keep my image fresh, and to keep up my billing with the public and the impresarios. An artist should keep his appearances to a minimum, to try to ensure that his public still wants to come and see him. You can never be certain. The important thing in bullfighting has always been to leave behind an impression.

I say again that the epidemic of vulgarity which poisoned bullfighting in the mid-1990s served to reaffirm me even more in my convictions and to raise my personal profile. I noticed how people's respect for me went up during that time, and especially the older toreros as well. My morale was boosted by the way people spoke about me, for instance toreros like Luis Fuentes Bejarano, Pepín Martín Vázquez, and even the great Antonio Ordóñez.

After he had seen me perform in a special 'corrida Goyesca' in his bullring in Ronda, the maestro Ordóñez invited me to lunch in Madrid. He brought a book with him, which he dedicated to me in his own hand, saying that I was a model torero, and that I must carry on being so, and not to let him down. I was very moved by the thought that someone as significant as Ordóñez, who has been the idol of many generations of toreros, should tell me that he admired and respected me. At that moment, I wouldn't have changed places with anybody. It was one of the best things that ever happened to me.

When I began, I set myself the target of being a torero who was complete in all respects and the very best in all the stages of a corrida. But when I realised what this would mean, I settled for being a 'torero for toreros', that I might be respected by my colleagues of the same generation, of the next generation, and if possible, because it is the most difficult respect to achieve, those of past generations too. That is the most an artist can aspire to, and that's why those words of Ordóñez were so important to me, because in the world of bullfighting, he was a god.

THE RIVALS: FACT AND FICTION

I like the idea that I played the part of a counterbalancing force during such strange times. As a result, a number of young novilleros emerged who wanted to take after me, wishing to follow in my footsteps in my way with the bulls. To be aware that those up-and-coming toreros had the same admiration for me that I had held for Curro Vázquez and for the stars of yesteryear – that is something worth more than I can say.

Some say that, if it wasn't for the example I set, the later success of toreros like José Tomás and *el Juli* would be hard to understand, and they were the ones who finally got things back to normal after the madness of the 1990s. I am not convinced that this is true, but if it is, it would give me great satisfaction to think that my example served a purpose. The best way to end my career, which I had already marked out for myself, was to be remembered for having a purity of style and for having passed on the code of behaviour, which I inherited and which must not be lost, for future generations.

During the two decades I was active, I was able to learn this and pass it on while working alongside several generations of toreros, from those who began their careers in the 1950s, right up to others who began in the twenty-first century. I have drawn my own conclusions by seeing things from this perspective.

Antoñete was one of the oldest toreros I worked with. I couldn't view him objectively, because we didn't get on, and I must admit that I probably didn't appreciate him as much as he deserved: I only saw his failings. But, at the age of more than fifty, as well as deserving more attention than I gave him, the maestro with – famously – a white streak in his hair was capable of some marvellous things. Above all, I admired his elegance in the ring.

Curro Romero had the same noble bearing, that presence, although when I appeared with him, it annoyed me very much when the public went crazy at the tiniest thing he did. Now, looking back, I recognise that those 'tiny things' were amazing touches of real quality and pure art. I loved his way of following the charging bull round and pushing his chest out. Now that we are both retired, I enjoy his natural charm in speaking and the way he conducts himself.

With *Rafael de Paula*, it was the opposite to *Antoñete*. Because I admired him tremendously, whatever he did was okay with me. The subtlety of his movements, the elegant, lifting waist movement, the gypsy-like depth in everything he did, has never been equalled.

I also frequently appeared with the stars of the 1970s, among them some great toreros: José Maria *Manzanares*, for his sheer class; *Niño de la Capea*, for his awe-inspiring dignity; and the godfather at my alternativa, Dámaso González, for his 'temple', the smoothness of his action. He had the best right hand in the business, and tremendous guts, but aesthetically, in all honesty, he was only average.

Contrary to what most people say, I liked Julio Robles less with the capote than with the muleta, which he used punishingly on the bulls. Ortega Cano was an excellent torero, with great depth, perhaps the greatest depth I've ever seen. It's a shame that he has been plagued by problems in his later years, because they detract from his real qualities as a torero. As for Luis Francisco Esplá, who had very different ideas from mine, I recognise that he had extraordinary intelligence and sought to introduce an old-fashioned, traditional style with the bulls at the end of the twentieth century. He was neither a stylist nor a 'gladiator', but his feeling for the corrida and its setting showed the public a very different facet of the fiesta, which helped him to establish his own identity. He's a very sincere man.

The torero who has impressed me most is Paco Ojeda, for the outstanding fearlessness with which he stood up to a charging bull. When I was just a novillero, I saw him one year in Madrid with a nasty animal which threatened to catch him several times, but he wouldn't move, and finally the bull gave him a cornada. They said he was a rough diamond, but it was his courage that was untamed, the way he let the horns brush his chest to terrify the bulls into making them do what he wanted.

And of course, Curro Vázquez, my Curro. He is a torero unlike any other. With his easy manner and apparent fragility before going on to produce great depth and commitment, so much subtlety and harmony, he was a marvel. He had a divine gift and I couldn't take my eyes off him when he was in the ring.

It is true that I had several rivals among the generation of the 1980s. *Espartaco* was the Number One I had to take on. He was up there right at the top, sitting firmly upon the throne, and he was the one to beat. He wasn't exactly my mirror image artistically, but he was what drove me on in my early years. On the basis of his age, his natural rival should have been *Yiyo*, but that was not to be. To tell the truth, I couldn't really compete with him either, because our careers were at different stages: *Espartaco* was at the height of his profession when I had just started, and there were many other differences between us too, not just the generation gap.

He didn't think of me as a rival to compete against, either. On the contrary, he froze me out of certain billings, despite his fixed smile and warm embraces, like the unenthusiastic ones he gave me one time in Granada when I cut more ears than him. The next day, I found out that he'd had me removed from all the corridas we were supposed to appear in together that year. But he was at the top, and therefore he could do that sort of thing.

César Rincón got on the wrong side of me the year of his four exits from Las Ventas on shoulders. I can't forgive him for the going-over he gave me in the September fair of my adopted hometown of Talavera, because in bars and streets all through the next winter, the locals were endlessly pulling my leg about it. That put me off him, and when his career wound down, I was not sympathetic.

Rincón stood up for the classic style during what I refer to as the crazy years. For example, he revived the idea of calling the bull from a distance, which had been forgotten under the influence of Ojeda. And because there was a time when the Colombian was everywhere, like the flavour of the month, I had to come back at him by giving more. Sadly, it only lasted a couple of seasons because a serious attack of hepatitis prevented him from keeping up the pressure. But César had guts and was as tough as old boots, and he didn't give in so easily.

On another tack, artistically speaking, I was very impressed by Julio Aparicio. Trying to follow his example was good for the development of my own personal style, and the same thing happened later with *Morante de la Puebla*, who also impressed me very much. For me, Curro Vázquez, Aparicio and *Morante* are my references for the sublime elegance that dreams are made of.

My most obvious rival was Enrique Ponce, and I appeared more times with him than with any other torero. It wasn't a genuine rivalry, though. We are very different both as toreros and as individuals, and we look at things differently. We each wanted to be better than the other, but in different ways, with scarcely any points of comparison.

There were others who stimulated me more, because Enrique didn't like challenges. I enjoyed pushing him hard on his home ground, Valencia, and in Linares, where he now lives. But he avoids confrontation, because that's not the way he is. He went his own way, and in his own manner he had many more triumphs than I ever did. He always led the way home, cutting loads of ears, but I could never keep up that consistency, because after all, that's just the way I am. But on a good day it was another story...

Tongue in cheek I said to him once, 'Be honest, Enrique. Even in your dreams you couldn't do what I can do when I'm wide awake.'

Ponce is a fantastic torero. The best and worst thing about him is that he has consistently kept up at the same level and at the same rhythm. That's very difficult to achieve, but it can also work against you if the public gets used to looking upon what you do as normal, even if it isn't.

During all the years we were together, there was friction between us on a few occasions, mainly because of the differences in our characters. I remember that once, because he got the wrong end of the stick about something silly that happened when we were in Almeria, he started to bad-mouth me behind my back. I heard about it immediately, and the next day when we were on together in Linares, I decided to dedicate a bull to him. I took him into the middle of the ring beyond the painted lines, so no one could hear, and I dared him to repeat to my face the things I believed he had been saying about me. But he didn't take it as I expected, he didn't even blank me. He went so far as to invite me to dinner after the corrida. That's how he is, he doesn't show his feelings, and he doesn't want to know about problems of any kind.

The supposed rivalry with Ponce was something our supporters wanted: not us. My people, thousands of them, were prepared to stand by me through thick and thin, although I confess I didn't give them much to go on and sometimes I even worked against them. I was such an idiot at the time that I didn't dedicate enough time or kindness to them.

We toreros are very egocentric and we expect everything to revolve around us in the way we want it to. My fans travelled great distances following me on the road and spent a fortune doing it to see me. When I finally realised what was happening, I was sorry and at least began to give then some of my time and a few words together after the corrida, before I set off again. Some of them came twenty or thirty times a year to see me, making their holiday arrangements to fit in with my appearances. I spent more time with some of them, the most dedicated ones, and sometimes even had dinner with them.

Some got to know me and my ways, and they knew well enough that, if things had gone badly for me in the ring, I wouldn't hang around. The fact that they could be so considerate like that also helped to teach me how to behave with other people.

I have never been a sociable individual, which isn't good for someone in the public eye. I keep myself to myself a lot, and I find it hard to deal with others. When I was active in my profession, tension and other worries made this even worse. I have never been what is called nowadays 'politically correct', and I have always spoken my mind, even when it wasn't the right time to do so.

There is a lot of cynicism out there in dealing with the public. I saw some of my colleagues wearing a permanent smile, and prepared even to hug a lamp post if need be, but I just couldn't do any of that. My mother and then my wife criticised me for not being more friendly, even towards people I knew, but when I tried to, it all seemed so false. That's how I earned a reputation for being offhand.

Nowadays, I come out of my shell a bit more; I overdo it sometimes. This startles some people, and the better they know me, the more surprised they get. When I'm relaxed, I have a very mischievous side which only a very few people have seen. To tell the truth, even I don't know what I'm like really. It could be either the way other people see me, or just how I am feeling at the time.

Other toreros who were my contemporaries, *Jesulín de Ubrique* for example, were very good at public relations, and, despite everything, he was a great torero. He was a classic, although he seems exactly the opposite. He has a lot of courage, and enormous technical skills, but he lost himself in the jungle that he built up around himself. I never wanted, or thought it was necessary, to compete with him. We were fighting two different battles, and if he had no respect for himself, why should I?

By contrast, the torero who got under my skin the most was Rivera Ordóñez, which may surprise some people. Really. Francisco was arrogant and stuck-up, and was even more so in the early days when he exploded upon the scene wanting to take on the world. I was one of the toreros he had to try to displace, and I made it clear that I wasn't going to move over.

Time went by, and as we were both high-spirited young fighting cocks, we were always sparring with one another. Even more so after the afternoon he confirmed his alternativa in Madrid during that unforgettable San Isidro of 1996, when Ponce and I took turns in an exchange of cape passes on one of my bulls, and I didn't invite him to join in. Among other things, it was because it wasn't his place to do so.

It wasn't that which annoyed Francisco, so much as later when Enrique and I sat down on the estribo, the ledge in the ring fence, while he made a circuit of the ring. He thought it showed disrespect and he told me that he wanted to give us both a good kick in the balls. We were talking about it a few days later and we almost had a punch-up because we were both so worked up and squaring up to each other. Fortunately, things calmed down, and ever since then we've got on very well together, and whenever there was a problem, we always talked it out, face-to-face, man to man.

That friendly rivalry carried on through a period at the end of the 1990s when we both appeared together quite often. At the time, he liked to work close to the bull, and often got caught, so they put together a bill and called us the 'three tenors' with Ponce, Francisco and me. Until, one day in Leganés, we were joined by José Tomás in a corrida of eight bulls, and that changed things.

I think he is the only torero I could never get the better of. Our careers overlapped just as he was taking off in a big way, and as happened in Colombia with Rincón, I could see José Tomás coming up fast. It happened in Arles, before he'd become famous. I was with Ponce behind the fence, watching him tackling with great courage a very difficult, very dangerous bull. But he stood his ground and resisted all the charges without moving his feet. It was a real eye-opener.

'This boy is a wild man,' said Ponce.

'He's not wild, it's just that he's got a massive pair of balls. Bigger than yours and mine put together.'

Since that day, I've nothing but great respect for José Tomás, although he really got to me for a while. He was a torero with the same ideas as mine about the bulls, but much more courage.

I knew that I could never reach the same level, and I had to use all my resources to compete with him, to avoid being put in the shade by him and losing out before I started. Because I could never match his courage.

MY DESCENT INTO HELL

My time up in the clouds ended on the same day I was carried out on shoulders through the Puerta del Príncipe of the Maestranza bullring in Seville in 1997. That archway overlooking the River Guadalquivir is one of the ambitions that all toreros dream about. Finally, I too got to pass through it.

I was very keen to triumph in that bullring, considered a temple by many. Las Ventas is very impressive because of its size, and the demanding nature of its public, even though I'd appeared there on many occasions. Once I began to become very successful, I was less impressed by the venue than by the responsibility I had to succeed. But in La Maestranza, I felt as if I were under the microscope, because the Seville public knows how to spot the smallest details.

Although they are less harsh than in Madrid, they know what they are looking at, and even though they make less noise, they are more demanding. Whoever they are, the chances are that they will either have faced bulls themselves, or have seen them close up in the countryside. As if that's not enough, there will always be someone who heckles you with a witty remark from the seats, and so you keep your head down, unless you're feeling very confident.

The first time I appeared there as a full matador, nothing went right for me, but José María *Manzanares* gave me a good piece of advice, 'José, just be yourself. Don't try and be someone different just because you are in Seville.'

It was true that, like all outsiders who want to get on the same wavelength as the Sevillanos, I wanted to show them my 'artistic' side, but what I did was pretentious, instead of doing what I felt inside. So, then I did what the maestro said and tried to act naturally, although I risked being more dry and unemotional than they like down there.

Even like that, it wasn't easy to get accepted in La Maestranza. I was ready for anything, to die if necessary, as Antonio Ordoñez used to say, a feeling you should experience several times a year if you wanted to be at the top. I tried everything, but I never quite pulled it off, because I just cut single ears, or I would ruin a good faena by messing up the kill.

Years went by, and in that jokey way they have down there, many of the Sevillanos started calling me 'Pepito' instead of *Joselito*, suspicious of the reports of my successes elsewhere, but never in Seville. And of course, there was the fact that I wasn't from around those parts, but from Madrid... But at last I got my revenge. The day was perfect, the sun was shining, not a trace of wind. It was 14th April... Everything pointed to me having a major triumph in La Maestranza at last.

The first bull charged well, and I was able to do things the way I liked, so I started to hear cries of 'Bieeeen!', stretching out the word, which is typical of a favourable response from the Seville crowd, drawn out and husky sounding because it comes from deep down. And I killed well, with a good sword.

When I cut two ears from that first bull – and you need three to qualify for an exit by the Puerta del Príncipe – that got me off to a good start. As I was making a circuit of the ring with the ear of my second bull, I was on top of the world. At last I had cracked it. After ten years waiting for this moment, I had finally got my self-esteem back, I had arrived: I was going to exit by the Puerta del Príncipe. It had been a long time since a torero from Madrid did that.

As I went out that magical gate, instead of looking across at the River Guadalquivir, all I could see was my cuadrilla minibus waiting for me, but it was parked too close for me to enjoy being carried out on shoulders for as long as I would have wanted. Fortunately, when they reached the car, the guys who were carrying me swung round to the right and carried me all the way to the Hotel Colón, through the streets of Seville lined with springtime blossom.

Physically, being carried on shoulders can be uncomfortable. Especially if it lasts as long as on that occasion. But when you are surrounded by an admiring crowd, it feels wonderful. Because I didn't feel any pain, in that Seville sunset. I didn't even feel the damage to the ligament of my right hand which I'd hurt in making the swordthrust to that last bull.

That year of 1997, I had many good afternoons, but after injuring my hand, I lost confidence with the sword, and I didn't cut many ears. Although I had some great faenas, there were still more than twenty important fairs when I didn't go out on shoulders, and where I could have come out winning.

It took me a long time to get better, because the doctors couldn't find out what was wrong. I had a really bad time. I had terrible pains in my thumb, so I couldn't even do up the buttons of my shirt. My muscles became affected by too many painkillers.

By the following winter, they finally worked out that the ligament was severed, and I had surgery, only about a month before the start of the season of 1998. I cut short the rehabilitation period so that I could appear in the Fallas Fair in Valencia, but I wasn't back in shape yet, either physically or mentally. I began to go downhill again, and couldn't do anything about it. This time, the battles with the impresarios were causing me more problems than my injury.

The impresarios were determined to continue forcing us toreros to be televised in live broadcasts. In 1992, when Canal Plus began to televise all the corridas of San Isidro, Ponce, Rincón and I tried to put a stop to it by signing an exclusive contract direct with TVE, Spanish Television. But, as so often happens, the others backed down, and I found myself holding out alone in the dispute. And out of the corridas in Madrid too.

After that, my father and I got into a tug-of-war between the impresarios and the television companies which we had hopes of winning. Then, in early 1998, the TV company Vía Digital entered the frame, with offers of so much more money that the impresarios lost the plot.

The impresario in charge of Seville, that fine fellow Diodoro Canorea, had signed up with Enrique for my appearances in the April Fair. To help him out, we gave way on some good dates which he could televise without me on national television. But while we were away in America, we found out that, without consulting us, he had signed another exclusive contract for all the corridas on pay-per-view TV.

When my father called him up, very concerned, Canorea apologised, saying that he had forgotten our deal, and offered to pay us compensation. It wasn't about the money, but respect. Contrary to what was said at the time, I hadn't refused to allow my corridas to be televised. I said that I wanted to control the use of my image by appearing on TV only two or three times a year in important bull-rings, rather than wearing it out with almost daily exposure. And, of course, I didn't want others to tell me what to do and when to appear for their own personal profit.

The subsequent experience with televised corridas was dreadful. Over a couple of years, between regional, national and especially independent companies, they televised more than three hundred events a year, most of them of poor quality, following boring, tasteless toreros like *Jesulín* and Co.

The easiest thing for me would have been to accept it, to let them televise me whenever they wanted to, and for me to send out invoices for hundreds of millions of pesetas, which is what others did. But I refused to, out of self-respect, and because I could see that this game of cards was doing the fiesta a great deal of harm.

One of the hardest things in life is to say no, and many of my contemporaries didn't go along with me in this fight. We were beginning to get somewhere, and were close to an agreement to make a common front, but the bad guys were already planning to divide and conquer.

I think my position was very correct, not just defending my own interests, but also those of the other toreros, against the crooks who didn't respect us. We couldn't accept conditions being imposed upon us without consultation, and even less that the payments for image rights were so badly shared out, because, apart from those at the top, the others hardly got to see a few crumbs from a pie which was worth millions.

So many televised corridas affected the smaller impresarios too because they realised that, when the events they were organising in small villages coincided with televised corridas, the public didn't turn out to buy their tickets. Turning corridas into mass entertainment on television was a tremendous mistake, benefitting only a few. As is typical of this business, no one was thinking of the long term. 'Devil take the hindmost' was the motto of those promoting it.

With that in mind, on the morning of the day of my first corrida of the 1998 April Fair, Enrique presented to the legal authorities the contract we'd signed with Canorea. In black and white, it specified that the corrida would only be held on the condition that no TV cameras were present.

There was a hell of a rumpus in the offices of La Maestranza, because Vía Digital had already moved in their camera equipment. Discussions went on all morning, and the TV commentator even had the stupid idea of making the TV screens go black for my bulls. In the end, the corrida wasn't broadcast. What it came down to was that my father and I had taken on the network of interests formed by the communications groups: Telefónica, with Vía Digital, and the Prisa media group, with Canal Plus. Suddenly, we received a broadside from the media, and bombs began to rain down on us in the press.

THE PRESS AND MY FALL FROM GRACE

As I've said, I had very few successes the year before because of injury, and the critics turned against me, and then 1998 wasn't going well for me either, neither with the sword or the muleta, so the critics began to give me a hard time.

Until that moment, my relations with journalists had been very normal, with some of them in favour of me, and others against. One or two, such as Vicente Zabala for example, took an intense dislike to me because of my failure to dedicate to the King that time, and my republican banderillas; others were very much under the influence of certain impresarios, but, on the whole, I was well treated. It would be wrong to say that I had a bad press in general.

Among the heavyweights, Joaquín Vidal wrote some good stuff about me from when I started as a becerrista. But when I got to the top, he was always critical. Especially after the time he interviewed me on a ranch in Badajoz. When we finished the interview, he began to outline to me his personal view of bullfighting, practically telling me what I should do. He even stood up to demonstrate: foot forward, muleta like this... So I told him that, if I did such peculiar things in front of a bull, I would fall flat on my backside. I suppose he got annoyed, poor chap.

The highly regarded Alfonso Navalón was the most aggressive of the critics, and also kept hammering away at me mercilessly. I didn't mind what he said about me as a matador, but as he did with all toreros, this piece of work kept digging into my personal life and picked up on all the nasty made-up rumours doing the rounds.

In the early days, he got on very well with Enrique. And as he had a herd of toros bravos, he used to invite the boys from the Madrid School up to his heifer trials, called 'tientas'. In one of them, showing off to a group of aficionados from Logroño who were present, he was laying down the law that toreros should always use the real sword when making passes, and to demonstrate his point, he caught hold of the dummy swords of José Luis Bote and myself and broke them in half. He couldn't break *Fundi*'s one because it was made of aluminium. My one had been a present from my father.

They tell me that I looked at him like I was going to kill him. I was fearless in those days and was certainly ready to give him a punch on the nose, but because the teachers had ingrained in us that we should learn how to behave in public, I held back. He was quite happy to play that nasty trick on a couple of kids as part of his silly joke. That's when I realised what a scumbag he really was.

In the beginning, Navalón wrote some good things about me as well, when I was having those early successes in Madrid, but I think he did it to take away the spotlight from Paco Ojeda and *Espartaco*, who were big at the time. He was just using the image of a poor guy like me to get at them.

Later, when I was successful, this same individual asked Enrique as a favour to have me appear with his bulls in a small village.

But because he was in the habit of being so dismissive and insulting to toreros, we decided to put him to the test by suggesting that he 'shave' the bulls first, which means cutting off the tips of their horns. He agreed at once. That champion of high standards of integrity in the fiesta, the avowed enemy of fraud, constantly having a go at toreros, was in an instant prepared to go against everything he supposedly stood for. Dignity went out of the window. Obviously, we didn't fight his bulls, and, from that moment on, he attacked me at every opportunity.

Reporters in the media who had previously been more or less favourable towards me changed overnight, because of their reliance on the companies they worked for; this is what happened to me with Manolo Molés, who worked for the powerful Prisa media group. The year that Canal Plus began to televise corridas, I noticed in his commentaries a growing bitterness towards me. I caught him on the way out of a press conference and told him that I could take his criticism, but when I was good, would he please not say the opposite.

I told him, 'If it's just for the sake of saying something, we can all do that, but if you've nothing good to say about me, I would prefer that you leave me out of it.'

And for a while, he didn't mention me, even when I had a big triumph.

As far as I know, I have never given money to the press. In America, yes, because that's how it works out there. In Spain, that sort of thing changed a long time ago. That's not to say that I haven't had dealings with some journalists, as happens in other activities too, but nothing so significant as to try to influence their judgement.

The reverse is true: the interests of the media groups have had an influence on me. For example, I know for certain that, when I stood up against the impresarios in Madrid, a well-known wheeler-dealer who had shares in the Lozanos' business was responsible for mounting a campaign against me in one of the newspapers he owned. It was the critic on that same paper who confirmed this to us.

The lack of sufficient training because of my injury, and the attacks against me in the media, depressed me and took away my enthusiasm for appearing with the bulls. When the 1998 season started, I began to think of retiring. I didn't tell anyone, but what had been an idea became a conviction as the weeks went by.

I ordered a white and silver suit from my tailor, like the one I wore when I first put on a suit of lights in that little village in Castile. It was like a symbolic closing of the circle, to be worn on the last day of my career, which I felt was near at hand.

To throw people off the scent and to avoid suspicion, I wore it beforehand, such as in the corrida that I thought would be my farewell appearance in Madrid. Surprised to see me dressed in a different way from usual, a journalist asked me about it while we were waiting to make the opening parade in Las Ventas. And I told him – tongue firmly in cheek – that, because I was so bad and everyone wanted me to retire, I was getting used to the idea of dressing like a banderillero, in case I needed to change my category.

Wearing that suit, I cut my last ear in Las Ventas, but even so my season didn't recover that year. Even the regional press commented before my appearances that I was going through a bad patch, which was enough to put the public off, even before the bull came into the ring.

Everything was against me, but, above all, I was feeling very low. I was at rock bottom, and what's worse, I felt bored and didn't have the stomach for a fight. I was the only one who knew about my plans to retire, because I didn't even say anything to Enrique. I didn't want the public to say goodbye to me out of pity, because I was some poor little chap. I couldn't bear that. If I was bad, I preferred that they should swear at me if they wanted to.

At the beginning of September, on the way to Palencia, I finally told my father about my decision. I cheered him up. My idea was to retire without any prior announcement in the last fair of the year, the Pilar of Zaragoza. But a few weeks before, in Valladolid, something happened which speeded things up a bit.

It was a few days after the alternativa of *el Juli*, who was booked to appear there with Ponce and me in a sell-out corrida. When the time came for the parade, the place was packed to the rafters, and then the skies opened and a deluge of heavy rain fell, which left the ring in a terrible state. It was impossible to go on.

El Juli, who was appearing with us for the first time, was mad keen to go ahead, but we two old hands knew that the conditions were impossible, that it would be putting the lives of our people in danger in that mud-bath. Enrique Ponce urged me to take charge, and, as the senior matador, it was up to me to tell the authorities that we were not prepared to proceed. We waited a bit, while they tried to clean up the ring, and in that time the pressures built up for us to go on, including being harassed by high-up politicians from the local government of Castilla and Leon, and, without saying anything to me, Ponce went back on his word and left me looking like an idiot. Once again, *Joselito* was the bad guy in the movie.

In the end, the corrida went ahead. It was two against one. But that messy business annoyed me so much that I decided I'd had enough. The next day, I was due to appear with six bulls in Seville, and I told Joaquín Ramos that, although it would be a pain in the arse, he would have to make a long detour and go by way of Talavera that very night to pick up the white and silver suit.

The corrida in La Maestranza was the 'chronicle of a death foretold'. The contract had been signed since February, so they could announce it in the list of events for the complete season in their ring. When it was put forward, I was very pleased with the idea of a solo corrida in Seville, but I realised at the time that it could be a double-edged sword, because it was so many months away, and I didn't know how I'd be feeling when the time came. I was right, because, when the day arrived, I was an absolute wreck.

Even so, the night before, I tried to build myself up by whatever means possible. In the car, and then in bed, I tried to get my spirits up by thinking that I would cut a tail, that I was going to end my career on a high note with a major triumph. Or that, even if there weren't any ears, the public would carry me out of the ring on shoulders anyway, in tribute to my long and successful career.

But that 26th September dawned cold and overcast. The little mental strength that I had gathered up overnight vanished when I went for a walk around the streets. And when I began to dress in the white and silver traje de luces, I didn't even grease down my hair, but left it loose, like when I was a becerrista. I was going to end as I had begun. I went out like someone who knew that the last parade I would ever make would end in a monumental disaster.

With the first four bulls, nothing I tried worked out. I was trying to give myself some encouragement under my breath, but I couldn't climb out of the deep hole I was in. When the fifth bull came out, it looked as if things were going to get better at last, because I received it with some good verónicas, which the public cheered. But, at the end of the series, the bull tore the capote from my hands and I had to run for the fence to make my escape.

Halfway there, I stopped. I suddenly thought that, if the bull caught me and gave me a cornada, I would be taken to the infirmary with honour, and I wouldn't have to go though the shame of walking back across the ring of Seville after another painful disaster. But someone ran in to save me and stopped the bull from doing what I wanted it to do.

I finished off the rest of the corrida with about as much finesse as a butcher. Everything was awful, except for the dedication I made to my father in the sixth. Enrique stepped out into the ring smiling, because he thought that I was going to wish him a happy birthday. But his face changed when I explained to him that this was the end of the line, that this would be the last bull I ever killed in my life, and that I had no words to tell him how grateful I was for everything he'd done for me ever since I was a child.

The walk back across the ring at the end of the corrida was like crossing a desert as wide as the one I felt inside me. Worst of all, the public didn't even show their anger – no whistles, no insults, no thrown cushions. I offered a picture of someone so desolate that, for the first time in my life, I felt that I'd made people feel sorry for me in a bullring. More than anything else, that's what really screwed me up.

The atmosphere in the hotel room was like a funeral parlour. The faces of my supporters, who had come in their hundreds from all corners of the world, were the picture of misery. But I felt okay.

At last I was able to breathe normally by coming to terms with my decision. Artistically I was at an all-time low, but as a human being – contented. Now all that had to be done was to cancel the few remaining contracts left. Out of respect for my public, I couldn't carry on in the state I was in.

The next day, the press wiped the floor with me, logically enough. Some of them even seized the opportunity to rubbish my whole career. Lots of my enemies had been waiting for this moment: impresarios, journalists, some of my contemporaries. So I made myself scarce, to deprive them of the pleasure of finding something to get their teeth into.

As I expected, none of that worried me. The only thing which churned my guts was what the celebrated Joaquín Vidal wrote in *El País*, daring to make a joke out of the intimate, heartfelt dedication I had made to my father. The two of us were alone in the middle of the ring at La Maestranza, at a very important moment in both our lives, and that arsehole said that we looked like 'a drug dealer selling a dose to a junkie'. Fortunately, I never came face-to-face with the sonofabitch again in this life.

8

WAKING FROM A DREAM

For several months after that day in Seville, I did absolutely nothing. I kept off the radar, and had them cut my hair in a very short crew cut, so I wouldn't even be tempted to go back to bullfighting. I hadn't cut my coleta in La Maestranza – cutting off the traditional pigtail worn by all toreros is a definitive sign of retirement from the profession. So the usual bunch of gossip-mongers began speculating again, and making up weird stories about me.

Some said that I'd joined the Hare Krishnas, and was meditating in Tibet. Others, probably after reading Vidal's article in *El País*, swore blind that I had entered a detox clinic to shake off a supposed drugs habit.

As always, the truth was very different, and much more straightforward: I locked myself away in my house doing nothing, and, at the beginning of 1999, I began the preparations for my wedding with Adela, scheduled for the month of June that year.

It was like taking a sabbatical year away from all the pressure, time to relax and give my mind a rest. I turned to the work of running my ranches, but without trying too hard, and I did some travelling, but not too much of that either. After all, when I was working with the bulls I was travelling around for many years, and I knew most parts of Spain, France and the Americas. Not just the bullrings and hotels either, like some of my contemporaries.

It came down to the fact that I had stopped bullfighting because I needed to stop and take a breather. Caught up in the whirlwind of the bullfight calendar, I didn't know how to do that – and I didn't want to – until I was forced out by circumstances. I had been working in the world of the bulls since the age of thirteen – seventeen seasons on the trot – and the time had come to sort out my life and, above all, my head. You can't be working with the bulls unless both mind and body are on the ball. This warrior needed a rest.

But at the end of the summer, I began to think about the bulls again. One morning in the middle of September, for no particular reason, I got out of bed, put on a tracksuit, and went down to the practice bullring. And then, step by step, I saw myself walking into the ring like in those first days in Bullfighting School. And then, suddenly, I had a capote in my hands, and I was giving practice passes.

It had been a year since I'd done that. I hadn't even worked with the cows of my own herd. The first few times it happened, I thought it was just a good excuse to get back into an exercise regime. But I couldn't keep lying to myself: this was just an unconscious way of getting back to doing what I enjoyed most in life.

In November, the bull-breeder Domingo Hernández rang me to say that he was going to set up a 'tienta de machos', a test of young bulls. I thought he was just inviting me to come along and have a look, so I said yes, delighted, just tell me the time and date, and I would come along to the ranch in Salamanca. I didn't have anything better to do.

But two or three weeks later, he called me back and knocked me sideways, 'Hi José, when are you coming to test my bulls?'

'What are you saying, Domingo? You know I don't do that anymore.'

'But I want you to do it for me; that's why I called before.'

'Why me? I haven't gone near bullfighting for over a year.'

'You're not telling me you've forgotten what to do. Come off it, think it over and call me back.'

And so I went, of course I went. I upped my training, and then I got to work a few bulls in my friend's ranch in Salamanca, and, since then, I have a special affection for him, because he's the one who whetted my appetite again.

Since the end of October, my father had been in America with José Tomás, who he'd been managing after my retirement. After thinking about it for a while, I decided to call him on the phone to tell him I was going to try myself out on a few more bulls, and that, if all went well, I was thinking I might make a comeback the following year. I told him all this, and he cut me off!

I dialled again four or five times, but he wouldn't even answer the phone. A week later, he finally picked up and, to avoid him doing the same again, I got him talking, asked how it was going with José Tomás. He answered perfectly normally, until I reminded him of my plans and he didn't give an answer. I went on about it and he finally told me what he thought: that it was a silly idea, and that I didn't need to make a comeback.

But, of course, I did. The reason had been nagging away inside me since that last day, because I didn't think that was the sort of ending that my career deserved. And because I felt that there were still things I wanted to say with the bulls.

Enrique just pointed out the problems and the negatives, so I asked Joaquín Ramos to look out for tientas and possible contracts for me. I asked him to tell my father that I was going back to the bulls with or without him. When he came back to Spain, after a few more rows about it, Enrique had no choice but to accept the fact.

I made my comeback on 2nd April in the Castellón Fair, in a mano a mano with José Tomás, with the ring packed. A year and a half after Seville, I put on the same white and silver suit as I wore on the last day, as a symbol that I was starting over. Like on my first day.

I did nothing special on that first day, but I had the same old feelings back. The same nerves, the same uncertainty that I felt the first time I put on a suit of lights in Salas de los Infantes. I had killed several bulls during my run-up to the big day, and I was confident of my abilities and my responsibilities, but, as I waited to make the parade in that eastern town, that wasn't what worried me, so much as facing the crowd and convincing them again what I was capable of.

Luckily, everything went well in Castellón, and once back in the ring with a bull, I felt for sure that I had definitely got back the will to succeed, which I'd lost in that awful year of 1998. *Joselito* was back! From nought to a hundred in ten seconds.

At the same time, I knew that, this time, it wasn't going to be easy. The 'wise guys', as always, when they realised that Enrique Martín Arranz was now the manager of both of us, started to put out the story that my father and myself planned to exploit José Tomás, by taking advantage of his growing fame and drawing power at the box office. Anticipating this, because I already knew how their minds worked, I invited José Tomás to a tentadero at my ranch to explain to him how I saw things.

'Look, José, people are going to say all sorts of things, but I am coming back to the bulls because I think there are still things I have left unsaid. There are some places where I am a bigger draw than you, and I'll put myself forward when the time comes to talk about the choice of bulls and the money. There are other places where it will be the other way around. Yours is yours, and mine is mine; neither of us is going to take anything away from the other. If that's okay with you, they can say whatever they want.'

José Tomás understood perfectly, although, later, the situation which I'd anticipated changed radically, because he was at a higher level than me. He made a sensational impression in the ring and worked closer to the bulls than anyone had ever done before or since. And because there was no let up, not a single day, I was put in the shade most times we appeared together. You could tell just by looking at my face.

This has happened to me many times before, when other matadors had a better day than me, but my character and self-respect always ensured I didn't give up the fight. But the crushing triumphs of José Tomás just kept on coming, like a steam hammer.

I had nothing new to show anyone, but I did want to show myself that I could compete with him. He really had me very screwed up.

Only now and again the odd bull came out which I could put on a good show with, and it felt like a small victory. I realise now that, if it weren't for the fact that I have such a competitive nature, the phenomenon of José Tomás wouldn't have affected me so much, and my comeback would have been different.

The truth is that, during the eighteen months I was away from the ring, the spectacle had moved on in leaps and bounds, but I'd remained the same person I was in September 1998. I had recharged my batteries, but I hadn't kept up with the new superstars. José Tomás and *el Juli* had given bullfighting a kick up the backside in that time. They were marching to a new drum, and there were new faces in charge now: but I was going nowhere. The public was no longer watching out for me, because they'd moved on to the new boys who had taken over. I couldn't handle that. I just couldn't put my ego and arrogance to one side, and get used to the idea that I was no longer the top dog.

When I woke up to the new situation, a few months after my comeback, I tried to take the pressure off, to cool it, to play down the obsession I had with the competition. I needed to look for another source of inspiration more in tune with where I was at this point in my career, like, for example, going for a more stylish touch, a different feeling, and using the body language that experience brings.

I wasn't ready to give up the struggle, because I still had to keep faithful to my convictions, my ideas about freedom and independence, and the new leaders were no longer my problem. I would do better to compete against my own self and make my performances better every time.

A RACE AGAINST PAIN

One of the great moments of that last stage in my career was the faena I gave to a bull of José Luis Cobo in the Quito Fair, December 2001. Over there in Ecuador, which is on the equator, the corridas begin at twelve midday. As *El Cordobés* used to say – it's like having bulls for breakfast. When I arrived at the bullring that morning, I hadn't slept, because the night before, after dinner with some friends, things got a bit out of hand, and it turned into a wild party which went on beyond dawn.

It was the serious business of dressing for the corrida in my traje de luces which cured my hangover and cleared my mind, so, when I arrived at the bullring, I was in a good mood, with all my pores open, and my wrists supple, to allow the movements which I felt welling up inside me to come out naturally. And, as often happens on the best occasions, the perfect bull came out, sweet as a nut and smooth as silk, so I could do wonderful things with the capote and the muleta.

I knew that animal was excellent as soon as it came into the ring, and so I allowed myself the luxury of behaving like a veteran torero, with something I had seen other old maestros do before me. When it was time for the kill, I brought all my friends from the previous night's escapades out into the centre of the ring, hiding behind hats and sunglasses, and I dedicated the bull to them, very soberly, with the words that they had to learn how to be 'a dog by night, as well as a dog by day'.

That was quite a faena, the one in Quito. So much so that, for the first time in my life, Enrique, my father (or 'bato,' as the gypsies say), had to think hard, going over and over in his mind every detail of the faena, looking for something to pick up on at the end of the corrida, sitting in the cuadrilla bus, on the way back. At last he found one – a chest pass in which the bull had touched the muleta. What a guy!

At last I had found my way back, and I loved it, but the next spring in Nîmes, I had a bad injury which had me laid up for several months. My delight was short-lived. The triple fracture of the head of the femur brought things to a dead halt, which meant that, once again, I had to go back and start anew.

The break in my career did me more harm than the serious injury, because it nearly ended my dreams. It is always the bull before anything else which messes up all the best-laid plans of toreros. That one took me off the scene for almost an entire season. On the other hand, a positive consequence was that I was very pleased with my own dogged persistence which allowed me to get better sooner than the doctors had predicted.

The bull in Nîmes caught me in a moment of foolishness as I was leading it up to the picador – it wasn't even a proper pass. I was careless and, as the bull turned on me unexpectedly, it caught me in the thigh (without a cornada, though) and hardly lifted me off the ground. But it turned me in the air, and when I fell back onto the sand I heard a horrible dry crack, like a splitting bone. For an instant, I thought I would end up in a wheelchair. I couldn't move, and I couldn't feel my right leg.

My wife was more than a thousand kilometres away at a corrida in Talavera when she received a series of confused messages. As always happens, first they said it was a cornada, but then it became blown up out of all proportion until the story was that I'd actually been killed by a bull. We already had our daughter Alba, and Adela had a really bad time until she finally got to speak to Enrique.

Meanwhile, they'd taken me to hospital, and left me on a stretcher while they waited for the results of tests. I still couldn't move, and my father tried to calm me down, but it didn't help that I could hear him talking to a doctor in the next room, who was saying that he wasn't sure whether to send me to the USA or Russia to be operated on by a specialist. I was gripped by a terrible anxiety. What could it be that was so wrong with me that they needed to take me that far away? What was going to happen to me?

But, as has been the case so many times before when I was caught by a bull, I was very lucky. At that very moment, the duty doctor appeared, a traumatologist who just happened to be a specialist in injuries to the hip.

When I landed on the rock-hard sand of the Roman amphitheatre of Nîmes, the head of my femur had broken into three pieces, and the trochanter had split. I learnt that this is the part of the femur head to which the muscles are attached. I didn't have to be sent off anywhere, because they operated on me right there and then, and inserted various plates and screws to repair the damage.

Once the morning sunshine had driven away all the dragons I saw flying around the room that night, the doctors told me that the process of recovery would be very slow; that I wouldn't be able to walk for six months; and that, with a bit of luck, and a painful convalescence, I might be able to think about going back to the bulls after a year. Even so, they warned me not to expect too much. It was the middle of May and I was taken back home in an ambulance in complete despair.

In July, as was my custom, because it coincided with San Fermín in Pamplona, I went to spend a beach holiday at Isla Antilla. I was limping badly, but they recommended me to move my leg in the water to build up the muscles, and to get some sunshine on my huge scar, to make it heal more quickly.

I was in a lot of pain, but, after four days on the beach, I asked Joaquín to get fourteen or fifteen bulls ready for me to fight behind closed doors, and to pick another six for me to face solo in the Feria of Zaragoza in October that year.

Everyone panicked, saying that the injury had driven me crazy. It was true: I was crazy to get back to the bulls. I had such a bad time in those first days of rehabilitation, but I had to bite the bullet and put up with the pain. I knew that it was the only way I was going to be able to carry on through this painful process. I am sure that, if I'd settled down to follow the slow path the doctors wanted, I would've been stuck with a limp, and I would never have got back to fighting bulls again.

All through the summer, I desperately pushed myself through the exercises, drawing the strength to put up with the pain from somewhere deep down inside me. Although I worked hard at rehabilitation, some days I couldn't help being miserable because I seemed to be moving backwards. I spent the nights in tears, but, the following morning, I'd go back to working like a donkey with Doctor Sorando, who, as well as being a traumatologist, is also a breeder of bulls; he helped me enormously and kept my head above water.

Two weeks before my return to the ring, in one of the first tentaderos that I'd organised to get back in condition, I could hardly walk. I was still dragging my right leg when, as part of my training, I killed eighteen bulls in three days before the 11th October, which was the date I'd set myself as a target.

In the end, I was able to appear in Zaragoza, which was the most important thing. Only the first of the six bulls let me do anything more or less decent, because it charged smoothly. I was a long way from being one hundred per cent, and I had a few bad moments. I didn't have what was needed to try to do more with the others, which needed a greater effort from me.

But that was not the main issue. My success that day was not measured in ears, but in the satisfaction of having triumphed over the last challenge in my professional career.

Two days later, I went back to Nîmes, to appear in a charity event. In the morning, I went to see Bernard, the doctor who operated on me, and he was surprised to see me walking already, and that my recovery was so complete.

'It's going so well,' I said, 'that the day before yesterday I killed six bulls in Zaragoza.'

He thought I was joking at first, but when I showed him the photos and newspaper cuttings, he couldn't believe it. In May, he'd told me that I needed six months before I could walk, but now he saw with his own eyes that, in just five months, I'd managed to recover well enough to appear with the bulls again.

ANOTHER SECRET FAREWELL

They took out the plates and screws that same winter. The fractures had grown together again perfectly, and I was able to start the 2003 season feeling good, once more back in top-notch physical condition. But the year off had reduced my appeal at the box office, and I was now less important than other star performers. If I was once the cock of the north, I was now a trussed chicken.

I didn't like that feeling. I was still appearing in the important fairs, but in the less important corridas, which were not what I'd been used to. I knew at once that this was a cast-iron sign that my career was taking a dive, and that I had to be honest with myself that the time had come for me to pack up and go home without a fuss. In the world of the bulls, if you're not on top, or fighting to be on top, it's best to get out.

At the end of August, after appearing in Las Ventas for the last time, and after cutting another ear in Seville, something happened which I had been expecting since the spring. It was in Calahorra, in the Rioja region, and this nutcase had been giving me a hard time from the seats all through the corrida.

I don't know if he was drunk, but he was calling me all sorts of names, personal, disrespectful stuff, even when I wasn't actually performing out in the ring; he must have had some kind of a fixation on me. I didn't even answer him back, as I would have done before, because the bulls were bad, so I didn't have the option to shut him up by ramming a triumph down his throat.

But it was that pain in the arse punter who made me finally make up my mind to retire. I began to think that perhaps he was right, and that the public was beginning to find me boring. After all, I was only making up numbers in the billing, I wasn't the main attraction, and to carry on like that would have been hitting absolute rock bottom.

In the middle of September in the Guadalajara Fair, I told the members of my cuadrilla that they should start looking out for another matador for next season, that I would be cutting back on the number of my corridas, and that they would earn better money elsewhere.

I didn't want to tell them the truth so as not to make it drawn out. I wanted to avoid the news getting out and have long-faced crowds saying goodbye to me in the corridas that were left, as happened in that dreadful corrida in Seville. I didn't want pity or excuses. The only ones who knew the real truth were my wife and my parents.

That 13th October 2003, once more in Zaragoza, I knew exactly what was going to happen, this time for sure – the last day of my career. My whole family was there, happy in the knowledge that all the doubts and suffering of so many years were finally coming to an end. Although the corrida left much to be desired, as was normal for me that year, I was happy too.

There were no nerves or worries on that day. The definitive farewell had been decided and thought through. The bulls were from a good ranch, El Pilar, and I cheered myself up with the thought that there was a chance that my final corrida would produce a good faena.

For the last time, Antonio Pedrosa dressed me in my tobacco-brown and gold traje de luces; he had been my sword handler for this last period. But Joaquín Ramos, my faithful friend, was also in the room. I enjoyed every step of that magical ritual of putting on the silk and gold, without getting carried away by the sentiment of the moment. No tears, either. It was all very emotional and touching, but I bore it well, hoping only for just a little bit of luck to close the last page of the adventure that was my life with the bulls.

I arrived at the ring very relaxed. It was autumn, and a north wind was blowing hard as the cuadrilla bus drove through the streets of Zaragoza. But since the bullring is covered now, the wind wasn't going to spoil my farewell in a setting where I'd always been well received, ever since my days as a novillero.

Unlike that autumn day in Seville in 1998, this time the stars were in my favour, because, to crown things, the last bull of my career as a matador did me the great favour of charging steady and true, a classy animal. That day belonged to me; it was all down to me and my skills as a bullfighter. I enjoyed every moment, every step, every pass, expressing in the ring the calmness and satisfaction I felt inside.

I did everything slowly, very slowly, savouring the passes with a nostalgic hunger, in a countdown as my days as a torero ebbed out of me. Only a handful of the thousands of spectators filling up the seats knew that this was the last time they would see *Joselito* in a suit of lights in a bullring.

After I killed that wonderful animal with a single sword thrust, and did a circuit of the ring of Zaragoza with the two ears, I went into the callejón and breathed a sigh of relief, as if a great weight had been lifted off me. Now everything was really at an end. If I didn't actually 'cut my coleta', it's only because I will remain a torero until the day I die.

They carried me out on shoulders, but I hardly smiled. In the photos of that last triumph, my face reflects an air of melancholy. You could always read me like a book. As before, and in the same relaxed manner, I didn't overdo the celebrations that night either.

I had a big table reserved in a restaurant in the centre of town, away from the eyes of the public, and only for those I wanted near me at this private and personal time: my family, my cuadrilla – both former and current members – the office staff, my old friends Julia and Juan, and of course my loyal group of followers, and Curro and *el Chino*, two of the 'strongmen' who travel around the ferias carrying out the toreros on their shoulders.

We had a good dinner, we laughed a lot, we made toasts all round, and I told them all the news that I was retiring. There were kisses, tears, hugs, congratulations... Everyone who loved me was there, those who had been with me, suffered with me, enjoyed the high spots with me since the early days: Juanín Cubero, the picador Emiliano Sánchez, Joaquín... It was a great evening, with no difficult moments. After a few drinks, they all went out on the town around the streets of Zaragoza, but I went back to the hotel with Adela, my wife. Because that night was really hers, not mine.

I didn't announce my retirement publicly until the following year. There were rumours, but I didn't care if people knew or not. That winter, I spent two or three months doing nothing, just trying to get used to the idea that I had become an ordinary citizen again, and that I was starting a new life very different from the old one.

The first year, I wasn't very aware of the changes, because I was still doing things in the world of the bulls – going around bullrings, receiving tributes and awards, giving talks to clubs and universities... I was still a torero, but I didn't have to stand in front of a bull any more. It was even less obvious the next year, because in 2004 I decided to manage César Jiménez, a young torero from Fuenlabrada with the right qualities to make it to the top, but who had lacked sound management.

I went with César everywhere, trying to realise our hopes together, but the experience of being a manager didn't really appeal to me. I felt that, unconsciously, I was stealing his thunder. Many people who had followed me started following him too, probably to spend more time with me now that I was out and about less often.

Although I tried hard to keep to my role of just being by his side, so as not to put him in the shade, he felt very uncomfortable about the way things turned out, and it became even worse when the boys in the press got the brilliant idea of suggesting that he was imitating me in the ring.

Apart from that, as I later realised, worst of all was that the ideas and advice I was giving César were really about me and what had worked for me when I was active, instead of thinking about him and the way he did things. We were very different, and I didn't really know how to put myself in his shoes.

I didn't like to get on his back either, telling him to get closer to the bull and to put his life on the line on those days when it was important. I remembered how my father treated me, never speaking to me in the ring, and on only one occasion in Las Ventas, did I decide to do that with Jiménez.

During the banderillas, I told him to close his eyes and allow the tricky bull he was working with to pass by very close to his legs, and that ten painful minutes could turn this into a major success, but ten minutes of indecision could ruin it.

He already had the guts and a natural ability to do it, and he won his exit on shoulders this time, but I walked back to the hotel on my own feeling very uncomfortable, that it was unforgiveable to have made him take a risk which could have turned out very differently.

That old saying in Spanish says it all: 'You can read the bulls very well from the other side of the fence'. But if you know what you're looking at, if you have already felt it before in the ring yourself, you can also be scared stiff behind the fence. When it's you standing out there in front of the bull, you can make up your own mind what you want to do and how much you want to take risks. But it seems inhuman to ask someone else to put his life in danger.

The office side of management was handled by Joaquín, because I had a very short temper, and I was hopeless at it. He did all the negotiating with the impresarios, and I looked after the torero, and was with him on the days of the actual corrida. Even so, I managed to have several major bust-ups, which almost ended in coming to blows, if an impresario tried to go back on what he'd agreed to.

All of this meant that I didn't enjoy being in management. I was used to moving around in the profession on a higher level than the one where César found himself, higher in every respect, and I found it very difficult to come to terms with that.

I was going through difficult personal problems at the time, and the second year we were together, I'm sorry to say I paid less attention to him. I didn't have the time to combine both things, and I had to make a decision between my own private life and the professional career of César Jiménez. The choice was simple, but I waited until the end of the season before I stepped down.

Despite everything – because all experiences in life can teach you something – I learnt a great deal from that period in management, not just in dealing with impresarios, but also artistically. From my position behind the fence, I began to see the bulls from a different perspective, to take in technical details which I hadn't noticed before when I was performing, and which would have been easy for me to include if I had.

In the handful of charity events that I've appeared in since my retirement, I've had a chance to put into practice some of the things I learnt while with César and I've noticed that my style has improved; I was seeing things much more clearly then, and my ideas were fresher, too.

It's also true that, without having the pressures of a long career, and with less demanding animals, it was easier for me to be free to express my new knowledge, and the feelings that life had brought me.

I sometimes wonder how far I could have got with all the stuff that I've picked up in my years of inactivity. But it's just a mad thought, which I shrug off immediately. Although I am still relatively young, I have no wish whatsoever to put on the 'spangly suit' again.

More than that, I don't think I am up to it. In plain language, I haven't got the balls to put my arse on the line again. And I know it.

I would have to have a major overhaul, shut myself away from everything else and prepare myself mentally and physically in order to try, just to try, to summon up enough strength to stand in front of a bull again. It's one thing to want to do something, but it's altogether quite different to be able to do it. I don't feel it's possible right now. Just look at the daredevil toreros of today and the amazing things they do in the ring. I don't think I could do that, and to be just another face in the crowd isn't worth leaving the house for.

As well as lacking the nerve – and there have never been toreros with more nerve that this modern bunch – I see a lack of personality in them, and that is what makes the difference between the very few outstanding ones and the rest. Maybe that's because of the times we live in, but I've noticed a certain similarity in all of them and especially that they lack that small spark of rebellion they need when they're up against the closed shop of the bull business.

Today's young guys think differently. If you listen to them talking, they say things which I find shocking, such as that so-and-so in his early twenties is looking for an easy life in how his career is run. The business of the bulls was never easy; it should be a constant battle. A quiet life and security are not good for toreros.

A BRACELET FROM BOSNIA

If you risk your life in front of a bull, you have the right – I would say the obligation – to defend your interests and what you have earned in the ring, and to do this with the same courage and determination. And if you are really powerful, you should also think of those who are not as lucky as you, and have no means to defend themselves.

Someone who has been at the top in bullfighting should leave a legacy for future generations, and at least try to leave the fiesta in a better state than they found it when they began. Even if we spilt our blood on the sand, we should be prepared to pay back some of what the art has given us. That's why I was always poking my nose into stuff that didn't concern me, although my own career was already sorted out.

One of my great aims was to tackle the unfair distribution of image rights among toreros, and put an end to the impresarios imposing terms on them for television rights. My father and I were trying to do this in 1992, when Ponce and Rincón backed out of the exclusive deal that we signed with Spanish Television.

I came back to it fighting at the end of the 1990s, with a group of other fellow toreros, when Vía Digital entered the frame. And because of various fishy deals, it opened up a division within the Asociación de Matadores, effectively the matadors' trade union, until things reached a point where a parallel organisation was set up, directed by the impresarios themselves, who took it upon themselves to punish that soul of integrity, Luis Francisco Esplá.

In the year 2000 when I made my comeback, José Tomás and I thought we were powerful enough to finally win the battle, even if *el Juli* didn't join us. But, after a disastrous press conference we held with my father, which others did their utmost to undermine, we found ourselves still on the outside.

Our claims were lawful and logical. We were not asking for more money for the transmissions, but we wanted to decide for ourselves when our images could be used and to oblige the TV companies to provide space for bullfighting in their news broadcasts, so as to present the true image of toreros, not the damaging, irrelevant misrepresentation offered in glossy magazines. But, once again, no one joined us and the press came down on us from a great height.

The problem was, as I've said before, we were up against a network of economic interests made up of a large number of individuals, but they didn't include the main protagonists. With hardly any support, I felt that José Tomás and I were like two imbeciles fighting windmills, against a faceless enemy, and we didn't know where the next attack would come from.

He has done very well now, keeping up the struggle on his own. But because at that time there was a great deal of interest in having bullfighting on TV, the year 2000 would have been the perfect moment to bring in an arrangement which would've been valid for the situation today.

Some of those who abandoned us have finally realised that we were right. But they are still stuck without a solution to a problem which has got worse with 'the crisis', with companies which prefer to make bigger profits for themselves by selling off the fiesta to pay-per-view channels, when it should be sold on free-to-view, so that it would be seen as it should be by millions of viewers.

Since my own future with the bulls became clear, I've always been keen to think about the overall future of bullfighting, to protect and maintain its traditions so that our children can enjoy it in the best possible circumstances. That's why my father and I had the idea of creating the Joselito Foundation with the profits of the Benefiencia corrida of 1993, and which we later topped up with other fees.

The initial investment didn't pass through our hands but via the Community of Madrid as organisers of the event, who paid the box-office receipts direct to the Foundation without charge – the first time in history that such a thing was started by a torero.

The Foundation is run by a board formed of representatives of all political parties from the Community and others designated by me, like my father; so far, it has accomplished several interesting activities.

First, we set up two cultural awards to do with bullfighting: one an essay prize for more or less recognised professionals, and the other for a piece of research by university students, both well supported and with a guarantee of publication by our partners, the publishers Espasa-Calpe.

But even in a world supposedly as honourable as that of culture, you discover things which make the devious intriguers of the bull business look like beginners. After the first four editions of the essay prize, which were won, if my memory serves me correctly, by the philosopher Víctor Gómez Pin, Father Lezama, and the writers Víctor Diusabá and Germán San Nicasio, one member of the jury, behind our backs, decided to interfere with one of the basic principles of the competition so as to award a prize to a work which had already been rejected the previous year.

The 'winner', a writer from Valencia who was using a pseudo-nym, called me in all innocence to thank me before the award had been made public, and she asked me also to say thank you on her behalf to the gentleman who had made the necessary corrections for her to win the prize of six million pesetas.

The swindle was so obvious that I immediately told the woman not to bother to turn up to collect the prize because I was going to refuse to give it to her. But bearing in mind the sum we were talking about, she decided to turn up anyway, and in the end to avoid further ado, I went to the awards ceremony and presented her with the cheque. But I made certain that, from that day on, the literary prize of the Joselito Foundation would be abandoned.

We also organised and funded for ten consecutive years a Course of Taurine Journalism at the public university of Madrid, the Universidad Complutense, and this has turned out well, helping many young journalists to find work. Unfortunately, in 2011, instead of supporting the scheme, someone in the bull business set up a similar one in parallel, but with very different ulterior motives. I felt so cheated that I chose to drop out of the one which bore my name.

I also dropped out of supporting the competition for youngsters called *Madrid busca un torero* ('Madrid is looking for a torero'), which was held three years running in the new Palacio Vistalegre bullring. The people who were running it introduced a mystifying selection system which was both political and kowtowing to bull-business interests, and resulted in them choosing boys who were not as good as many of those who'd been eliminated in the initial trials.

When I saw them with calves, anyone with a minimum under-standing of these things could have realised that the majority had neither the desire, nor the ability, to be toreros. After being taught in that very demanding Madrid School of Bullfighting of the early 1980s, the unfair selection methods, and the elaborate untaurine bureaucracy handling the money of my Foundation, did nothing but put me right off.

To add insult to injury, one imbecile from the Federation of Bullfighting Schools went so far as to question my credibility in something for which I was not only putting up the money, but also giving my full attention to. Because of these cases of ingratitude, and obnoxious wheeler-dealings, at this moment the Joselito Foundation is virtually inactive. I've dropped everything.

Well, almost everything, because I'm still involved in the project in Guadalajara to raise the standards of performance in bullfighting, where intensive instruction is given, similar to the Casa de Campo of old, to a selection of outstanding pupils from different bullfighting schools. But, even here, I am near to blowing up. We receive a small grant from the local government of Guadalajara, and the politicians there are trying to smear us with their backbiting slime by involving us in their silly games of revenge.

Not all our work has gone wrong like this. I am very proud of our support for the victims of the war in the Balkans in the mid-1990s.

When he heard of the existence of the Foundation, I had a visit from Paco Gallardo, a sergeant in the Spanish Legion who was sent to Bosnia and was a first-hand witness to the urgent needs of the Muslims cut off in Mostar, which was the zone controlled by the Spanish troops as part of the international intervention force.

He was from Malaga, and was a keen aficionado: he had set up a bullfight club in the camp at Medjugorje to relieve tension among his companions at arms. He described to me with great passion the tragic situation of those poor souls who had been displaced by the war, and especially the ruinous state of the hospital where the medicines were kept, with rats running around everywhere and the doctors operating without anaesthetics.

I was so impressed by what he told me that I gave my word to appear in a corrida to try to alleviate the disastrous situation, even if it was just by a little. The Community of Madrid gave the soldiers permission to use Las Ventas, but we couldn't fully agree on everything, because, although they are the owners of the ring, under pressure from the Lozanos, who were out to teach me a lesson, they could only give permission for us to hold a minor event, a 'festival', not a corrida, which is what I wanted. The income from a festival would not be enough.

In the end, the Madrid politicians used the profits from that year's Beneficiencia corrida to send an aid package to the conflict zone, which comprised several intensive care units. And in order to keep my word given to Sergeant Gallardo, I ended up killing six bulls for the cause in San Sebastián de los Reyes.

Even so, we still had problems. What we wanted was to buy the medicines and charter a plane to take them directly to Bosnia with the help of Médecins Sans Frontières. But one of the bosses in the NGO, who was violently opposed to bullfighting, as well as putting other obstacles in our way, refused to let the people know that the gift had been made possible by a spectacle which – according to him – was violent and bloody.

So we gave them the takings of that day in which I had unselfishly risked my life in front of six bulls, and we allowed them to deal with the gift as they saw fit. That's the way things are in this hypocritical world.

Paco Gallardo, that brave and dedicated Legionnaire, felt very disappointed by the way in which his idea had been dealt with. So, to thank me, he brought from Mostar a present which I shall treasure for ever: a bracelet made from the strap of one of the pallets used for transporting the aid package, which a Bosnian child had engraved with my name.

FOLLOWING IN THE LAST FOOTSTEPS OF JUAN BELMONTE

We should go back to the time shortly after my final retirement, because, three years after that, I lived through some of the most critical moments of my entire life. After two years spent travelling around Spain receiving tributes and managing César Jiménez, in which I was unconsciously avoiding facing up to the realities of my new situation, I needed to deal with all the business affairs of my various ranches which I hadn't want to get involved with.

I had to do some serious thinking, because the ranches and various kinds of cattle that I had acquired were now my only source of income, and I needed to find ways to produce more and do better, in order to get a return on my investment. Enrique had separated from my mother, and re-married in Mexico, leaving me running the business. Overnight and almost without my realising it, my life-long support was suddenly missing. I was stunned, and felt unable to deal with the new situation.

It was this fundamental change in my daily routine that brought home the fact that I really had left behind the active life of a bull-fighter. That's when I felt the enormous loss that all toreros suffer when they finally hang up their suit of lights. It was the same for me as for other toreros who I've talked to about it; that sudden change is very traumatic.

You move from all to nothing, from being the centre of attention to being the same as anyone else. You have dedicated all your adolescence and youth to the bulls, more than half your lifetime, but suddenly it's over and you don't know what to do about it. You've got ranches, herds of cattle, cars... You've got everything, but – so what? The truth is that nothing you possess is as attractive to you as bullfighting, and you have to be very strong to be able to make up for the loss.

Enrique was no longer at my side and I was without Joaquín, who had fulfilled his role as sword handler so well that I had got used to the idea that whatever problem I had outside the ring would be sorted out by someone else, and so the silliest little thing that I had to do now seemed enormous, a mountain which I couldn't manage to climb on my own.

I wasn't a torero anymore. I was a farmer, who just like so many others in Spain, had to work hard every day to make his farming business break even, at what was a very difficult time for people in the countryside. It all seemed impossible.

Just to make a phone call to buy a truckload of grain, for example, seemed an impossible task. Anything that was simple and straightforward would be put off for tomorrow. I couldn't face up to reality, and that hurt me even more.

In bed at night, I felt like a loser, because I knew that I hadn't been up to the job. I would make up my mind to definitely deal with it in the morning...and the same process would happen all over again: in the early morning, I wouldn't call anyone because it was too early; by mid-morning, I wouldn't do it because I thought that whoever it was that I wanted to speak to would be on a coffee-break; at one or two o'clock, it was a bad time because they'd be having lunch; and so on until night time, and, back in my room, I tortured myself with thoughts of what a wimp I was. The fact is that I always found an excuse for not facing up to things.

Anxiety and misery were always with me. I moved on from tormenting myself with these thoughts to being unable to get to sleep, waking up in the middle of the night, never getting any rest as things whirled around in my head in a terrible vicious circle.

I was in such a bad way that I came close to doing something really stupid, and I thought of a thousand different ways of doing it. It's true: I thought very seriously about killing myself, like Juan Belmonte, because there came a time when I didn't care about anything: my daughters, my wife, my farms... My mother advised me to go back to bullfighting, which might help. But that wasn't what it was all about. Going back to the bulls might prove a distraction for a year or two, but it wouldn't sort out the stuff in my head.

And that's how it was that, as I sank deeper and deeper into depression, two months after the end of the 2006 season, when I left César, I had to put myself into the hands of the doctors.

I had been resisting it for a while, but I had to bite the bullet if I wanted to avoid losing all that I held most dear. My father had to drive me to Madrid on the first day, in case I did something silly on the motorway. When I arrived at the consultant's surgery, I held nothing back, I told the doctor everything that was happening to me, and promised her that I was prepared to take whatever pills were necessary to get me out of the terrible state I was in.

It didn't come to that because the doctor thought quite rightly that it was better to try all the other possibilities before falling back on powerful medication. For three months, twice a week, all she did was listen to me.

I talked a lot, because I needed to, telling her my life story since childhood, just like I am doing in this book now. Until the day came that, after baring my soul and spewing out all that I had kept inside me, the doctor told me we could stop, because I was cured. At last I'd grown to accept that I could no longer count on the support of Enrique, as I had done for so many years, and the time had come to face life's struggles on my own without the tower of strength who'd always been there for me ever since the death of my biological father.

I also think that my retirement from the bullring had removed the one possibility for expressing myself in the best way I know how, which was with the capote and the muleta. There was no longer a torero and his public; I was a performer who no longer had a stage to act on. I had been wrapped up inside myself for three years, although I was travelling around, and being seen in public, but I had no one to express my feelings to.

I was cured because the doctor let me express myself again, but this time, in words. Something similar is happening to me now as I tell my story in these pages; it is an experience which will leave me feeling re-energised. Luckily, the illness which took me to the edge of the abyss has been defeated, but I don't think I will ever lose my inherent touch of madness.

Now I work like a slave. I get up at dawn and work far into the night running my farms, which, the way things are, produce much less than they should. Sometimes I think of all the times I have risked my life just to end up having to work as hard as all those who work themselves to death every day for wages, just to survive.

The herd of toros bravos, the ganadería, keeps me going. It has become my passion and my favourite way of keeping fit. I began breeding bulls about a year after taking the alternativa, when, on 10th August 1987, I bought my first stock from Lora Sangrán and branded them with the number '1' which used to belong to Luis Miguel *Dominguín*. But I didn't really get involved seriously until I had retired from the ring. I now have two separate brands, which appear on the posters as *Toros del Tajo* and *Ganadería de la Reina* and come from the same bloodline of Domecq. Tajo is the River Tagus, which runs through Talavera de la Reina.

Being a breeder of toros bravos is not easy, because genetics is a tricky business. When everything works out well, that's great, but the results don't depend solely on you, and it's more usual that it all goes wrong if you don't keep on top of things. It's not possible to know everything there is to know about a ganadería, or at least I find it impossible.

Some breeders say they have a bad time on the day when their bulls are taken to the bullring, but it's much worse for the guy waiting in the hotel to face them. What worries the breeder is that his prestige and finances are at stake, but that's very different from the torero, because what's at stake is his life.

I accept that the job can be very nerve-wracking, because you're on a knife-edge from the time the bull leaves the ranch, is unloaded at the bullring, passes the vets' inspection, is separated into the corrals, and then is fought in the ring, at the same time hoping that the toreros don't get injured... Last year, my bulls caught several top matadors, probably just through bad luck, but that made me suffer terribly.

You can't compare one triumph with another, not by a long chalk. As a breeder, it's fantastic to see an animal which you've bred charge well, but that can never be the same as to create emotion with your caping of the bull, getting twenty passes out of it, leaving on shoulders through the main gate of a first-class ring... That is heavenly.

Apart from those differences, a ganadería is also something creative, or at least instinctive, because, as a breeder, you try to use genetics to mould your animals to get them to charge the way you want them to, in pursuit of an ideal which can't always be achieved. Success doesn't lie in your own hands, because you're always at the mercy of your bulls and what the toreros want to do, or are capable of doing, with them.

My experience as a torero has given me the knowledge to appreciate details which other breeders may miss, the sort of detail which can only be seen by facing an animal. Even though I have to admit that, because of the tensions going on during a bullfight, toreros frequently fail to see the whole picture.

That's why, because I already know what it feels like to be in the line of fire, I never cape my own heifers in my tentaderos. From the outside, I am in a better position to calculate the ingredients I need to make the magical cocktail necessary for the sort of qualities I want to achieve.

My ideal bull should have the ability to be 'fixed', that is to say, to concentrate on the confrontation, on the man, and on the cloth in front of it. It should be steady in its charge, lower its head, push hard from its hindquarters, and never ease off the attack. And especially this: it should have an extra metre on the end of its charge as it comes out from every pass. That's the kind of bull I liked to work with, and what I want to achieve as a breeder.

I also try to bring out a touch of wildness, more aggression than is normal. A well-bred bull, if it charges and follows the cape, can contribute to the success of a torero who gives it twenty passes and drives the public into a frenzy. To do that, you have to be very committed and very firm, do everything well, but also in a short space of time.

On the other hand, with a bull which 'isn't a nuisance', as we toreros say, you have to be prepared to give it fifty passes, and spend a lot more time with it if you want to build up excitement and cut a maximum of a single ear, or maybe two if you're a real artist.

I like a bull which charges repeatedly and helps the torero, but it should always have an untamed, fierce quality because that means that the spectator won't have the depressing idea that he could come down into the ring himself. A true toro bravo increases admiration for a torero because it brings a sensation of wildness and a thrill which should always be present in the spectacle.

The bulls have given me everything in life; that's why I have nothing but respect for them, and that's why I breed them. As long as I am able, I will continue to give them my complete respect. The bull is a fighter which is pitted against you, but it can also help you; it is a majestic opponent which gives you an opportunity to express yourself in the ring. It is both your enemy and your friend. It's like a sign flashing 'danger!' and it attracts you like a magnet.

That sense of risk is one of the things that's brought me most in this life. When I went through that incredibly deep depression, I had another 'doctor' to help me through it: one of my horses, sired by the famous *Cagancho* which belonged to the rejoneador, Hermoso de Mendoza.

It was one of the most bad-tempered animals you can imagine. It had already thrown and kicked four or five men on the ranch, and I brought it home to get rid of its bad habits. At first, it began playing up with me, too, but I managed to get the better of it in very risky situations.

The adrenalin of those dangerous moments in the saddle on that horse brought me back to earth. To tame that animal was such a challenge that I needed to be physically fit, and I had to overcome my fear and self-doubt every time I got onto its back.

I finally succeeded in showing it who was the boss, controlling its temperament and getting on the right side of it, which made me feel like a new man, like in the bullring. That horse will die of old age in the stables with my eternal gratitude for the therapy it gave me, forcing me to control myself first, in order to control the horse.

The feeling that you are taking a risk every time in a corrida – like throwing yourself into space without a parachute – all that gives you a fantastic feeling of freedom. Because, in the face of danger, it's you alone who must make the decisions.

FROM A THIEF TO A GENTLEMAN

How can you explain all this to someone who is an anti, who is opposed to the bulls? How can you explain to them what a toro bravo is, and what it means to us? It's hard to make yourself heard by someone who doesn't want to listen, who is locked up in their own prejudices and preconceptions.

It's difficult to explain to those people that the corrida is an artform in which death is present in order to honour life? I think of myself as an artist because I can communicate emotion through the bull and by risking my life. Bullfighting is a ritual form of sacrifice in which you are moved by the animal's power as you take its life, even though you are prepared to pay for it with your own blood, pain or even death.

We toreros have enormous respect for the bull, and because of its imposing majesty and wildness, the worst insult you could make to it is to take pity on it. That's why I've always tried to be honest and to act out of purity, giving it the chance to win the fight.

I tried to communicate this in the Catalan Parliament a couple of years ago, when I was invited to take part in the sessions they organised to debate the prohibition of bullfighting there. But they didn't want to listen.

It all seemed very strange on that wintry, cold and wet day in Barcelona. Immediately upon my arrival, I was met in the doorway to the building by two boys protesting against the bulls, holding a placard and with their faces painted red. There were two, just two of them. Curious, I approached them, offered them a cigarette, and they confessed that they were being paid fifty euros to be there.

I had never taken part in a parliamentary session before. I awaited my turn in the corridor, and, when they called me in, I explained to the Catalan Deputies present what my ideals and views about bullfighting were, in terms of the emotions and as art. I don't think they understood me or wanted to understand me. The one who really didn't understand it was me, because, when they asked me their questions in Catalan, they didn't even have the common decency to provide a translator for me. Only the representatives of the Partido Popular and of the Ciutadans party spoke to me in Spanish.

I couldn't reply to the others because I didn't understand what they were saying. When I left the room, someone translated for me the contents of their questions, which had nothing to do with what I had said to them. It was all in Double Dutch, talking at cross purposes. If it weren't for what happened later, I would say that the whole thing was nothing short of a farce. Because the manipulative skullduggery, using an Act of Declaration, resulted in a ban of a part of Catalan culture which some people aren't happy with. And that's not right.

I felt I had been used and made to look foolish for taking part in this game in which the cards had been marked by local nationalism. I was there for no good reason other than to justify with my presence the fiction of a supposed freedom of expression, to give a speech which they didn't want to listen to, because the matter had already been decided. The whole show was a nasty little deception cooked up by the Catalan politicians.

I know perfectly well that nothing which happened in the Catalan Parliament had anything to do with the protection of animals. I also know that there is a movement which is trying to put an end to corridas by any means possible, and that their militants are well-organised and funded by groups from a number of overseas countries.

Even so, I believe that, in Spain, there are many more of us in favour of the corrida than those against. The problem is that we don't have the same numbers of militants because we have never felt the need to defend ourselves. No one has taken the necessary steps, and even fewer from inside the world of the bulls, which is constantly aware of the threat.

The future of the fiesta de los toros is uncertain because the naive arguments of the antis, by the do-gooders and the fun-lovers, are gathering strength among young people in cities: not those in the countryside, where there's a more sensible and realistic approach to nature. I have no problem with the welfare of animals, but I believe more in the welfare of human beings, especially when you look at all the disasters in the world, with hunger and misery not far from our own front doors.

A terrible hypocrisy surfaces when talking about these things. For instance, some people say that seeing a corrida can 'damage the sensitivities of minors', so they try to ban them from entry to a bullring. I have been going to bullrings from a very early age, and I don't feel traumatised by it: quite the opposite, in fact.

There are horrendous things that a child sees every day on television – deaths are commonplace, scenes of violence on the news come into our homes at every mealtime. Then there's the aggressiveness of the gossip magazines, the lack of respect for individual dignity which is a daily occurrence in children's programmes. Kids are used to killing off their enemies in video games, and they see from time to time how an unbalanced teenager can break into a school building and cause a massacre. They've made us grow accustomed to that sort of thing and we accept it as normal.

We're living in strange times in which the media decide for us what is good and what is bad. And the bulls are very high up on the blacklist, as something brutal which should be stopped. The worst thing about all this is that people accept it without questioning.

I have seen fourteen or fifteen-year-old kids riding motorbikes at more than two hundred kilometres an hour on a race circuit, and no one puts their hands up in horror, but, if a boy capes a calf, they see that as inhuman, a crime against the innocence of childhood. Television doesn't show the great faenas of a corrida, but they repeat ad nauseam the scenes of cornadas and accidents in village fiestas; I don't know if it's because of morbid interest or simply an anti-taurine message designed to cause alarm and scandal among people.

With all this negative imagery it's not easy to get to the real meaning of bullfighting. We need to take over the media to offer a more positive image, so that people can understand the traditions and who it is that's maintaining them.

The world of the bulls is deeply rooted in a long list of human values which are still very necessary in today's society: endeavour, self-sacrifice, responsibility, courage, loyalty, honesty, commitment, friendship... It is important to let the public know that there still exist a few madmen out there who call themselves 'toreros' and present these sets of values for public view.

The media want to paint an image of us as playboys, country bumpkins, chauvinist pigs, bloody and violent, but, in real life, we toreros are like ordinary people, and different only when we are doing our job. I have never been in a fight and I hate violence, which you won't find, either in the ring or among the spectators, during the celebration of a spectacle which is bloody but not cruel.

In all the bullrings I have been to, which must be several hundred, I've never seen the sort of acts of violence which are a daily occurrence in a football stadium. The stuff that a kid can see and hear in a football match is unbelievable. But the worst thing is that often it's the kid's father who encourages him to copy what he is doing, thereby making yet another little hooligan to vent his frustrations on others.

I am convinced that bullfighting, on the other hand, is a perfect place to learn. For a child, the ring is like a reflection of life itself, the drawing pad where lessons can be learned which are relevant to daily life. My own example is a good case in point.

There's nowhere to hide out there in the ring, and there's no way you can blame someone else for your failures, or escape your responsibilities; there are no 'kicking the ball away' or comfort zones. It's just you, on your own, in front of the bull. That is the big difference and it's the most important lesson to be learned from this art form.

Now that they are growing up and beginning a more difficult part of their education, I am trying to encourage in my daughters the values which were so important for me to progress and eventually succeed. I want them to understand that you have to make an effort to get things in life, and that they have to get them by themselves by having a good education and a healthy respect for the basic rules of behaviour. That's why I took them to La Guindalera, so they could see for themselves where I came from, and so they know their own roots.

I try to give them a lot of affection, lots of kisses and the warmth that I missed out on, but I still have many doubts about how best to educate them. I'm not sure at what point their freedom ends and mine to guide their upbringing begins. I'm not sure of the boundaries between parental discipline and allowing children to develop their own personality.

With children, it's important to give them room to stand up for themselves and still have the possibility of learning from their own mistakes. After all, the little tearaway that I was when I was thirteen was able to accept his own responsibilities. There were many reasons that I could have given myself to go with the flow, but, to escape from it, I had deep inside me a determination to win through, which led me to bullfighting and to those who taught me about it.

My childhood was very different from that of my daughters: it was another world and another time. It's difficult for me to compare that experience with nowadays. Today's comfortable circumstances have nothing to do with the hand-to-mouth existence of the 1970s in the neighbourhood where I grew up. But I also believe that there are timeless values which are, perhaps, more necessary than ever at a time when everything seems so much easier.

I don't want to make the same mistakes that my father made with me. Luckily, I have Adela by my side to keep us pulling in the same direction with Alba and Claudia and to help me deal with the doubts that I have myself.

The way things are today, there are even more dysfunctional families like the one I grew up. Some believe that this sort of thing doesn't have any effect on a child's education. But, from my own experience, I know that such instability can cause traumas which scar you for life.

That's what I worry about now – my daughters. And my daily grind to provide a better life for them than the one I had. That's what I think about every hour of my day. Then, one afternoon in the spring of 2011, I received a phone call from a journalist who wanted to arrange an interview because, according to her, I had just been awarded the national Fine Arts Gold Medal.

I was in the shade of a holm oak tree, with my father and a friend who was about to sell me a machine for feeding my domestic cattle. It was just after three in the afternoon, in the middle of the countryside. I had been at it since seven o'clock, rushing all over the place, so it wasn't a good time for a wind-up. I more or less told them to piss off, and went on talking about the deal.

But the poor girl called me back ten minutes later, apologising if she had interrupted me, but she insisted that it had been confirmed and that the news was true that I had been awarded the Gold Medal.

I still wasn't convinced, even when two or three friends rang up to congratulate me, until the Culture Minister herself, Ángeles González-Sinde, told me the news in her own words at six that evening.

I thanked her, but I didn't feel any different. Like so many other important moments in my life, I didn't get over-excited because I thought, sincerely and without any false modesty, that it was a recognition which I deserved, and which had been a long time coming. The truth is that I already had the best reward, which was to have made a dream come true by giving over my heart and soul to my passion, through dedicating my life to the bulls.

I am aware that this medal is extraordinarily important, above all because, on previous occasions, I know that awarding the medal to a torero puts them on the same level as other creative artists. But without wishing to appear pretentious, the fact that they were making the award to me meant nothing short of public recognition of what I'd already known for a long time: that I was an artist.

I went to receive the medal some months later. It was presented to me by King Juan Carlos, who was very kind towards this so-called 'republican'. As he offered his hand, he said some words to me which I found very touching, and for which I thanked him from the bottom of my heart, 'José, this Medal is truly deserved. I am delighted that it is for you.'

I couldn't see his eyes, because His Majesty was hiding a recent black eye behind a pair of sunglasses, which, just for a moment, reminded me of the sunglasses I used to wear during my wild times in La Guindalera.

Who could have told the young punk that I was then, that small-time crook in a black leather jacket who stole watches and radio cassettes in vacant lots, that, in a short while, they would put a card in front of him with 'Excelentísimo Señor' in front of his name? Truth to tell, I still don't know which of the two is the real *Joselito*, the real deal.